ME

ELTON JOHN

MACMILLAN

First published 2019 by Macmillan
an imprint of Pan Macmillan
The Smithson, 6 Briset Street, London EC1M 5NR
Associated companies throughout the world
www.panmacmillan.com

ISBN 978-1-5098-5331-1

9 8 7 6

A CIP catalogue record for this book is available from the British Library.

Typeset by Palimpsest Book Production Ltd, Falkirk, Stirlingshire
Printed and bound by CPI Group (UK) Ltd, Croydon, CR0 4YY

Visit **www.panmacmillan.com** to read more about all our books
and to buy them. You will also find features, author interviews and
news of any author events, and you can sign up for e-newsletters
so that you're always first to hear about our new releases.

This book is dedicated to my husband, David,
and to our beautiful sons Zachary and Elijah.
Special thanks to Alexis Petridis, without
whom this book would not have been possible.

prologue

I was onstage at the Latino club in South Shields when I realized I couldn't take it anymore. It was one of those supper clubs that were all over Britain in the sixties and seventies, all virtually identical: people dressed in suits, seated at tables, eating chicken in a basket and drinking wine out of bottles covered in wicker; fringed lampshades and flock wallpaper; cabaret and a compère in a bow tie. It felt like a throwback to another era. Outside, it was the winter of 1967, and rock music was shifting and changing so fast that it made my head spin just thinking about it: The Beatles' *Magical Mystery Tour* and The Mothers of Invention, *The Who Sell Out* and *Axis: Bold As Love*, Dr John and *John Wesley Harding*. Inside the Latino, the only way you could tell the Swinging Sixties had happened at all was because I was wearing a kaftan and some bells on a chain around my neck. They didn't really suit me. I looked like a finalist in a competition to find Britain's least convincing flower child.

The kaftan and the bells were Long John Baldry's idea. I was the organ player in his backing band, Bluesology. John had spotted all the other r'n'b bands going psychedelic: one week you'd go and see Zoot Money's Big Roll Band playing James Brown songs, the next you'd find they were calling themselves Dantalian's

Chariot, wearing white robes onstage and singing about how World War Three was going to kill all the flowers. He'd decided we should follow suit, sartorially at least. So we all got kaftans. Cheaper ones for the backing musicians, while John's were specially made at Take Six in Carnaby Street. Or at least, he thought they were specially made, until we played a gig and he saw someone in the audience wearing exactly the same kaftan as him. He stopped in the middle of a song and started shouting angrily at him – 'Where did you get that shirt? That's *my* shirt!' This, I felt, rather ran contrary to the kaftan's associations with peace and love and universal brotherhood.

I adored Long John Baldry. He was absolutely hilarious, deeply eccentric, outrageously gay and a fabulous musician, maybe the greatest 12-string guitarist the UK has ever produced. He'd been one of the major figures in the British blues boom of the early sixties, playing with Alexis Korner and Cyril Davies and The Rolling Stones. He had an encyclopedic knowledge of the blues. Just being around him was an education: he introduced me to so much music I'd never heard before.

But more than that, he was an incredibly kind, generous man. He had a knack of spotting something in musicians before anybody else could see it, then nurturing them, taking the time to build their confidence. He did it with me, and before that he'd done it with Rod Stewart, who'd been one of the singers in Steampacket, John's previous band: Rod, John, Julie Driscoll, Brian Auger. They were incredible, but then they split up. The story I heard was that one night after a gig in St-Tropez, Rod and Julie had an argument, Julie threw red wine over Rod's white suit – I'm sure you can imagine how well *that* went down – and that was the end of Steampacket. So Bluesology had got the gig as John's backing band instead, playing hip soul clubs and blues cellars all over the country.

It was great fun, even if John had some peculiar ideas about music. We played the most bizarre sets. We'd start out doing really hard-driving blues: 'Times Getting Tougher Than Tough', 'Hoochie Coochie Man'. The audience would be in the palm of our hand, but then John would insist we played 'The Threshing Machine', a sort of smutty West Country novelty song, the kind of thing rugby players sing when they're pissed, like ''Twas On The Good Ship Venus' or 'Eskimo Nell'. John would even sing it in an ooh-arr accent. And after that, he'd want us to perform something from the Great American Songbook – 'It Was A Very Good Year' or 'Ev'ry Time We Say Goodbye' – which enabled him to do his impersonation of Della Reese, the American jazz singer. I don't know where he got the idea that people wanted to hear him playing 'The Threshing Machine' or doing an imper- sonation of Della Reese, but, bless him, he remained absolutely convinced that they did, in the face of some pretty compelling evidence to the contrary. You'd look out at the front row, people who'd come to hear blues legend Long John Baldry, and just see a line of mods, all chewing gum and staring at us in complete horror: *What the fuck is this guy doing?* It was hilarious, even if I was asking myself the same question.

And then, catastrophe struck: Long John Baldry had a huge hit single. Obviously, this would usually have been the cause of great rejoicing, but 'Let The Heartaches Begin' was an appalling record, a syrupy, middle-of-the-road, *Housewives' Choice* ballad. It was a million miles from the kind of music John should have been making, and it was Number One for weeks, never off the radio. I'd say I didn't know what he was thinking, but I knew exactly what he was thinking, and I couldn't really blame him. He'd been slogging around for years and this was the first time he'd made any money. The blues cellars stopped booking us and we started playing the supper clubs, which paid better. Often we'd play two a night. They weren't interested in John's pivotal role in the British blues boom or his mastery of the 12-string guitar. They just wanted to see someone who'd been on television. Occasionally, I got the feeling they weren't that interested in music, full stop. In some clubs, if you played over your allotted time, they'd simply close the curtains on you, mid-song. On the plus side, at least the supper club audiences enjoyed 'The Threshing Machine' more than the mods did.

There was one other major problem with 'Let The Heartaches Begin': Bluesology couldn't play it live. I don't mean we refused to play it. I mean we literally *couldn't play it*. The single had an orchestra and a female chorus on it: it sounded like Mantovani. We were an eight-piece rhythm and blues band with a horn section. There was no way we could reproduce the sound. So John came up with the idea of putting the backing track on tape. When the big moment came, he'd drag a huge Revox tape machine onstage, press play and sing along to that. The rest of us would just have to stand there, doing nothing. In our kaftans and bells. While people ate chicken and chips. It was excruciating.

In fact, the only entertaining thing about the live performance of 'Let The Heartaches Begin' was that, whenever John sang it, women started screaming. Apparently overwhelmed by desire, they'd temporarily abandon their chicken and chips and run to the front of the stage. Then they'd start grabbing at the cord of John's microphone, trying to pull him towards them. I'm sure this kind of thing happened to Tom Jones every night and he took it in his stride, but Long John Baldry wasn't Tom Jones. Rather than bask in the adulation, he'd get absolutely furious. He'd stop singing and bellow at them like a schoolmaster: 'IF YOU BREAK MY MICROPHONE, YOU'LL PAY ME FIFTY POUNDS!' One night, this dire warning went unheeded. As they kept pulling at the cord, I saw John raise his arm. Then a terrible thud shook the speakers. I realized, with a sinking feeling, that it was the sound of a lust-racked fan being smacked over her head with a microphone. In retrospect, it was a miracle he didn't get arrested or sued for assault. So that was the main source of amusement for the rest of us during 'Let The Heartaches Begin': wondering if tonight would be the night John clobbered one of his screaming admirers again.

It was the song that was playing when I had my sudden moment of clarity in South Shields. Ever since I was a kid, I'd dreamed of being a musician. Those dreams had taken many forms: sometimes I was Little Richard, sometimes Jerry Lee Lewis, sometimes Ray Charles. But whatever form they had taken, none of them had involved standing onstage in a supper club outside of Newcastle, not playing a Vox Continental organ, while Long John Baldry alternately crooned to the accompaniment of a tape recorder and angrily threatened to fine members of the audience fifty pounds. And yet, here I was. Much as I loved John, I had to do something else.

The thing was, I wasn't exactly swimming in other options. I didn't have a clue what I wanted to do, or even what I could do. I knew I could sing and play piano, but I clearly wasn't pop star material. For one thing, I didn't look like a pop star, as evidenced by my inability to carry off a kaftan. For another, I was called Reg Dwight. That's not a pop star's name. 'Tonight on *Top of the Pops*, the new single by . . . Reg Dwight!' It obviously wasn't going to happen. The other members of Bluesology, they had the kind of names you could imagine being announced on *Top of the Pops*. Stuart Brown. Pete Gavin. Elton Dean. Elton Dean! Even the sax player sounded more like a pop star than me, and he had absolutely no desire to be one: he was a serious jazz buff, killing time with Bluesology until he could start honking away in some free impro-visational quintet.

Of course I could change my name, but what was the point? After all, not only did I think I wasn't pop star material, I'd liter-ally been told I wasn't pop star material. A few months before, I'd auditioned for Liberty Records. They had put an advert in the *New Musical Express*: LIBERTY RECORDS WANTS TALENT.

But, as it turned out, not my talent. I'd gone to see a guy there called Ray Williams, played for him, even recorded a couple of songs in a little studio. Ray thought I had potential, but no one else at the label did: thanks but no thanks. So that was that.

In fact, I had precisely one other option. When I'd auditioned for Liberty, I'd told Ray that I could write songs, or at least half write songs. I could write music and melodies, but not lyrics. I'd tried in Bluesology and the results could still cause me to wake up at night in a cold sweat: 'We could be such a happy pair, and I promise to do my share'. Almost as an afterthought, or a consolation prize after rejecting me, Ray had handed me an envelope. Someone responding to the same advert had sent in some lyrics. I had a feeling Ray hadn't actually read any of them before he passed them on to me.

The guy who wrote them came from Owmby-by-Spital in Lincolnshire, hardly the pulsating rock and roll capital of the world. He apparently worked on a chicken farm, carting dead birds around in a wheelbarrow. But his lyrics were pretty good. Esoteric, a bit Tolkien-influenced, not unlike 'A Whiter Shade Of Pale' by Procol Harum. Crucially, none of them made me want to rip my own head off with embarrassment, which meant they were a vast improvement on anything I'd come up with.

What's more, I found I could write music to them, and I could write it really fast. Something about them just seemed to click with me. And something about him just seemed to click with me, too. He came down to London, we went for a coffee and we hit it off straight away. It turned out that Bernie Taupin wasn't a country bumpkin at all. He was extremely sophisticated for a seventeen-year-old: long-haired, very handsome, very well read, a huge Bob Dylan fan. So we'd started writing songs together, or rather, not together. He would send me the lyrics from Lincolnshire, I'd write the music at home, in my mum and step-dad's flat in Northwood Hills. We'd come up with dozens of songs that way. Admittedly, we hadn't actually managed to get any other artists to buy the bloody things yet, and if we committed to it full-time, we'd be broke. But other than money, what did we have to lose? A wheelbarrow full of dead chickens and 'Let The Heartaches Begin' twice a night, respectively.

I told John and Bluesology I was leaving after a gig in Scotland, in December. It was fine, no hard feelings: like I said, John was an incredibly generous man. On the flight home, I decided I should change my name after all. For some reason, I remember thinking I had to come up with something else really quickly. I suppose it was all symbolic of a clean break and a fresh start: no more Bluesology, no more Reg Dwight. As I was in a hurry, I settled for pinching other people's names. Elton from Elton Dean, John from Long John Baldry. Elton John. Elton John and Bernie Taupin. *Songwriting duo* Elton John and Bernie Taupin. I thought it sounded good. Unusual. Striking. I announced my decision to my now ex-bandmates on the bus back from Heathrow. They all fell about laughing, then wished me the best of luck.

one

It was my mum who introduced me to Elvis Presley. Every Friday, after work, she would pick up her wages, stop off on the way home at Siever's, an electrical store that also sold records, and buy a new 78. It was my favourite time of the week, waiting at home to see what she would bring back. She loved going out dancing, so she liked big band music – Billy May and His Orchestra, Ted Heath – and she loved American vocalists: Johnnie Ray, Frankie Laine, Nat King Cole, Guy Mitchell singing 'she wears red feathers and a huly-huly skirt'. But one Friday she came home with something else. She told me she'd never heard anything like it before, but it was so fantastic she had to buy it. As soon as she said the words Elvis Presley, I recognized them. The previous weekend I'd been looking through the magazines in the local barber shop while I was waiting to have my hair cut, when I came across a photo of the most bizarre-looking man I'd ever seen. Everything about him looked extraordinary: his clothes, his hair, even the way he was standing. Compared to the people you could see outside the barber shop window in the north-west London suburb of Pinner, he might as well have been bright green with antennae sticking out of his forehead. I'd been so transfixed I hadn't even bothered to read the accompanying article, and by the time I got home I'd forgotten his name. But that was it: Elvis Presley.

As soon as Mum put the record on, it became apparent that Elvis Presley sounded the way he looked, like he came from another planet. Compared to the stuff my parents normally listened to, 'Heartbreak Hotel' barely qualified as music at all, an opinion my father would continue to expound upon at great length over the coming years. I'd already heard rock and roll – 'Rock Around The Clock' had been a big hit earlier in 1956 – but 'Heartbreak Hotel' didn't sound anything like that either. It was raw and sparse and slow and eerie. Everything was drenched in this weird echo. You could barely understand a word he was singing: I got that his baby had left him, after that I completely lost the thread. What was a 'dess clurk'? Who was this 'Bidder Sir Lonely' he kept mentioning?

It didn't matter what he was saying, because something almost physical happened while he was singing. You could literally *feel* this strange energy he was giving off, like it was contagious, like it was coming out of the radiogram speaker straight into your body. I already thought of myself as music mad – I even had a little collection of my own 78s, paid for with record tokens and postal orders I got on birthdays and at Christmas. Until that moment, my hero had been Winifred Atwell, a big, immensely jolly Trinidadian lady who performed onstage with two pianos – a baby grand on which she played light classical and a battered old upright for ragtime and pub songs. I loved her sense of glee, the slightly camp way she would announce, 'And now, I'm going to my *other* piano'; the way she would lean back and look at the audience with a huge grin on her face while she was playing, like she was having the best time in the world. I thought Winifred Atwell was fabulous, but I'd never experienced anything like *this* while listening to her. I'd never experienced anything like this in my life. As 'Heartbreak Hotel' played, it felt like something had changed, that nothing could really be the same again. As it turned out, something had, and nothing was.

And thank God, because the world needed changing. I grew up in fifties Britain and, before Elvis, before rock and roll, fifties Britain was a pretty grim place. I didn't mind living in Pinner – I've never been one of those rock stars who was motivated by a burning desire to escape the suburbs, I quite liked it there – but the whole country was in a bad place. It was furtive and fearful and judgemental. It was a world of people peeping around their curtains with sour expressions, of girls being sent away because they'd Got Into Trouble. When I think of fifties Britain, I think of sitting on the stairs of our house, listening to my mum's brother, Uncle Reg, trying to talk her out of getting divorced from my dad: 'You can't get divorced! What will people think?' At one point, I distinctly remember him using the phrase 'what will the neighbours say?' It wasn't Uncle Reg's fault. That was just the mindset of the times: that happiness was somehow less important than keeping up appearances.

The truth is that my parents should never have got married in the first place. I was born in 1947, but I was effectively a war baby. I must have been conceived while my father was on leave from the RAF – he had joined up in 1942 at the height of World War Two and elected to stay on after the war ended. And my parents were definitely a war couple. Their story sounds romantic. They met the same year my dad joined up. He was seventeen, and had worked in a boatbuilding yard in Rickmansworth that specialized in making narrowboats for canals. Mum was sixteen, her maiden name was Harris, and she delivered milk for United Dairies on a horse and cart, the kind of job a woman would never have done before the war. My dad was a keen amateur trumpet player, and while he was on leave, he apparently spotted my mum in the audience while he was sitting in with a band playing at a North Harrow hotel.

But the reality of Stanley and Sheila Dwight's marriage wasn't romantic at all. They just didn't get on. They were both stubborn and short-tempered, two delightful characteristics that it's been my huge good fortune to inherit. I'm not sure if they ever really loved each other. People rushed into marriage during the war – the future was uncertain, even by the time of my parents' wedding in January 1945, and you had to seize the moment – so maybe that had something to do with it. Perhaps they had loved each other once, or at least thought they had, in the time they snatched together. Now they didn't even seem to like each other. The rows were endless.

At least they subsided when my dad was away, which he often was. He was promoted to flight lieutenant, and was regularly posted abroad, to Iraq and Aden, so I grew up in a house that seemed to be filled with women. We lived with my maternal grandmother, Ivy, at 55 Pinner Hill Road – the same house I was born in. It was the kind of council house that had sprung up all over Britain in the twenties and thirties: three bedrooms, semi-detached, red brick on the ground floor and white-painted render on the top floor. The house actually had another male occupant, although you wouldn't really have noticed. My grandfather had died very young, of cancer, and Nan had remarried, to a guy called Horace Sewell, who'd lost a leg in World War One. Horace had a heart of gold, but he wasn't what you would call one of life's big talkers. He seemed to spend most of his time outside. He worked at the local nursery, Woodman's, and when he wasn't there, he was in the garden, where he grew all our vegetables and cut flowers.

Perhaps he was just in the garden to avoid my mother, in which case I couldn't really blame him. Even when Dad wasn't around, Mum had a terrible temper. When I think back to my childhood, I think of Mum's moods: awful, glowering, miserable silences that descended on the house without warning, during which you walked on eggshells and picked your words very carefully, in case you set her off and got thumped as a result. When she was happy she could be warm and charming and vivacious, but she always seemed to be looking for a reason not to be happy, always seemed to be in search of a fight, always had to have the last word; Uncle Reg famously said she could start an argument in an empty room. I thought for years that it was somehow my fault, that maybe she never really wanted to be a mother: she was only twenty-one when I was born, stuck in a marriage that clearly wasn't working, forced to live with her mum because money was so tight. But her sister, my auntie Win, told me she was always like that – that when they were kids it was as if a dark cloud used to follow Sheila Harris around, that other children were scared of her and that she seemed to like that.

She definitely had some deeply weird ideas about parenting. It was an era when you kept your kids in line by clobbering them, when it was generally held that there was nothing wrong with children that couldn't be cured by thumping the living daylights out of them. This was a philosophy to which my mother was passionately wedded, which was petrifying and humiliating if it happened in public: there's nothing like getting a hiding outside Pinner Sainsbury's, in front of a visibly intrigued crowd of onlookers, for playing havoc with your self-esteem. But some of Mum's behaviour would have been considered disturbing even by the standards of the time. I found out years later that when I was two, she'd toilet-trained me by hitting me with a wire brush until I bled if I didn't use the potty. My nan had, understandably, gone berserk when she found out what was going on: they didn't speak for weeks as a result. Nan had gone berserk again when she saw my mother's remedy for constipation. She laid me on the draining board in the kitchen and stuck carbolic soap up my arse. If she liked to scare people, she must have been overjoyed by me, because I was fucking terrified of her. I loved her – she was my mum – but I spent my childhood in a state of high alert, always trying to ensure that I never did anything that might set her off: if she was happy, I was happy, albeit temporarily.

There were no problems like that with my nan. She was the person I trusted the most. It felt like she was the centre of the family, the only one who didn't go out to work – my mum had graduated from driving a milk cart during the war to working in a succession of shops. Nan was one of those incredible old working-class matriarchs: no nonsense, hard-working, kind, funny. I idolized her. She was the greatest cook, had the greenest fingers, loved a drink and a game of cards. She'd had an incredibly hard life – her father had abandoned her mother when she was pregnant, so Nan was born in a workhouse. She never talked about it, but it seemed to have left her as someone nothing could faze, not even the time I came howling down the stairs with my foreskin caught in my trouser zip and asked her to get it out. She just sighed and got on with it, as though extracting a small boy's penis from a zip was the kind of thing she did every day.

Her house smelt of roast dinners and coal fires. There was always someone at the door: either Auntie Win or Uncle Reg, or my cousins John and Cathryn, or else the rent man, or the man from Watford Steam Laundry, or the man who delivered the coal. And there was always music playing. The radio was almost per-manently on: *Two-Way Family Favourites, Housewives' Choice, Music While You Work, The Billy Cotton Band Show*. If it wasn't, there were records playing on the radiogram – mostly jazz, but sometimes classical.

I could spend hours just looking at those records, studying the different labels. Blue Deccas, red Parlophones, bright yellow MGMs, HMVs and RCAs, both of which, for reasons I could never figure out, had that picture of the dog looking at the gramophone on them. They seemed like magical objects; the fact that you put a needle on them and sound mysteriously came out amazed me. After a while, the only presents I wanted were records and books.

I can remember the disappointment of coming downstairs and seeing a big box wrapped up. Oh God, they've got me Meccano.

And we had a piano, which belonged to my nan. Auntie Win used to play it, and eventually so did I. There were a lot of family myths about my prodigious talent at the instrument, the most oft-repeated being that Win sat me on her lap when I was three, and I immediately picked out the melody of 'The Skaters' Waltz' by ear. I've no idea whether that's actually true or not, but I was definitely playing piano at a very young age, around the time I started at my first school, Reddiford. I'd play stuff like 'All Things Bright and Beautiful', hymns I'd heard in assembly. I was just born with a good ear, the way some people are born with a photographic memory. If I heard something once, I could go to the piano and, more or less, play it perfectly. I was seven when I started lessons, with a lady called Mrs Jones. Not long after that, my parents began wheeling me out to play 'My Old Man Said Follow The Van' and 'Roll Out The Barrel' at family gatherings and weddings. For all the records in the house and on the radio, I think an old-fashioned sing-song was the form of music my family loved the most.

The piano came in useful when my dad was home on leave. He was a typical British man of the fifties in that he seemed to regard any display of emotion, other than anger, as evidence of a fatal weakness of character. So he wasn't tactile, he never told you he loved you. But he liked music, and if he heard me playing the piano, I'd get a 'well done', maybe an arm around the shoulder, a sense of pride and approval. I was temporarily in his good books. And keeping in his good books was vitally important to me. If I was marginally less terrified of him than I was of my mother, it was only because he wasn't around as much. At one point, when I was six, my mum had made the decision to move us away from Pinner and all her family, and go with my dad to Wiltshire – he had been posted to RAF Lyneham, near Swindon. I can't remember much about it. I know I enjoyed playing in the countryside, but I also recall feeling quite disorientated and confused by the change, and falling behind at school as a result. We weren't there for long – Mum must have realized she had made a mistake very quickly – and after we came back to Pinner, it felt like Dad was someone who visited rather than lived with us.

But when he did visit, things changed. Suddenly, there were all these new rules about everything. I would get into trouble if I kicked my football off the lawn into the flower bed, but I would also get in trouble if I ate celery in what was deemed to be The Wrong Way. The Right Way to eat celery, in the unlikely event that you're interested, was apparently not to make too loud a crunching sound when you bit into it. Once, he hit me because I was supposedly taking my school blazer off incorrectly; sadly, I seem to have forgotten The Right Way to take off a school blazer, vital though this knowledge obviously was. The scene upset Auntie Win so much that she rushed off in tears to tell my nan what was going on. Presumably worn down by the rows over potty training and constipation, Nan told her not to get involved.

What *was* going on? I haven't got a clue. I've no more idea of what my father's problem was than I have about my mother's. Maybe it had something to do with him being in the forces, where there were rules about everything as well. Maybe he felt a bit of jealousy, like he was shut out of the family because he was away so much: all these rules were his way of imposing himself as the head of the household. Maybe that was the way he had been brought up, although his parents – my grandad Edwin and grandma Ellen – didn't seem particularly fierce. Or maybe both my parents just found dealing with a child difficult because they'd never done it before. I don't know. I do know that my dad had an incredibly short fuse and that he didn't seem to understand how to use words. There was no calm response, no 'now come on, sit down'. He would just explode. The Dwight Family Temper. It was the bane of my life as a kid, and it remained the bane of my life when it became apparent it was hereditary. Either I was genetically predisposed to losing my rag, or I unconsciously learned by example. Whichever it was, it has proved a catastrophic pain in the arse for me and everyone around me for most of my adult life.

Had it not been for Mum and Dad, I would have had a perfectly normal, even boring fifties childhood: *Muffin the Mule* on TV and Saturday morning children's matinees at the Embassy in North Harrow; the Goons on the radio and bread and dripping for tea on a Sunday night. Away from home, I was perfectly happy. At eleven, I moved up to Pinner County Grammar School, where I was conspicuously ordinary. I wasn't bullied, nor was I a bully. I wasn't a swot, but I wasn't a tearaway either; I left that to my friend John Gates, who was one of those kids that seemed to spend their entire childhood in detention or outside the headmaster's office, without the range of punishments inflicted on him making any difference at all to the way he behaved. I was a bit overweight, but I was all right at sport without any danger of being a star athlete. I played football and tennis – everything except rugby. Because of my size, they put me in the scrum, where my main role involved being repeatedly kicked in the balls by the opposing team's prop. No thanks.

My best mate was Keith Francis, but he was part of a big circle of friends, girls as well as boys, people I still see now. I occasionally have class reunions at my house. The first time, I was really nervous beforehand: it's been fifty years, I'm famous, I live in a big house, what are they going to think of me? But they couldn't have cared less. When they arrived, it might as well have been 1959. No one seemed to have changed that much. John Gates still had a twinkle in his eye that suggested he could be a bit of a handful.

For years, I lived a life in which nothing really happened. The height of excitement was a school trip to Annecy, where we stayed with our French pen pals and gawped at the sight of Citroën

2CVs, which were like no car I'd ever seen on a British road – the seats in them looked like deckchairs. Or the day during the Easter holidays when, for reasons lost in the mists of time, Barry Walden, Keith and I elected to cycle from Pinner to Bournemouth, an idea I began to question the wisdom of when I realized that their bikes had gears and mine did not: there was a lot of frantic pedalling up hills on my part, trying to keep up. The only danger any of us faced was that one of my friends might be bored to death when I started talking about records. It wasn't enough for me to collect them. Every time I bought one, I kept a note of it in a book. I wrote down the titles of the A and B sides and all the other information off the label: writer, publisher, producer. I then memorized the lot, until I became a walking musical encyclopedia. An innocent enquiry as to why the needle skipped when you tried to play 'Little Darlin'' by The Diamonds would lead to me informing everyone within earshot that it was because 'Little Darlin'' by The Diamonds was on Mercury Records, who were distributed by Pye in the UK, and that Pye were the only label that released 78s made from new-fangled vinyl, rather than old-fashioned shellac, and needles made from shellac responded differently to vinyl.

But I'm not complaining at all about life being dull – I liked it that way. Things were so exhausting at home that a dull life outside the front door seemed oddly welcome, particularly when my parents decided to try living together full-time again. It was just after I started at Pinner County. My dad had been posted to RAF Medmenham in Buckinghamshire and we all moved into a house in Northwood, about ten minutes away from Pinner, 111 Potter Street. We were there for three years, long enough to prove beyond any doubt that the marriage wasn't working. God, it was miserable: constant fighting, occasionally punctuated by icy silences. You couldn't relax for a minute. If you spend your life waiting for the next eruption of anger from your mum, or your dad announcing another rule that you'd broken, you end up not knowing what to do: the uncertainty of what's going to happen next fills you with fear. So I was incredibly insecure, scared of my own shadow. On top of that, I thought I was somehow responsible for the state of my parents' marriage, because a lot of their rows would be about me. My father would tell me off, my mother would intervene, and there would be a huge argument about how I was being brought up. It didn't make me feel very good about myself, which manifested in a lack of confidence in my appearance that lasted well into adulthood. For years and years, I couldn't bear to look at myself in the mirror. I really hated what I saw: I was too fat, I was too short, my face just looked weird, my hair would never do what I wanted it to, including not prematurely fall out. The other lasting effect was a fear of confrontation. That went on for decades. I stayed in bad business relationships and bad personal relationships because I didn't want to rock the boat.

My response when things got too much was always to run upstairs and lock the door, which is exactly what I used to do when my parents fought. I would go to my bedroom, where I kept everything perfectly neat and ordered. It wasn't just records I collected, it was comics, books, magazines. I was meticulous about everything. If I wasn't writing down the details of a new single in my notebook, I was copying all the different singles charts out of *Melody Maker*, the *New Musical Express*, *Record Mirror* and *Disc*, then compiling the results, averaging them out into a personal chart of charts. I've always been a statistics freak. Even now, I get sent the charts every day, the radio chart positions in America, the box office charts for films and Broadway plays. Most artists don't do that; they're not interested. When I'm talking to them, I know more about how their single's doing than they do, which is crazy. The official excuse is that I need to know what's going on because, these days, I own a company that makes films and manages artists. The truth is that I'd be doing it if I was working in a bank. I'm just an anorak.

A psychologist would probably say that, as a kid, I was trying to create a sense of order in a chaotic life, with my dad coming and going and all the reprimands and rows. I didn't have any control over that, or over my mother's moods, but I had control over the stuff in my room. Objects couldn't do me any harm. I found them comforting. I talked to them, I behaved as if they had feelings. If something got broken, I'd feel really upset, as if I'd killed something. During one particularly bad row, my mother threw a record at my father and it smashed into God knows how many pieces. It was 'The Robin's Return' by Dolores Ventura, an Australian ragtime pianist. I remember thinking, 'How can you do that? How can you break this beautiful thing?'

My record collection exploded when rock 'n' roll arrived. There were other exciting changes afoot, things that suggested life might be moving on, out of the grey post-war world, even in suburban north-west London: the arrival in our house of a TV and a washing machine, and the arrival in Pinner High Street of a coffee bar, which seemed unimaginably exotic – until a restaurant that served Chinese food opened in nearby Harrow. But they happened slowly and gradually, a few years between them. Rock 'n' roll wasn't like that. It seemed to come out of nowhere, so fast that it was hard to take in how completely it had altered everything. One minute, pop music meant good old Guy Mitchell and 'Where Will The Dimple Be?' and Max Bygraves singing about toothbrushes. It was polite and schmaltzy and aimed at parents, who didn't want to hear anything too exciting or shocking: they'd had enough of that to last them a lifetime living through a war. The next, it meant Jerry Lee Lewis and Little Richard, these guys who sounded unintelligible, like they were foaming at the mouth when they sang and who your parents hated. Even my mum, the Elvis aficionado, bailed out when Little Richard showed up. She thought 'Tutti Frutti' was just a terrible noise.

Rock and roll was like a bomb that wouldn't stop going off: a series of explosions that came so thick and fast it was hard to work out what was happening. Suddenly, there seemed to be one incredible record after another. 'Hound Dog', 'Blue Suede Shoes', 'Whole Lotta Shakin' Goin' On', 'Long Tall Sally', 'That'll Be The Day', 'Roll Over Beethoven', 'Reet Petite'. I had to get a Saturday job to keep up. Luckily, Mr Megson at Victoria Wine was looking for someone to help out in the back of the shop, putting empty beer bottles in crates and stacking them up. I think there was a vague idea of my saving up some money, but I should have realized that idea was doomed to failure from the start: Victoria Wine was next door to another record shop. Mr Megson might as well have just put the ten bob he paid me straight into their till and cut out the middleman. It was an early example of what turned out to be a lifelong attitude to shopping: I'm just not very good at keeping money in my pocket if there's something I want to buy.

Sixty years on, it's hard to explain how revolutionary and shocking rock and roll seemed. Not just the music: the whole culture it represented, the clothes and the films and the attitude. It felt like the first thing that teenagers really owned, that was aimed exclusively at us, that made us feel different from our parents, that made us feel we could *achieve* something. It's also hard to explain the extent to which the older generation despised it. Take every example of moral panic pop music has provoked since – punk and gangster rap, mods and rockers and heavy metal – then add them all together and double it: that's how much outrage rock and roll caused. People fucking *hated* it. And no one hated it more than my father. He obviously disliked the music itself – he liked Frank Sinatra – but more than that, he hated its social impact, he thought the whole thing was morally wrong: 'Look at the way they dress, the way they act, swivelling their hips, showing their dicks. You are *not* to get involved.' If I did, I was going to turn into something called a wide boy. A wide boy, in case you don't know, is an old British term for a kind of petty criminal – a confidence trickster, someone who does a bit of wheeler-dealing or runs the odd scam. Presumably already alive to the thought that I might go off the rails thanks to my inability to eat celery in the correct way, he resolutely believed that rock and roll was going to result in my utter degradation. The mere mention of Elvis or Little Richard would set him off on an angry lecture in which my inevitable transformation into a wide boy figured heavily: one minute I'd be happily listening to 'Good Golly Miss Molly', the next thing you knew, I was apparently going to be fencing stolen nylons or duping people into playing Find-the-Lady on the mean streets of Pinner.

There didn't seem much danger of that happening to me – there are Benedictine monks wilder than I was as a teenager – but my father was taking no risks. By the time I started at Pinner County Grammar School in 1958, you could see the way people dressed was changing, but I was expressly forbidden from wearing anything that made me look like I had some connection to rock and roll. Keith Francis was cutting a dash in a pair of winkle-picker shoes that had pointed toes so long the ends of them seemed to arrive in class several minutes before he did. I was still dressed like a miniature version of my father. My shoes were, depressingly, the same length as my feet. The closest I got to sartorial rebellion was my prescription glasses, or rather, how much I wore my prescription glasses. They were only supposed to be used for looking at the blackboard. Labouring under the demented misapprehension that they made me look like Buddy Holly, I wore them all the time, completely ruining my eyesight in the process. Then I had to wear them all the time.

My failing eyesight also had unexpected consequences when it came to sexual exploration. I can't remember the exact circumstances in which my dad caught me masturbating. I think I was attempting to dispose of the evidence rather than engaged in the act itself, but I do remember I wasn't as mortified as I should have been, largely because I didn't really know what I was doing. I was a real late developer when it came to sex. I wasn't really interested in it at all until I was well into my twenties, although I made an impressively concerted effort to make up for lost time after that. But at school, I'd listen to my friends talking about it, and it would just leave me really bemused: 'Yeah, I took her to the cinema, got a bit of tit.' How? Why? What was that supposed to mean?

So I think what I was doing was more about experiencing a pleasant sensation rather than a frantic expression of my burgeoning sexuality. Either way, when my dad caught me, he came out with the well-worn line about how if I kept Doing That, I would go blind. Obviously, boys across the country were given exactly the same warning, realized it was a load of rubbish and blithely ignored it. I, on the other hand, found it preying on my mind. What if it was true? I'd already damaged my eyesight with my misguided attempt to look like Buddy Holly; maybe this would finish it off. I decided it was better not to take the risk. While plenty of musicians will tell you that Buddy Holly had a massive impact on their lives, I'm probably the only musician that can say he inadvertently stopped me wanking, unless Holly happened to walk in on The Big Bopper doing it while they were on tour or something.

But despite all the rules about clothes and warnings about my sure-fire descent into criminality, it was too late for my dad to tell me not to get involved in rock and roll. I was already in it up to my neck. I saw *Loving You* and *The Girl Can't Help It* at the cinema. I started going to see live shows. A big crowd from school headed up to the Harrow Granada every week: me, Keith, Kaye Midlane, Barry Walden and Janet Richie were the most devoted, regular members, along with a guy called Michael Johnson, who was the only person I'd met who seemed just as obsessed as me about music. Sometimes, he even seemed to know things I didn't. A couple of years later, it was he who came to school brandishing a copy of 'Love Me Do' by The Beatles, whoever they were, claiming that they were going to be the biggest thing since Elvis. I thought that was laying it on a bit thick until he played it to me, when I decided he might have a point: another musical obsession was sparked.

A ticket for the Granada was two and sixpence or five bob if you wanted the posh seats. Either felt like good value, because they packed the shows with singers and bands. You would see ten artists in a night: two songs from each until the headlining act, who would do four or five. Everybody seemed to play there, sooner or later. Little Richard, Gene Vincent, Jerry Lee Lewis, Eddie Cochran, Johnny And The Hurricanes. If by any chance someone declined to grace the Harrow Granada with their presence, you could get the tube up to London: that's where I saw Cliff Richard And The Drifters at the Palladium, before his backing band changed their name to The Shadows. Back in the suburbs, other, smaller venues started putting on bands: the South Harrow British Legion, the Kenton Conservative Club. You could easily see two or three gigs a week, as long as you had the money. The funny thing is, I can't recall ever seeing a bad gig, or coming home disappointed, although some of the shows must have been terrible. The sound must have been dreadful. I'm pretty certain that the South Harrow British Legion in 1960 wasn't in possession of a PA system capable of fully conveying the brutal, feral power of rock and roll.

And when my dad wasn't around, I played Little Richard and Jerry Lee Lewis songs on the piano. They were my real idols. It wasn't just their style of playing, although that was fabulous: they played with such aggression, like they were assaulting the keyboard. It was the way they stood up while they played, the way they kicked the stool and jumped on the piano. They made playing the piano seem as visually exciting and sexy and outrageous as playing the guitar or being a vocalist. I'd never realized it could be any of those things before.

I was inspired enough to play a few gigs at local youth clubs, with a band called The Corvettes. It was nothing serious; the other members were all still at school too – they went to Northwood, the local secondary modern – and it only lasted a few months: most of the gigs we played, we got paid in Coca-Cola. But suddenly, I had an idea what I wanted to do with my life and it didn't involve my father's plans for me, which centred around either joining the RAF or working in a bank. I would never have dared say it aloud, but I quietly decided he could stick both those plans up his arse. Maybe rock and roll had changed me in the rebellious way Dad feared after all.

Or maybe we never really had anything in common, except football. All the happy childhood memories of my dad are related to that: he came from a family of football fanatics. Two of his nephews were professional players, both for Fulham in south-west London – Roy Dwight and John Ashen. As a treat, he would take me to watch them from the touchline at Craven Cottage, in the days when Jimmy Hill was their inside right and Bedford Jezzard was their highest scorer. Even off the pitch, Roy and John seemed like incredibly glamorous figures to me; I was always slightly in awe when I met them. After his career ended, John became a very astute businessman with a thing for American cars – he'd turn up to visit us in Pinner with his wife, Bet, parking an unreal-looking Cadillac or a Chevrolet outside the house. And Roy was a fantastic player, a right-winger who transferred to Nottingham Forest. He played for them in the 1959 FA Cup Final. I watched it at home on TV, with a supply of chocolate eggs I'd saved from Easter in anticipation of this momentous event. I didn't eat the chocolate so much as cram it in my mouth in a state of hysteria. I couldn't believe what was happening on the screen. After ten minutes, Roy scored the opening goal. He was already on the verge of a call-up for England. Now he'd surely sealed his fate: my cousin – *an actual relative of mine* – was going to play for England. It seemed as unbelievable as John's taste in cars. Fifteen minutes later, they were carrying him off on a stretcher. He'd broken his leg in a tackle and *that* was what sealed his fate. His football career was basically over. He tried, but he was never the same player again. He ended up becoming a PE teacher at a boys' school in south London.

My dad's team were the substantially less glamorous and awe-inducing Watford. I was six when he first took me to see them play. They were toiling away at the bottom of something called the Third Division South, which was as low as you could get in the football league without being thrown out entirely. In fact, not long before I started going to Watford games, they had played so badly that they actually had been thrown out of the football league; they were allowed to stay after applying for re-election. Their ground at Vicarage Road seemed to tell you all you needed to know about the team. It only had two very old, very rickety, very small covered stands. It doubled as a greyhound racing track. If I'd had any sense, I would have taken one look at it, considered Watford's recent form, and opted to support a team that could actually play football. I could have saved myself twenty years of almost unmitigated misery. But football doesn't work like that, or at least it shouldn't. It's in your blood: Watford were my dad's team, therefore Watford were my team.

And besides, I didn't care about the ground, or the hopelessness of the team, or the freezing cold. I loved it all straight away. The thrill of seeing live sport for the first time, the excitement of getting the train to Watford and walking through the town to the ground, the newspaper sellers that came round at half-time and told you the scores in other games, the ritual of always standing in the same spot on the terraces, an area by the Shrodells Stand called The Bend. It was like taking a drug to which you instantly became addicted. I was as obsessive about football as I was about music: when I wasn't compiling my chart of charts in my bedroom, I was cutting football league ladders out of my comics, sticking them to my wall and making sure the scores on them were completely up to date. It's one addiction I've never shaken, because I've never wanted to, and it was hereditary, passed on to me by my dad.

When I was eleven, my piano teacher had put me forward for the Royal Academy of Music in central London. I passed the exam, and for the next five years that was my Saturday: studying classical music in the morning, Watford in the afternoon. I preferred the latter to the former. At the time, the Royal Academy of Music seemed to smell of fear. Everything about it was intimidating: the huge, imposing Edwardian building on Marylebone Road, its august history of turning out composers and conductors, the fact that anything that wasn't classical music was expressly forbidden. It's completely different today – whenever I go there now, it's a really joyful place; the students are encouraged to go off and do pop or jazz or their own writing as well as their classical training. But back then, even talking about rock and roll at the Royal Academy would have been sacrilege, like turning up to church and telling the vicar that you're really interested in worshipping Satan.

Sometimes the Royal Academy was fun. I had a great teacher called Helen Piena, I loved singing in the choir and I really enjoyed playing Mozart and Bach and Beethoven and Chopin, the melodic stuff. Other times, it seemed like a real drag. I was a lazy student. Some weeks, if I'd forgotten to do my homework, I didn't bother to turn up at all. I'd ring from home, putting on a voice and saying I was ill, and then – so my mum didn't realize I was dodging – take the train up to Baker Street. Then I'd go and sit on the tube. I'd go round and round the Circle Line for three and a half hours, reading *The Pan Book of Horror Stories* instead of practising Bartók. I knew I didn't want to be a classical musician. For one thing, I wasn't good enough. I don't have the hands for it. My fingers are short for a piano player. If you see a photo of a concert pianist, they've all got hands like tarantulas. And for another, it just wasn't what I wanted out of music – having everything regimented, playing the right notes at the right time with the right feeling, no room for improvisation.

In a way, it's ironic that I ended up being made a Doctor and an Honorary Member of the Royal Academy years later – I was never going to win an award for star pupil while I was there. But in another way, it isn't ironic at all. I'd never, ever say the Royal Academy was a waste of time for me. I'm really proud to have gone there. I've done benefit gigs and raised money for a new pipe organ for them; I've toured with the Royal Academy Symphony Orchestra in Britain and America; I pay for eight scholarships there every year. The place was full of people I'd end up working with, years later, when I became Elton John: the producer Chris Thomas, the arranger Paul Buckmaster, harpist Skaila Kanga and percussionist Ray Cooper. And what I learned there seeped into my music: it taught me about collaboration, about chord structures and how to put a song together. It made me interested in writing with more than three or four chords. If you listen to the *Elton John* album, and virtually every album I made afterwards, you can hear the influence of classical music and of the Royal Academy on it somewhere.

It was while I was studying at the Royal Academy that my parents finally got divorced. In fairness to them, they had tried to make their marriage work, even though it was obvious they couldn't bear each other; I suspect because they wanted to give me stability. It was completely the wrong thing to do, but they made an effort. Then, in 1960, my father was posted to Harrogate in Yorkshire, and while he was there, Mum met someone else. And that was the end of that.

My mum and I moved in with her new partner, Fred, who was a painter and decorator. It was a really hard time financially. Fred was a divorcee too; he had an ex-wife and four children, so money was really tight. We lived in a horrible flat in Croxley Green, with peeling wallpaper and damp. Fred worked really hard. He did window cleaning and odd jobs on top of his decorating: anything to make sure we had food on the table. It was tough on him and it was tough on my mum. Uncle Reg had been right – there really was a stigma around getting divorced in those days.

But I was so happy they'd got divorced. The daily friction of my mum and dad being together was gone. Mum had got what she wanted – rid of my father – and, for a while at least, it seemed to change her. She was happy, and that happiness trickled down to me. There were fewer moods, less criticism. And I really liked Fred. He was generous and big-hearted and easy-going. He saved up and got me a drop-handlebar bike. He thought it was funny when I started saying his name backwards and calling him Derf, a nickname that stuck. There weren't any more restrictions on what I wore. I started calling Derf my stepdad years before he and Mum got married.

Best of all, Derf liked rock and roll. He and Mum were really supportive of my music career. I suppose there was an added incentive for my mum, because she knew that encouraging me would infuriate my father, but, for a while at least, she seemed to be my biggest fan. And Derf got me my first paying gig, as a pianist in the Northwood Hills Hotel, which wasn't a hotel at all, it was a pub. Derf was having a pint there when he learned from the landlord that their regular pianist had quit, and suggested they give me a try. I would play everything I could think of. Jim Reeves songs, Johnnie Ray, Elvis Presley, 'Whole Lotta Shakin' Goin' On'. Al Jolson numbers: they loved Al Jolson. But not as much as they loved old British pub songs that everyone could sing along to: 'Down At The Old Bull And Bush', 'Any Old Iron', 'My Old Man', the same things my family liked to have a sing-song to after a couple of drinks. I made really good money. My pay was only a pound a night, three nights a week, but Derf would come with me and take a pint pot around and collect tips. Sometimes I could end up with £15 a week, which was a massive amount for a fifteen-year-old kid to be making in the early sixties. I saved up and bought an electric piano – a Hohner Pianette – and a microphone so I could make myself better heard over the noise of the pub.

As well as earning me money, the pub pianist's job had another important function. It made me pretty fearless as a performer, because the Northwood Hills Hotel was by no stretch of the imagination Britain's most salubrious venue. I played in the public bar, not the more upscale saloon next door, and virtually every night, when enough booze had been consumed, there would be a fight. I don't mean a verbal altercation, I mean a proper fight: glasses flying, tables being pushed over. At first I'd try and keep playing, in the vain hope that music might soothe the situation. If a burst of 'Bye Bye Blackbird' failed to work the intended magic, then I would have to turn to a group of travellers who regularly came to the pub for help. I'd become friendly with one of their daughters – she'd even asked me around to their caravan for dinner – and they would make sure I was all right when the pub kicked off. And if they weren't in that night, I would have to deploy my last resort option. This involved climbing out of the window next to the piano and coming back later when things had calmed down. It was terrifying, but at least it made me mentally tough when it came to playing live. I know artists who've been completely destroyed by the experience of playing a bad gig to an unappreciative audience. I've played bad gigs to unappreciative audiences as well, but they've never impacted on me too deeply. If I don't actually have to stop performing and climb out of a window in fear of my life, it's still an improvement on how I started out.

Up in Yorkshire, my dad met a woman called Edna. They got married, moved to Essex and opened a paper shop. He must have been happier – they had four more sons, all of whom adored him – but he didn't seem any different to me. It was like he didn't know any other way to behave around me. He was still distant and strict, still moaning about the terrible influence of rock and roll, still consumed by the idea that I was going to turn into a wide boy and bring disgrace on the Dwight family name. Getting on the Green Line bus to Essex to visit him was the reliable low point of any week. I stopped going to Watford with him: I was old enough to stand on The Bend by myself.

Dad must have gone berserk when he found out I was planning on leaving school before sitting my A-levels, to take up a job in the music business. He really didn't think it was a suitable career for a boy with a grammar school education. To make matters worse, it was his own nephew who got me the job: my cousin Roy, he of the goal in the FA Cup, who had stayed on good terms with my mum after the divorce. Footballers always seemed to have links with the music industry and he was friends with a guy called Tony Hiller, who was the general manager of the Mills Music publishing company in Denmark Street, Britain's answer to Tin Pan Alley. Via Roy, I found out that there was a job going in the packing department – it wasn't much, the pay was £4 a week, but it was a foot in the door. And I knew I had no chance of passing my A-levels anyway. Somewhere between the Royal Academy, practising playing the piano like Jerry Lee Lewis and climbing out of the window of the Northwood Hills Hotel on a regular basis, my schoolwork had started to slide.

I say he must have gone berserk, because I honestly can't remember his reaction. I know he wrote to my mum demanding that she stop me, but you can imagine how that went down: she was absolutely delighted. Everyone else seemed pleased for me – Mum and Derf, even my school headmaster, which seemed almost miraculous. Mr Westgate-Smith was a very stern, strict man. I was absolutely terrified when I went to see him, to explain about the job. But he was really wonderful. He said he knew how much I loved music, he knew about the Royal Academy, and that he would let me leave if I promised to work hard and give everything I had to the project. I was amazed, but he meant it.

He could easily have refused; I would have gone anyway, but I would have left school under a cloud. Instead he was really supportive. Years later, after I became successful, he used to write to me telling me how proud he was of what I'd done.

And in a perverse way, my dad's attitude helped me, too. He never changed his mind about my career choice. He never said well done. Not long ago, his wife Edna wrote to me and told me that he was proud of me in his own way; it just wasn't in his make-up to express it. But the fact that he never expressed it instilled in me a desire to show him that I'd made the right decision. It made me driven. I thought the more successful I got, the more it proved him wrong, whether he acknowledged it or not. Even today, I still sometimes think that I'm trying to show my father what I'm made of, and he's been dead since 1991.

two

With perfect timing, I arrived at my first job in Denmark Street just as Denmark Street went into terminal decline. Ten years before, it had been the centre of the British music industry, where writers went to sell their songs to publishers, who'd in turn sell them to artists. Then The Beatles and Bob Dylan had come along and changed everything. They didn't need the help of professional songwriters: it turned out they *were* professional songwriters. More bands started appearing with a songwriter in their ranks: The Kinks, The Who, The Rolling Stones. It was obvious that was how things were going to be from now on. There was still just about enough work to keep Denmark Street going – not every new band could write their own material and there was still an army of vocalists and easy-listening crooners who sourced their songs the old-fashioned way – but the writing was on the wall.

Even my new job at Mills Music seemed like a throwback to a bygone era. It had nothing to do with pop at all. My duties consisted of parcelling up sheet music for brass bands and taking the packages to the post office opposite the Shaftesbury Theatre. I wasn't even in the main building: the packing department was round the back. That it couldn't have been less glamorous was underlined when Chelsea's star midfielder Terry Venables and a handful of his teammates unexpectedly turned up there one afternoon. They were being pursued by the press – there was a scandal at the time about them going out drinking after a game against the manager's orders – and had opted to hide out in my new workplace. They knew Mills Music well – they were footballing friends, like my cousin Roy – and had clearly realized that the packing department was literally the last place in London you would look if you were searching for someone famous.

But I had a ball. It was a foot in the door of the music industry. And even if Denmark Street was on its last legs, it still held a magic for me. There was a kind of glamour there, albeit fading glamour. There were guitar shops and recording studios. You would get your lunch at the Gioconda coffee bar or the Lancaster Grill on Charing Cross Road. You wouldn't see anybody famous in there – they were restaurants for people who couldn't afford any better – but there was a buzz about them: they were full of hopefuls, would-bes, would-never-bes, people who wanted to be spotted. People, I suppose, like me.

Back in Pinner, my mum, Derf and I had moved out of the rented flat in Croxley Green, with the damp and the peeling wallpaper, into a new place, a few miles away in Northwood Hills, not far from the pub whose window I'd scrambled out of on a regular basis. Frome Court looked like an ordinary detached suburban house from the outside, but inside it was divided up into two-bedroom flats. Ours was 3A. It felt like a home, unlike our previous residence, which had felt like a punishment for Mum and Derf both getting divorced: you've done something wrong, so you have to live here. And I was playing the electric piano I'd bought with the proceeds from my pub gig in a new band, started by another ex-member of The Corvettes, Stuart Brown. Bluesology were much more serious. We had ambition: Stuart was a really good-looking guy, convinced he was going to be a star. We had a saxophone player. We had a set full of obscure blues tracks by Jimmy Witherspoon and J. B. Lenoir that we rehearsed in a Northwood pub called the Gate. We even had a manager, a Soho jeweller called Arnold Tendler: our drummer, Mick Inkpen, worked for him. Arnold was a sweet little man who wanted to get into the music business, and had the terrible misfortune to pick Bluesology as his big investment opportunity after Mick convinced him to come and see a gig. He sank his money into equipment for us and stage outfits – identical polo neck jumpers, trousers and shoes – and got absolutely no return, unless you counted us constantly moaning at him when things went wrong.

We started playing gigs around London, and Arnold paid for us to record a demo at a studio in a prefabricated hut in Rickmansworth. By some miracle, Arnold managed to get the demo to Fontana Records. More miraculous still, they put out a single, a song I'd written – or rather, the only song I'd written – called 'Come Back Baby'. It did absolutely nothing. It was played a couple of times on the radio, I suspect on the less salubrious pirate stations where they would play anything if the record label bunged them some dosh. There was a rumour it was going to be on *Juke Box Jury* one week, and we duly crowded round the television. It wasn't on *Juke Box Jury*. Then we put out another single, also written by me, called 'Mr Frantic'. This time, there wasn't even a rumour it was going to be on *Juke Box Jury*. It just vanished.

Towards the end of 1965, we got a job with Roy Tempest, an agent who specialized in bringing black American artists over to Britain. He had a fish tank full of piranhas in his office, and his business practices were as sharp as their teeth. If he couldn't get The Temptations or The Drifters to cross the Atlantic, he would find a handful of unknown black singers in London, put them in suits and book them on a nightclub tour, billed as The Temptin' Temptations or The Fabulous Drifters. When anyone complained, he would feign ignorance: 'Of course they're not The Temptations!

They're The Temptin' Temptations! Completely different band!'
So Roy Tempest effectively invented the tribute act.

In a sense, Bluesology got off lightly in their dealings with him.
At least the artists for whom we were employed as a backing band
were the real thing: Major Lance, Patti LaBelle And The Blue
Belles, Fontella Bass, Lee Dorsey. And the work meant I could
stop parcelling up brass band music for a living and become a
professional musician. I didn't really have a choice. There was no
way I could hold down a day job and work to the schedule of gigs
that Tempest set up. Unfortunately, the pay was terrible. Bluesology
got fifteen quid a week, out of which we had to pay for petrol for
the van and food and lodgings: if you played too far away from
London to drive home after the gig, you would book into a B&B
at five bob a night. I'm sure the stars we were backing weren't
getting much more. The workload was punishing. Up and down
the motorway, night after night. We played the big regional clubs:
the Oasis in Manchester, the Mojo in Sheffield, the Place in Hanley,
Club A Go Go in Newcastle, Clouds in Derby. We played the
cool London clubs: Sybilla's, The Scotch of St James, where
The Beatles and the Stones drank whisky and Coke, and the
Cromwellian, with its remarkable barman, Harry Heart, a man
almost as famous as the pop stars he served. Harry was very camp,
talked in Polari and kept a mysterious vase full of clear liquid on
the counter. The mystery was solved when you offered to buy him
a drink: 'Gin and tonic, please, and have one for yourself, Harry.'
He'd say, 'Ooh, thank you, love, bona, bona, just one for the pot,
then.' And he'd pour out a measure of gin, throw it into the vase
and drink out of it between serving people. The real mystery was
how a man who apparently drank a large vase full of neat gin on
a nightly basis remained vertical as the evening wore on.

And we played the most bizarre clubs. There was a place in
Harlesden that was basically someone's front room, and a place in
Spitalfields where, for reasons I never quite established, they had

a boxing ring instead of a stage. We played a lot of black clubs, which should have been intimidating – a bunch of white kids from the suburbs trying to play black music to a black audience – but somehow never was. For one thing, the audiences just seemed to love the music. And for another, if you've spent your teens trying to play 'Roll Out The Barrel' while the clientele of a Northwood Hills pub beat the living shit out of each other, you don't scare that easily.

In fact, the only time I felt uneasy was in Balloch, just outside Glasgow. We arrived at the venue to discover the stage was about nine feet tall. This, it quickly transpired, was a security measure: it stopped the audience trying to climb onstage and kill the musicians. With that particular avenue of pleasure closed off to them, they settled instead for trying to kill each other. When they arrived, they lined up on either side of the club. The opening note of our set was clearly the agreed signal for the evening's festivities to begin. Suddenly, there were pint glasses flying and punches being thrown. It wasn't a gig so much as a small riot with accompaniment from an r'n'b band. It made Saturday night in the Northwood Hills look like the State Opening of Parliament.

We played two gigs a night, almost every night – more if we tried to supplement our income by playing our own shows. One Saturday, Roy booked us to play an American services club in Lancaster Gate at 2 p.m. Then we got in the van and drove to Birmingham, and played two shows he had booked us there – at the Ritz and then the Plaza. Then we got back in the van again, drove back to London and played a show he'd booked us at Count Suckle's Cue club in Paddington. The Cue was a really cutting-edge black club that mixed soul and ska, one of the first places in London to book not just US artists but West Indian ones too. To be honest, my main memory of it isn't its groundbreaking cocktail of American and Jamaican music, but the fact that it had a food counter that served fantastic Cornish pasties. Even the most obsessive music fan develops a slightly different sense of priorities when it's six in the morning and they're starving to death.

Sometimes Roy Tempest got the bookings catastrophically wrong. He brought The Ink Spots over, apparently in the belief that, if they were a black American vocal group, they must be a soul band. But they were a vocal harmony group from a completely different era, pre-rock 'n' roll. They'd start singing 'Whispering Grass' or 'Back In Your Own Back Yard' and the audiences would just dissipate – they were wonderful songs, but not what the kids in the soul clubs wanted to hear. It was heartbreaking – until we got to the Twisted Wheel in Manchester. The audience there were such music lovers, so knowledgeable about black music's history, that they completely got it. They turned up with their parents' 78s for The Ink Spots to sign. At the end of the set they literally lifted them off the stage and carried them around the club on their shoulders. People talk about Swinging London in the mid-sixties, but those kids in the Twisted Wheel were so clued-up, so switched-on, so much hipper than anyone else in the country.

In truth, I didn't care about the money or the workload, or the occasional bad gig. The whole thing was a dream come true for me. I was playing with artists whose records I collected. My favourite was Billy Stewart, an absolutely enormous guy from Washington DC, signed to Chess Records. He was an amazing singer, who had turned his weight problem into a kind of gimmick. His songs kept alluding to it: 'she said I was her pride and joy, that she was in love with a fat boy'. He had a legendary temper – it was rumoured that when a secretary at Chess took too long to buzz him into the building he had expressed his irritation by pulling a gun and shooting the door handle off – and, we quickly discovered, a legendary bladder. If Billy asked for the van to pull over on the motorway because he needed to pee, you had to cancel whatever plans you had for the rest of the evening. You were there for hours.

The noise from the bushes was incredible: it sounded like someone filling a swimming pool with a fire hose.

Playing with these people was terrifying, and not merely because some of them were rumoured to shoot things when they lost their temper. Their sheer talent was scary. It was an incredible education. It wasn't just the quality of their voices, it was that they were fantastic entertainers. The way they moved, the way they spoke between songs, the way they could manipulate an audience, the way they dressed. They had such style, such panache. Sometimes they displayed some peculiar quirks – for some reason, Patti Labelle insisted on favouring the audience with a version of 'Danny Boy' at every gig – but you could learn so much about artistry by watching them onstage for an hour. I couldn't believe they were just cult figures over here. They'd had big American hits, but in Britain, white pop stars had seized on their songs, covered them and invariably been more successful. Wayne Fontana And The Mindbenders seemed to be the chief offenders: they'd re-recorded Major Lance's 'Um Um Um Um Um Um' and Patti LaBelle's 'A Groovy Kind Of Love' and vastly outsold the originals. Billy Stewart's 'Sitting In The Park' had flopped while Georgie Fame had the hit. You could tell this rankled with them, and understandably so. In fact, I got a good idea just how much it rankled with them when a mod in the audience at the Ricky-Tick club in Windsor made the mistake of shouting out 'We want Georgie Fame!' in a sarcastic voice, as Billy Stewart sang 'Sitting In The Park'. I've never seen a man that size move so fast. He jumped offstage, into the crowd, and went after him. The kid literally ran out of the club in fear for his life, as indeed you might if a trigger-happy twenty-four-stone soul singer had taken a sudden dislike to you.

In March 1966, Bluesology went to Hamburg – carrying our instruments on the ferry, then on a train – to play at the Top Ten Club on the Reeperbahn. It was legendary, because it was one of the places The Beatles had played before they were famous. They were living in the club's attic when they made their first single with Tony Sheridan. The set-up hadn't changed in the intervening five years. The accommodation for bands was still in the attic. There were still brothels with prostitutes sitting in the windows just down the street, and at the club you were still expected to play five hours a night, alternating with another band: an hour on, an hour off, while the clientele drifted in and out. It was easy to imagine The Beatles living the same life, not least because it looked suspiciously like the bed sheets in the attic hadn't been changed since John and Paul had slept in them.

We played as Bluesology and we also backed a Scottish singer called Isabel Bond, who'd relocated from Glasgow to Germany. She was hilarious, this sweet-looking dark-haired girl who turned out to be the most foul-mouthed woman I've ever met. She'd sing old standards and change the words so they were filthy. She's the only singer I've ever heard who could work the phrase 'give us a wank' into 'Let Me Call You Sweetheart'.

But I was so innocent. I barely drank and I still wasn't interested in sex, largely because I'd managed to get to the age of nineteen without gaining any real knowledge or understanding of what sex actually was. Aside from my father's questionable assertion that masturbating made you go blind, nobody had furnished me with any information about what you did or were supposed to do. I had no idea about penetration, no idea what a blow job was. As a result, I'm probably the only British musician of the sixties who went to work on the Reeperbahn and came back still in possession of his virginity. There I was, in one of Europe's most notorious fleshpots, every conceivable kink and persuasion catered for, and the raciest thing I did was buy a pair of flared trousers from a department store. All I cared about was playing and going to German record shops. I was totally absorbed by music. I was incredibly ambitious.

And, in my heart, I knew Bluesology weren't going to make it. We weren't good enough. It was obvious. We'd gone from playing obscure blues to playing the same soul songs that virtually every British r'n'b band played in the mid-sixties – 'In The Midnight Hour', 'Hold On I'm Coming'. You could hear The Alan Bown Set or The Mike Cotton Sound playing them better than us. There were superior vocalists to Stuart out there, and there were certainly far superior organ players to me. I was a pianist, I wanted to hammer the keys like Little Richard, and if you try and do that on an organ, the sound it makes can ruin your whole day. I didn't have any of the technical knowledge you need to play an organ properly. The worst instrument was the Hammond B-12 that was permanently installed on the stage of the Flamingo club in Wardour Street. It was an enormous wooden thing, like playing a chest of drawers. It was covered in switches and levers, draw bars and pedals. Stevie Winwood or Manfred Mann would deploy all of them to make the Hammond scream and sing and soar. I, on the other hand, didn't dare touch them because I had literally no idea what any of them did. Even the little Vox Continental I usually played was a technical minefield. One key had a habit of sticking down. It happened midway through a set at The Scotch of St James. One minute I was playing 'Land Of A Thousand Dances', the next my organ was making a noise that sounded like the Luftwaffe had turned up over London to give the Blitz another go. The rest of the band gamely continued dancing in the alley with Long Tall Sally and twisting with Lucy doing the Watusi while I attempted to fix the situation by panicking wildly. I was contemplating calling 999 when Eric Burdon, the lead singer of The Animals, got onstage. A man clearly blessed with the complex technical expertise I lacked – The Animals' keyboard player Alan Price was a genius on the Vox Continental – he thumped the organ with his fist and the key was released.

'That happens to Alan all the time,' he nodded, and walked off.

So we weren't as good as the bands who were doing the same thing as us, and the bands who were doing the same thing as us weren't as good as the bands who wrote their own material. When Bluesology were booked to play at the Cedar Club in Birmingham, we arrived early and found a rehearsal in progress. It was The Move, a local quintet who were obviously on the verge of big things. They had a wild stage act, a manager with the gift of the gab and a guitarist called Roy Wood who could write songs. We snuck in and watched them. Not only did they sound amazing, Roy Wood's songs sounded better than the cover versions they played. Only someone who was clinically insane would have said that about the handful of tracks I'd written for Bluesology. To be honest, I'd only written them because I absolutely had to, because we had one of our very infrequent recording sessions coming up and needed at least some material of our own. I wasn't exactly pouring my heart and soul into them, and you could tell. But I can remember watching The Move and having a kind of revelation. *This is it, isn't it? This is the way forward. This is what I should be doing.*

In fact, I might have left Bluesology sooner had Long John Baldry not come into the picture. We got the job with him because we were in the right place at the right time. Bluesology just happened to be performing in the south of France when Long John Baldry found himself without a backing band to play the Papagayo club in St-Tropez. His original idea was to form another band like Steampacket with himself, Stuart Brown, a boy called Alan Walker – who I think got the job because Baldry fancied him – singing, and a girl who had just arrived in London from the US, Marsha Hunt, taking the female vocalist's role. Bluesology were to be his backing band, at least after he'd revamped the line-up slightly: a couple of musicians he didn't like got the push and were replaced with ones he thought were better suited. It wasn't really what I wanted to do. I thought that line-up was a real step down for John. I knew how good Julie Driscoll and Rod were. I'd seen Rod playing with John at the Kenton Conservative Club when the band were still called The Hoochie Coochie Men and I was still at school, and he'd blown me away. And Brian Auger was a real musician's musician: he didn't seem like the kind of organist who'd ever require the lead singer of The Animals to climb onstage and offer a helpful thump in the middle of a show.

So I had my reservations. The line-up with Alan Walker and Marsha Hunt didn't last long anyway: Marsha looked incredible, this gorgeous, tall black girl, but she wasn't a great singer. Even so, I had to admit that, with Long John Baldry around, things suddenly got a lot more interesting. Indeed, if you ever feel your life is getting a little routine, a bit humdrum, I can wholeheartedly recommend going on tour in the company of a hugely eccentric six-foot-seven gay blues singer with a drink problem. You'll find things liven up quite considerably.

I just loved John's company. He'd pick me up outside Frome Court in his van, which came complete with its own record player, alerting me to his arrival by leaning out of the window and screaming 'REGGIE!' at the top of his voice. His life seemed packed with incident, often linked to his boozing, which I quickly worked out was self-destructive: the big clue came when we played the Links Pavilion in Cromer and he got so pissed after the show that he fell down a nearby cliff in his white suit. But I didn't realize that he was gay. I know it seems incredible in retrospect. This was a man who called himself Ada, referred to other men as 'she' or 'her' and continually gave you in-depth reports on the state of his sex life: 'I've got this new boyfriend called Ozzie – darling, he spins around on my dick.' But again, I was so naive, I honestly had no real understanding of what being gay meant, and I certainly didn't know that the term might have applied to me. I'd just sit there thinking, 'What? He spins around *on your dick*? How? Why? What on earth are you talking about?'

It was hugely entertaining, but none of it changed the fact that I didn't want to be an organist, I didn't want to be a backing musician and I didn't want to be in Bluesology. Which is why I ended up at Liberty Records' new offices, just off Piccadilly, prefacing my audition for the label by pouring out my woes: the stasis of Bluesology's career, the horror of the cabaret circuit, the tape machine and its role in our legendary non-performance of 'Let The Heartaches Begin'.

On the other side of the desk, Ray Williams nodded sympathetically. He was very blond, very handsome, very well dressed and very young. As it turned out, he was so young that he didn't have the power to give anyone a contract. The decision lay with his bosses. They might have signed me had I not chosen Jim Reeves's 'He'll Have To Go' as my audition piece. My logic was that everybody else would sing something like 'My Girl' or a Motown track, so I'd do something different and stand out. And I really love 'He'll Have To Go'. I felt confident singing it: it used to knock them dead in the Northwood Hills public bar. Had I thought twice, I might have realized that it wasn't going to muster much enthusiasm among people who were trying to start a progressive rock label. Liberty signed The Bonzo Dog Doo-Dah Band, The Groundhogs and The Idle Race, a psychedelic band fronted by Jeff Lynne, who went on to form the Electric Light Orchestra. The last thing they wanted was Pinner's answer to Jim Reeves.

Then again, maybe singing 'He'll Have To Go' was exactly the right thing to do. If I'd passed the audition, Ray might not have handed me the envelope containing Bernie's lyrics. And if he hadn't handed me Bernie's lyrics, I don't really know what would have happened, although I've spent a lot of time thinking about it, because it seems like such an incredible twist of fate. I should point out that Ray's office was chaos. There were piles of reel-to-reel tapes and hundreds of envelopes everywhere: he hadn't just been contacted by every aspiring musician and writer in Britain, but by every nutcase who'd seen Liberty's 'talent wanted' advert too. He seemed to pull the envelope out at random, just to give me something to take away, so the meeting didn't feel like a dead loss – I can't remember if he'd even opened it or not before he gave it to me. And yet that envelope had my future in it: everything that's happened to me since happened because of what it contained. You try and figure that out without giving yourself a headache.

Who knows? Maybe I would have found another writing partner, or joined another band, or made my way as a musician without it. But I do know my life and my career would have been very different, most likely substantially worse – it's hard to see how it could have turned out any better – and I suspect you wouldn't be reading this now.

L iberty Records weren't interested in the first songs that Bernie and I wrote together, so Ray offered to sign us to a publishing company he had set up. There was no money in it unless we actually sold some songs, but for the moment that didn't seem to matter: Ray really believed in me. He even tried to set me up with a couple of other lyricists, but it didn't work out with them the way it did with Bernie. The others wanted us to work together, writing the music and the lyrics at the same time, and I couldn't do that. I had to have the words written down in front of me before I could write a song. I needed that kick-start, that inspir- ation. And there was just a magic that happened when I saw Bernie's lyrics, which made me want to write music. It happened the moment I first opened the envelope, on the tube train home from Baker Street, and it's been happening ever since.

The songs were really flowing out of us. They were better than anything I'd written before, which admittedly wasn't saying much. Actually, only some of them were better than anything I'd written before. We wrote two kinds of songs. The first were things we thought we could sell, to Cilla Black, say, or Engelbert Humperdinck: big weepy ballads, jaunty bubblegum pop. They were awful – sometimes I shuddered at the thought that the weepies weren't that different from the dreaded 'Let The Heartaches Begin' – but that was how you made your money as a songwriting team for hire. Those big middle-of-the-road stars were your target market. It was a target we missed every time. The biggest name we managed to sell a song to was the actor Edward Woodward, who occasionally moonlighted as an easy-listening crooner. His album was called *This Man Alone*, a title that eerily predicted its audience.

And then there were the songs we wanted to write, influenced by The Beatles, The Moody Blues, Cat Stevens, Leonard Cohen, the kind of stuff we were buying from Musicland, a record shop in Soho that Bernie and I haunted so frequently that the staff would ask me to help out behind the counter when one of them wanted to get some lunch. It was the tail end of the psychedelic era, so we wrote a lot of whimsical stuff with lyrics about dandelions and teddy bears. We were really just trying on other people's styles and finding none of them quite fitted us, but that's how the process of discovering your own voice works, and the process was fun. Everything was fun. Bernie had moved to London and our friendship had really bloomed. We got on so well, it felt like he was the brother I'd never had, a state of affairs magnified by the fact that we were, at least temporarily, sleeping in bunk beds in my bedroom at Frome Court. We would spend the days writing – Bernie tapping out lyrics on a typewriter in the bedroom, bringing them to me at the upright piano in the living room, then scurrying back to the bedroom again as I started to set them to music. We couldn't be in the same room if we were writing, but if we weren't writing, we spent all our time together, in record shops, at the cinema. At night, we would go to gigs or hang around the musicians' clubs, watching Harry Heart drink his vase full of gin, chatting to other young hopefuls. There was a funny little guy we knew who – in keeping with the flower-power mood of the times – had changed his name to Hans Christian Anderson. The aura of fairy tale otherworldliness conjured by this pseudonym was slightly punctured when he opened his mouth and a thick Lancashire accent came out. Eventually he changed his first name back to Jon and became the lead singer of Yes.

We recorded both our types of song in a tiny four-track studio in the New Oxford Street offices of Dick James Music, which administrated Ray's own publishing company: it later became famous because it was where The Troggs were covertly recorded shouting and swearing at each other for eleven minutes while trying to write a song – 'you're talking out the back of your fuckin' arses!' 'Fuckin' drummer – I shit him!' – a recording that later got released as the notorious Troggs Tape. Caleb Quaye was the in-house engineer, a multi-instrumentalist with a joint permanently smouldering between his fingers. Caleb was very hip and he didn't let you forget it. He spent half his life guffawing at things Bernie or I had said or done or worn that indicated our desperate lack of cool. But, like Ray, he seemed to believe in what we were doing. When he wasn't rolling on the floor in hysterics or wiping tears of helpless mirth from his eyes, he was lavishing more time and attention on our songs than he needed to. Strictly against the company rules, we worked on them late into the night, calling in favours from session musicians Caleb knew, trying out arrangements and production ideas in secret, after everyone else from DJM had gone home.

It was thrilling, until we got caught by the company's office manager. I can't remember how he found out we were there – I think someone might have driven past and seen a light on and thought the place was being burgled. Caleb thought he was going to lose his job and, possibly out of desperation, played Dick James himself what we'd been doing. Instead of firing Caleb and throwing us out, Dick James offered to publish our songs. He was going to give us a retainer of £25 a week: a tenner for Bernie and fifteen quid for me – I got an extra fiver because I had to play piano and sing on the demos. It meant I could quit Bluesology and concentrate on songwriting, which was exactly what I wanted to do. We walked out of his office in a daze, too dumbfounded to be excited.

The only downside of this new arrangement was that Dick thought our future lay with the ballads and bubblegum pop. He worked with The Beatles, administering their publishing company Northern Songs, but at heart he was an old-fashioned Tin Pan Alley publisher. DJM was a strange set-up. Half the company was like Dick himself: middle-aged, more from that old Jewish showbiz world than rock and roll. The other half was younger and more fashionable, like Caleb, and Dick's son Stephen, or Tony King.

Tony King worked for a new company called AIR from a desk he rented on the second floor. AIR was an association of independent record producers that George Martin had started after he realized how badly EMI paid him for working on The Beatles' records, and Tony dealt with their publishing and promotion. To say Tony stood out in the DJM offices was an understatement. Tony would have attracted attention in the middle of a Martian invasion. He wore suits from the hippest tailors in London: orange velvet trousers, things made out of satin. He had strings of love beads around his neck and one or more of his collection of antique silk scarves fluttered behind him. His hair was dyed with blond highlights. He was an obsessive music fan, who'd worked for The Rolling Stones and Roy Orbison. He was friends with The Beatles. Like Long John Baldry, he was openly gay and he couldn't care less who knew it. He didn't walk so much as waft through the office: 'Sorry I'm late, dear, the telephone got tangled up in my necklaces.' He was hilarious. I was completely fascinated by him. More than that: I wanted to be like him. I wanted to be that stylish and outrageous and exotic.

His dress sense started to influence my own, with some

eyebrow-raising results. I grew a moustache. I bought an Afghan coat, but opted for the cheaper kind. The sheepskin wasn't cured properly and the ensuing stench was so bad my mother wouldn't let me in the flat if I was wearing it. Unable to stretch to the kind of boutiques Tony shopped at, I bought a length of curtain fabric with drawings of Noddy on it and got a seamstress friend of my mum's to make me a shirt out of it. For the adverts for my first single, 'I've Been Loving You', I wore a fake fur coat and a mock-leopardskin trilby hat.

For some reason, the sight of me clad in this striking ensemble failed to galvanize record buyers into the shops when the single was released in March 1968. It was a total flop. I wasn't surprised. I wasn't even disappointed. I didn't particularly want to be a solo artist – I just wanted to write songs – and my record deal had come about more or less by accident. Dick's son Stephen had been shopping demos of our songs around various labels in the hope that one of their artists would record them, someone at Philips had said they liked my voice and the next thing I knew, I had a deal to put out a few singles. I wasn't sure at all, but I went along with it because I thought it might be one way of getting some exposure for the songs Bernie and I were writing. We were really improving as songwriters. We had been inspired by The Band's rootsy Americana, and by a new wave of US singer-songwriters like Leonard Cohen, who we'd discovered in the imports section of Musicland. Something about their influence clicked with our writing. We'd started coming up with stuff that didn't feel like pastiches of other people's work. I'd listened to a song we'd written called 'Skyline Pigeon' over and over again and, thrillingly, I still couldn't think of anyone else it sounded like – we'd finally made something that was our own.

But Dick James had picked out 'I've Been Loving You' as my debut single, apparently after a long but ultimately fruitful search to find the most boring song in my catalogue. He managed to unearth something completely nondescript that Bernie hadn't even written the lyrics for, one that we'd earmarked for sale to a middle-of-the-road crooner. I suppose it was Dick's old-fashioned Tin Pan Alley roots showing. I knew it was the wrong choice, but I didn't feel like arguing. He was the Denmark Street legend who worked with The Beatles, and he'd given us a contract and got me a record deal when he should have thrown Bernie and me out on the street. The adverts claimed it was 'the greatest performance on a "first" disc', that I was '1968's great new talent' and concluded, 'YOU HAVE BEEN WARNED'. The British public reacted as if they'd been warned every copy was contaminated with raw sewage; 1968's great new talent went back to the drawing board.

There was one further, unexpected complication in my life at this point. I'd got engaged, to a woman called Linda Woodrow. We'd met in late 1967, at a gig Bluesology played at Sheffield's Mojo club. Linda was friends with the club's resident DJ, who was four foot eight and called himself the Mighty Atom. She was tall, blonde and three years older than me. She didn't have a job. I don't know where her money came from – I assumed her family were wealthy – but she was a woman of independent means. She was very sweet, interested in what I was doing. A post-gig conversation had turned into a meeting that felt suspiciously like a date, which had turned into another date, which had led to her coming down to visit Frome Court. It was an odd relationship. There wasn't much in the way of physicality, and we certainly never had sex, which Linda took as evidence of old-fashioned chivalry and romance on my part, rather than a lack of interest or willingness: in 1968 it still wasn't that unusual for couples not to sleep together before they were married.

But sexual or not, the relationship started to develop a momentum of its own. Linda decided to move to London and find a flat. Linda could afford one, and so we could move in together. Bernie could be our lodger.

I'd be lying if I said I didn't feel a sense of unease at all this, not least because Linda had started expressing misgivings about the music I was making. She was a big fan of an American crooner called Buddy Greco, and made it fairly clear she thought I would be better off modelling myself on him. But my unease was surprisingly easy to drown out. I liked the idea of moving out of Frome Court. And I suppose I was doing what I thought I should be doing at twenty – settling down with someone.

And so we ended up in a flat in Furlong Road, Islington: me, Bernie, Linda and her pet Chihuahua, Caspar. She got a job as a secretary, and the conversation increasingly turned to getting engaged. By now, the sound of alarm bells was hard to ignore, because the people closest to me kept ringing them. My mother was dead set against the idea, and you can get a pretty good sense of what Bernie thought from the lyrics of the song he subsequently wrote about that period, 'Someone Saved My Life Tonight'. It's hardly a glowing appraisal of Linda's multitude of good qualities: 'a dominating queen', 'sitting like a princess perched in her electric chair'. Bernie didn't like her at all. He thought she was going to screw up our music with all this stuff about Buddy Greco. He thought she was bossy – he was furious that, for some reason, she'd made him take down a Simon and Garfunkel poster he'd put up in his room.

A cocktail of stubbornness and my aversion to confrontation enabled me to blot the alarm bells out. We got engaged on my twenty-first birthday – I can't remember who asked who. A wedding date was set. Arrangements were being made. I started to panic. The obvious course of action was simply to be honest. But the obvious course of action didn't appeal – actually telling Linda how I felt was beyond me. So I decided to stage a suicide bid instead.

Bernie, who came to my rescue, has never let me forget the

exact details of my supposed attempt to end it all by gassing myself. Someone who really wants to kill themselves will commit the act in solitude, so as not to be stopped; they'll do it at the dead of night, or in a place where they're alone. I, on the other hand, did it in the middle of the afternoon in a flat full of people: Bernie was in his bedroom, Linda was having a nap. I'd not only put a pillow in the bottom of the oven to rest my head on, I'd taken the precaution of turning the gas to low and opening all the windows in the kitchen. It momentarily seemed quite dramatic when Bernie hauled me out of the oven, but there wasn't enough carbon monoxide in the room to kill a wasp. I'd expected the reaction to be one of terrible shock, followed by a sudden realization on Linda's part that my suicidal despair was rooted in unhappiness at our impending marriage. Instead the reaction was mild bemusement. Worse, Linda seemed to think that if I was depressed, it was because of the failure of 'I've Been Loving You' to light up the charts. Clearly, this would have been an ideal moment to tell her the truth. Instead, I said nothing. The suicide bid was forgotten, and the wedding remained in the diary. We started looking for a flat together in Mill Hill.

It took Long John Baldry to spell out what I already knew. We'd stayed good friends after my departure from Bluesology, and I had asked him to be my best man at the wedding. He seemed quietly entertained by the idea that I was getting married at all, but agreed. We arranged to meet at the Bag O' Nails club in Soho to talk over the details. Bernie tagged along.

There was something strange about John's mood from the minute that he arrived. He appeared preoccupied. I had no idea what with. I assumed something was going on in his personal life. Perhaps Ozzie had declined to spin around on his dick, or what-ever it was they did in private. It took a few drinks until he told me what the problem was, in no uncertain terms.

'Oh, fucking hell,' he erupted. 'What are you doing living with a fucking woman? Wake up and smell the roses. You're gay. You love Bernie more than you love her.'

There was an awkward silence. I knew he was right, at least up to a point. I didn't love Linda, certainly not enough to marry her. I did love Bernie. Not in a sexual way, but he was my best friend in the world. I certainly cared far more about our musical partnership than I did about my fiancée. But gay? I wasn't sure about that at all, largely because I still wasn't 100 per cent certain what being gay entailed, although thanks to a few frank conversations with Tony King I was getting a better idea. Maybe I was gay. Maybe that's why I admired Tony so much – I didn't just want to emulate his clothes and his sense of urbane sophistication, I saw something of myself in him.

It was a lot to mull over. Instead of doing that, I argued back. John was being ridiculous. He was drunk – yet again – and making a fuss about nothing. I couldn't possibly cancel the wedding. Everything was arranged. We'd ordered a cake.

But John wouldn't listen. He kept on at me. I'd ruin my life and Linda's too if I went through with it. I was a fucking idiot, and a coward to boot. As the conversation got more heated and emotional, it began attracting attention. People from adjoining tables became involved. Because it was the Bag O' Nails, the people from adjoining tables all happened to be pop stars, which lent everything an increasingly surreal edge. Cindy Birdsong from The Supremes chipped in – I'd known her back in the Bluesology days, when she'd been one of Patti LaBelle's Blue Belles. Then, somehow, P. J. Proby became embroiled in the conversation. I'd love to be able to tell you what the trouser-splitting, ponytail-wearing enfant terrible of mid-sixties pop had to say regarding my impending wedding, its potential cancellation and, indeed, whether or not I was a homosexual, but by then I was incredibly pissed, and the exact details are a little hazy, although at some point I must have given in and conceded that John was right, at least about the marriage.

In my memory, the rest of the night plays out in fractured images. Walking up the road to the flat as dawn was breaking – arm in arm with Bernie, for moral support – and the pair of us stumbling against cars and knocking dustbins over. A terrible row, during which Linda threatened to kill herself. A slurred conversation held through the locked door of Bernie's room – he'd made himself very scarce shortly after our arrival – about whether or not we thought Linda was actually going to kill herself. Another conversation through Bernie's door, asking if he'd mind unlocking it so I could sleep on the floor.

The next morning there was another row, and a desperate phone call to Frome Court. 'They're coming in the morning with a truck to take me home,' Bernie wrote in 'Someone Saved My Life Tonight'. That was a bit of poetic licence. There was no 'they' and no truck: only Derf in his little decorator's van. But Bernie and I did get taken home. Back to the bunk beds in Frome Court we went. Bernie stuck his Simon and Garfunkel poster on the wall. Neither of us ever saw Linda again.

three

In theory, Bernie and I were only back in Frome Court temporarily, until we found somewhere of our own. It slowly sank in that, in reality, we were going to be there for the foreseeable future. We wouldn't be getting anywhere of our own, because we couldn't afford anywhere of our own. We couldn't afford anywhere of our own because Britain's singers continued to prove implacably opposed to recording our songs. Occasionally, word would reach us that an artist's manager or producer was interested in something we'd written. You would get your hopes up and then . . . nothing. The rejections piled up. It's a no from Cliff, I'm afraid. Sorry, Cilla doesn't think it's quite right for her. No, Octopus don't want 'When I Was Tealby Abbey'. Octopus? Who the hell were *Octopus*? Literally the only thing I knew about them was that they didn't like our songs. We were being turned down by people we'd never even heard of.

Nothing was moving. Nothing was happening. It was hard not to get dispirited, although one advantage of living at Frome Court was that my mum was always on hand, armed with her patent method of snapping me out of despair. This involved a straight-faced suggestion that I abandon my songwriting career and go and work in a local shop instead: 'Well, you've got a choice, you know.

There's a job going in the launderette, if you like.' The launderette, you say? Hmm. Delightful as a career manning the tumble dryers sounds, I think I'll stick with songwriting for a bit longer.

So instead of moving out, we tried to make a bedroom with bunks in it look like an acceptable place for two grown men to live. I joined a *Reader's Digest* book club and gradually filled up the shelves with leather-bound editions of *Moby Dick* and *David Copperfield*. We got a stereo and two sets of headphones out of the Littlewoods catalogue – we could afford them because you paid in instalments. We bought a Man Ray poster from Athena in Oxford Street, then went next door to a shop called India Craft and bought some joss sticks. Lying on the floor, with our headphones on, our latest purchase from Musicland on the turntable and the air heady with incense smoke, Bernie and I could momentarily convince ourselves that we were artists living a bohemian existence at the cutting edge of the counterculture. Or at least we could until the spell was broken by my mum knocking on the bedroom door, asking to know what that bleedin' smell was and, by the way, what did we want for our dinner?

I had a little more money than Bernie, because Tony King had used his connections at AIR Studios and Abbey Road to get me work as a session musician. You got £3 an hour for a three-hour session, paid in cash if you were working at Abbey Road. Better yet, if the session went even a minute over the allotted time, the Musicians' Union rules meant that you got paid for a session and a half: nearly fifteen quid, the same as I earned in a week at DJM. The final bonus would be if I bumped into Shirley Burns and Carol Weston, the AIR Studios secretaries. They were so fabulous, always ready for a gossip, always happy to suggest my name if they heard of a job going. Something about me apparently brought out the maternal instinct in them, and they would quietly slip me their luncheon vouchers. So that meant a free meal on top of everything else – I thought I'd died and gone to heaven.

But forget the money: the session work was a fantastic experience. A session musician can't afford to be picky. Whenever work came in, whatever work it was, you accepted it. You had to work quickly and you had to be on point, because your fellow session players were some of the best musicians in the country. Frightening isn't an adjective you would normally associate with the Mike Sammes Singers, who did backing vocals for everyone – they looked like middle-aged aunties and uncles who'd arrived at the studio direct from a golf club dinner dance. But if you had to sing alongside them, they suddenly struck the fear of God into you, because they were so good at what they did.

And you had to be adaptable, because you were expected to play an incredible variety of music. One day you'd be singing backing vocals for Tom Jones, the next you'd be making a comedy record with The Scaffold, or arranging and playing piano with The Hollies, or trying to come up with a rock version of the theme from *Zorba the Greek* for The Bread and Beer Band, a project of Tony King's that never really got off the ground. You constantly met new people and made new contacts: musicians, producers, arrangers, record company staff. One day, I was recording with The Barron Knights when Paul McCartney suddenly walked into the studio. He sat in the control room and listened for a while. Then he went to the piano, announced that this was what he was doing in a studio nearby, and played 'Hey Jude' for eight minutes. That certainly threw what The Barron Knights were doing – making a novelty record about Des O'Connor taking part in the Olympic Games – into quite stark relief.

Sometimes a session was great because the music you were playing was incredible, but sometimes a session was great because the music you were playing was so terrible. I did a lot of covers albums for a label called Marble Arch: hastily knocked-out versions of current chart hits, released on compilations with titles like *Top of the Pops, Hit Parade* and *Chartbusters*, that were sold cheaply in supermarkets. Whenever my involvement in them comes up, people talk about it as a desperate low point in my career: the poor, undiscovered artist, reduced to anonymously singing other people's songs in order to earn a crust. I suppose you could look at it like that with the benefit of hindsight, but it certainly didn't feel that way at the time, because the sessions for the covers albums were screamingly, howlingly funny.

The instructions you would get from the producer Alan Caddy were fantastic – one completely insane request after another. 'Can you sing "Young, Gifted And Black"?' Well, that's not a song that makes an enormous amount of sense sung by a white guy from Pinner, but I'll give it a go. 'We're doing "Back Home" next – we need you to sound like the England World Cup Squad.' OK, there's only three singers here and one of us is female, so it's probably not going to sound *indistinguishable* from the original, but you're the boss. On one occasion, I was required to sound like Robin Gibb of The Bee Gees, a great singer but a man possessed of a unique vocal style: a kind of eerie, tremulous, nasal vibrato. I couldn't do it, unless I physically grabbed hold of my throat and wobbled it around while I was singing. I thought this was a real brainwave, but it caused absolute pandemonium among my fellow musicians. I stood there, wailing away, fingers clasped round my neck, desperately trying not to look across the studio, where the other session singers, David Byron and Dana Gillespie, were clinging on to each other and weeping with laughter.

Here's how much I enjoyed the sessions for the covers albums, this supposedly lamentable artistic nadir in my professional life: I went back and did one *after* my solo career took off. I assure you I'm not making this up. 'Your Song' was written, the *Elton John* album was out, I'd been on *Top of the Pops*, I was about to go to America for my first tour, and I went back into the studio and happily belted out shonky versions of 'In The Summertime' and

'Let's Work Together' for some terrible album sold in a super-market for fourteen and sixpence. It was, as usual, a hoot.

But the session work was far from the most important thing about my friendship with Tony King. He had a great circle of friends, like a little gang, mostly made up of gay men who worked in the music business. They were record producers, men who worked at the BBC, promoters and pluggers, and a Scottish guy called John Reid, who was young, ambitious, very confident and very funny. He was advancing through the music industry at an incredible rate. Eventually he was made the UK label manager for Tamla Motown, dealing with The Supremes, The Temptations and Smokey Robinson, a prestigious appointment that Tony commemorated with suitable gravitas by always referring to John thereafter as Pamela Motown.

Tony's group weren't particularly wild or outrageous – they had dinner parties, or went out to restaurants and pubs together, rather than haunting London's gay clubs – but I just loved their company. They were sophisticated and smart and very, very funny: I adored that camp sense of humour. The more I thought about it, the more I realized there was something odd about how completely at home I felt when I was with them. I'd never been a loner, I'd always had lots of friends – at school, in Bluesology, in Denmark Street – but this was different, more like a sense of belonging. I felt like one of the kids in *Mary Poppins*, suddenly being exposed to this magical new world. Twelve months after John Baldry had drunkenly announced that I was gay to everyone within earshot at the Bag O' Nails, I decided he was right.

As if to underline the point, my libido unexpectedly decided to show its face for the first time, like a flustered latecomer to a party that was supposed to have started ten years ago. At twenty-one, I suddenly seemed to be undergoing some kind of belated adolescence. There were suddenly a lot of quiet crushes on men. It clearly wasn't just his sense of humour and extensive knowledge of

American soul that made me find John Reid so captivating, for one. Of course, I never acted on any of them. I wouldn't have known how. I'd never knowingly chatted anyone up in my life. I'd never been to a gay club. I had no idea how you picked someone up. What was I supposed to say? 'Do you want to come to the cinema with me and maybe get your knob out later'? That's the main memory I have of the reality of my sexuality dawning on me. I don't recall feeling anxious or tormented. I just remember wanting to have sex, having absolutely no idea how to do it and feeling terrified that I might get it wrong. I never even told Tony I was gay.

Besides, I had other things on my mind. One morning, Bernie and I were called into a meeting at DJM with Steve Brown, who'd recently taken over from Caleb as the studio manager. He told us he'd listened to the songs we had been recording and thought we were wasting our time.

'You need to stop this rubbish. You're not very good at it. In fact,' he nodded, clearly warming to this disheartening theme, 'you're hopeless. You're never going to make it as songwriters. You can't do it at all.'

I sat there reeling. Oh, wonderful. This is it. The Northwood Hills launderette beckons. Maybe not; there was always the session work. But what about Bernie? The poor sod was going to end up back in Owmby-by-Spital, pushing his wheelbarrow full of dead chickens around again, the only evidence that he'd ever had a career in music one flop single he didn't actually write and a rejection note from Octopus, whoever they were. We hadn't even paid off the HP on the stereo.

As my mind raced, I became aware that elsewhere in the room, Steve Brown was still talking. He was saying something about 'Lady What's Tomorrow', one of the songs we'd written that we hadn't even bothered to try and sell. It was influenced by Leonard Cohen, and clearly Cilla Black wasn't going to be interested. But Steve Brown apparently was.

'You need to write more songs like that,' he continued. 'You need to do what you want to do, not what you think will sell. I'm going to talk to Dick and see if we can make an album.'

Afterwards, Bernie and I sat in the pub, trying to process what had just happened. On the one hand, I didn't have any great ambitions to be a solo artist. On the other, the opportunity to stop writing the weepies and bubblegum pop was too good to turn down. And we still thought releasing Elton John records was a good way of showcasing the kind of songs we liked. The more exposure our songs got, the more likely it was that another, more famous artist might hear them and decide to record one themselves.

There was one problem. The deal with Philips was for singles: they wanted a follow-up to 'I've Been Loving You', not an album. So Steve Brown recorded a new song that Bernie and I had written, following his instruction to stop trying to be commercial and do what we liked. It was called 'Lady Samantha', and it felt like a breakthrough. Admittedly, at this stage of my career, making a single that I could listen to without emitting an involuntary yell of horror would have constituted a breakthrough, but 'Lady Samantha' was a pretty good song. It sounded completely different from 'I've Been Loving You': it was weightier, hipper, more confident. Released in January 1969, it became what used to be called a 'turntable hit', which was a polite way of saying it was a single that got played on the radio a lot but no one actually bought.

In the aftermath of its failure, we discovered Philips weren't interested in renewing our deal: for some inexplicable reason, they seemed very resistant to financing an album by an artist who'd so far done nothing but lose them money. Dick James vaguely mentioned putting it out himself, setting up a proper label, rather than just licensing recordings out to other record companies, but he seemed more keen on talking about the Eurovision Song Contest. Much to Dick's delight, one of the attempts at middle-of-the-road songwriting we were supposed to have forgotten about had now been mooted as a potential UK entry. Lulu was going to sing six songs on her TV show and the British public were going to vote for a winner. To say Bernie greeted this news coolly was an understatement. He was appalled. Back then, Eurovision wasn't quite the orgy of embarrassment it is now, but still, it wasn't like Pink Floyd and Soft Machine were queuing up to get involved. Worse, he hadn't actually had anything to do with the song, even though it had his name on the credits. I'd knocked together the lyrics myself. It was 'I've Been Loving You' all over again. We were suddenly back where we started.

Bernie's worst fears were confirmed when we sat down in Frome Court to watch the Lulu show. Our song – *my* song – was completely undistinguished and forgettable, which was more than you could say for the rest of them. Every other songwriter seemed to have come up with an idea so horrendous you couldn't forget it if you tried. One was like something drunk Germans would slap their knees to in a Bavarian beer hall. Another featured the appalling combination of a big band and a bouzouki. Another was called 'March'. The title didn't refer to the month. The song was literally about marching, with an arrangement featuring a military brass band to ram home the point. Steve Brown was right. We really couldn't do this kind of thing at all, a fact underlined when our song came last in the public vote. The German oompah song won. It was called 'Boom Bang-A-Bang'.

The next day, we arrived at DJM to discover that the *Daily Express* had published an article helpfully explaining that our song had lost because it was self-evidently the worst of the lot. Dick wearily conceded that perhaps it might be better if we stopped wasting everybody's time and made our own album instead. If Philips wouldn't release it, then he would hire a press and promotions guy and start his own record label after all.

So we were sequestered in the little DJM studio, with Steve Brown producing and Clive Franks operating the tape machine.

Clive was the guy who recorded The Troggs Tape; years later, he ended up co-producing some of my albums, and he still works with me today, doing the sound engineering for my live shows. We collectively threw everything we could at the new songs. Psychedelic sound effects, harpsichords, backwards guitar solos courtesy of Caleb, flutes, bongos, stereo panning, improvised jazz interludes, trick endings where the songs faded out then suddenly back in again, the sound of Clive whistling. If you listened carefully, you could hear the kitchen sink being dragged into the studio. We might have been better off had we realized less is sometimes more, but you don't think like that when you're making your first album. There's a faint voice at the back of your mind telling you that you might never make another, so you may as well try everything while you have the chance. But, God, it was so much fun, such an adventure. The album was called *Empty Sky*. It came out on Dick's new DJM label on 6 June 1969. I can remember listening back to the title track and thinking it was the greatest thing I'd ever heard in my life.

Empty Sky wasn't a hit – it only sold a few thousand copies – but I could still sense things were starting to move, very gradually. The reviews were promising rather than great, but they were definitely an improvement on being told by the *Daily Express* that you couldn't write a song as good as 'Boom Bang-A-Bang'. Just as the album was released, we got a phone call to say that Three Dog Night had covered 'Lady Samantha' on their new album. Three Dog Night! They were American! An actual American rock band had recorded one of our songs. Not a light entertainer with a Saturday-night variety show on BBC1, not an entrant in the Eurovision Song Contest: a hip, successful American rock band. Bernie and I had a song on an album that was in the US Top Twenty.

And *Empty Sky* gave me material, which meant I could play live. The first gigs were pretty tentative. They were little pop-up shows; I was playing with any musicians I could find – usually Caleb and his new band Hookfoot – and I was still nervous: the last time I had been onstage, Long John Baldry had his tape recorder out and I was in a kaftan, suffering a complete collapse of the will to live. But the gigs got better the more comfortable I felt, and they really took off when I assembled my own band. I had met Nigel Olsson and Dee Murray lurking around DJM. Nigel was playing with a band called Plastic Penny, who had a big hit single in 1968 and, incredibly, had actually bought one of the songs Bernie and I had been trying to sell the previous year. It somehow seemed symbolic of our luck that they recorded it on an album that was released just as Plastic Penny's moment in the spotlight passed and their career went down the toilet. Dee, meanwhile, had been in The Mirage, a psychedelic band who released singles for years without getting anywhere. They were fantastic musicians and we clicked straight away. Dee was an incredible bass player. Nigel was a drummer from the Keith Moon and Ginger Baker school, a showman with a kit that took up most of our rehearsal space and had his name emblazoned across his twin bass drums. They could both sing. We didn't need a guitarist. The sound the three of us made was already huge and raw. Plus, there's something about performing in a trio that gives you a real freedom to play off the cuff. It didn't matter that we couldn't replicate the tricky arrangements of the album: instead we could stretch out and improvise, play solos, turn songs into medleys, suddenly launch into an old Elvis cover or a version of 'Give Peace A Chance'.

I started to think more about how I looked onstage. I wanted to be a frontman, but I was trapped behind a piano. I couldn't strut around like Mick Jagger, or smash my instrument up like Jimi Hendrix or Pete Townshend: bitter subsequent experience has taught me that if you get carried away and try and smash up a piano by pushing it offstage, you end up looking less like a lawless rock god and more like a furniture removal man having a bad day. So I thought about the piano players I'd loved as a kid, how they had managed to communicate excitement while stuck behind the old nine-foot plank, as I affectionately called it. I thought of Jerry Lee Lewis kicking his stool away and jumping on the keyboard, how Little Richard stood up and leaned back when he played, even the way Winifred Atwell would turn to the audience and grin. They all influenced my performances. It turned out that playing the piano standing up like Little Richard is bloody hard work when you have arms as short as mine, but I persevered. We didn't sound like anyone else, and now we didn't look like anyone else either. Whatever else might have been happening in pop as the sixties turned into the seventies, I was fairly certain there weren't any other piano-led power trios whose frontman was trying to mix the outrageousness and aggression of early rock and roll with Winifred Atwell's bonhomie.

As we toured around colleges and hippy venues like the Roundhouse, the gigs got wilder and the music got better, especially when we started playing the latest batch of songs Bernie and I had come up with. I confess, I'm not always the best judge of my own work – I am, after all, the man who loudly announced that 'Don't Let The Sun Go Down On Me' was such a terrible song that I would never countenance releasing it, of which more later – but even I could tell that our new material was in a different league to anything we'd produced before. They were easy songs to write – Bernie got the lyrics to 'Your Song' over breakfast one morning in Frome Court, handed them to me and I wrote the music in fifteen minutes flat – because, in a way, we'd already done all the hard work. The way they sounded was the culmination of the hours we'd previously put in trying to write together, the gigs I'd been playing with Nigel and Dee that had boosted my confidence, the years I'd spent at the Royal Academy much against my will, the nights on the club circuit in Bluesology. Something like

'Border Song' or 'Take Me To The Pilot' had a sort of funk and soulfulness that I'd picked up backing Patti LaBelle and Major Lance, but they also had a classical influence that seeped in from all those Saturday mornings where I'd been forced to study Chopin and Bartók.

They were also the product of the bedroom at Frome Court. At the time we were writing, two artists were constantly on the Littlewoods stereo. One was the rock/soul duo Delaney and Bonnie. I was completely obsessed with the way their keyboardist, Leon Russell, played. It was like he'd somehow climbed into my head and worked out exactly how I wanted to play piano before I did. He'd managed to synthesize all the music I loved – rock and roll, blues, gospel, country – into one, perfectly natural style.

And the other was The Band. We played their first two albums over and over again. Like Leon Russell's piano playing, their songs felt like someone switching a torch on and showing us a new path to follow, a way we could do what we wanted to do. 'Chest Fever', 'Tears Of Rage', 'The Weight': this was what we craved to write. Bernie went crazy for the lyrics. Ever since he was a kid, he'd loved gritty stories about old America, and that was what The Band told: 'Virgil Caine is the name and I served on the Danville train, 'til Stoneman's cavalry came and tore the tracks up again'. They were white musicians making soul music without covering 'In The Midnight Hour', or doing something that was just a pale imitation of what black artists did. It was a revelation.

When we played Dick the demos of the new songs, he was knocked out. Despite the sales of *Empty Sky*, he said he wanted another album. What's more, he was going to give us £6,000 to make it. That was a remarkable leap of faith. It was an incredible amount of money to spend on an album in those days, especially one by an artist who had barely sold any records yet. There's no doubting the belief Dick had in us, but I think his hand may also have been forced a little. Bernie and I had become friends with

Muff Winwood, Stevie's brother, who worked for Island Records and lived not far from Frome Court – I think we literally bumped into him on a train back to Pinner one day. We would go round to his house a couple of nights a week with a bottle of Mateus Rosé and a box of chocolates for his wife Zena – *very* sophisticated – play table football or Monopoly and pump Muff for advice about the music business. When he heard the new songs, he was really enthusiastic, and wanted to sign us to Island, a much bigger and cooler label than DJM. Word of a competitor got back to Dick, which might have galvanized him into getting his chequebook out.

Whatever the reason, the money meant we could move out of DJM into a proper studio, Trident in Soho. Steve Brown suggested we should get an outside producer: Gus Dudgeon, who'd produced David Bowie's 'Space Oddity', a number one single that we all loved the sound of. We could afford strings and an arranger, Paul Buckmaster, who had worked on 'Space Oddity' too. Paul arrived looking like D'Artagnan – he had long centre-parted hair, a goatee beard and a big hat. He seemed a bit eccentric, which, as it turned out, was a false first impression. Paul wasn't a bit eccentric. He was so eccentric as to suggest he might be genuinely nuts. He would stand in front of the orchestra and make noises with his mouth to indicate what he wanted them to do: 'I don't know how to describe what I want, but I want you to make a sound like this.' They got it exactly right. He was a genius.

But then everything about the sessions was weirdly magical. Me, Gus, Steve and Paul had planned everything out in advance – the songs, the sound, the arrangements – and it all just fell into place. I had barely touched a harpsichord before we hired one for 'I Need You To Turn To'; it was a really hard instrument to play, but I did it. I was petrified about playing live with an orchestra, but I psyched myself up, telling myself that this was it, something was finally coming to fruition. All those crappy clubs with Long

John Baldry and his tape recorder, all the session work, Derf carrying his pint pot round for tips at the Northwood Hills Hotel, Bernie and me escaping from Furlong Road and Linda's dreams of turning me into Buddy Greco: it was all leading up to this. And it worked. The whole album was done in four days.

We knew we'd made something good, something that would push us on to the next level. We were right. When it came out in April 1970 the reviews of *Elton John* were fantastic; John Peel played it and it crept into the bottom end of the charts. We started getting offers to play in Europe, although every time we went there something bizarre seemed to happen. In Paris, some genius booked us as the support act to Sérgio Mendes and Brasil '66. An audience expecting an evening of bossa nova showed their delight at having their musical horizons unexpectedly broadened by booing us off. We turned up in Knokke, Belgium to discover we weren't playing a gig at all: it was a televised song contest. We went to Holland to appear on a TV show and instead of getting us to perform, they insisted on making a film of me in a park, miming 'Your Song' into a microphone while surrounded, for some reason, by actors pretending to be paparazzi taking my photograph. They still show it on TV sometimes. I look absolutely furious, like I'm about to punch somebody – a fairly accurate representation of how I felt, but not really the ideal delivery for a tender ballad about blossoming love.

Back at home, though, a buzz was definitely building. In August, we played the Krumlin Festival in Yorkshire, which should have been a disaster. It was in a field in the middle of the moors. It was freezing cold, pouring with rain and completely disorganized. The stage was still being built when the festival was supposed to start, which gave the bands who were supposed to play time to start squabbling over the running order. I couldn't be bothered getting involved with that, so we just went on, handed out brandy to the crowd and tore the place apart while Atomic Rooster and

The Pretty Things were still backstage, arguing about who was the biggest star. I started seeing famous faces in the audiences at our London shows, which meant that word was getting about in the music business that we were worth checking out. A couple of weeks before we played Krumlin, Pete Townshend from The Who and Jeff Beck had turned up to our show at the Speakeasy club, which had taken over from the Cromwellian and the Bag O' Nails as London's big music industry hang-out. We got invited on *Top of the Pops* to play 'Border Song': our appearance didn't do much to help its sales as a single, but Dusty Springfield introduced herself to us in the dressing room and offered to mime backing vocals during our performance. My mouth just hung open. I'd travelled to Harrow to see her live with The Springfields when I was still at school, and hung around outside the stage door afterwards, just to get another glimpse of her: she walked past in a lilac top and mauve skirt, looking incredibly chic. I'd joined her fan club in the early sixties and stuck posters of her on my bedroom wall.

The only obstacle to our progress was Dick, who had got it into his head that we should go to America and play there. He had managed to sell the album to a US label called Uni – a division of MCA – and kept talking about how enthusiastic they were about it, how they wanted us to play some club shows. I couldn't see the point, and told him so. Something was starting to happen in Britain. The gigs were great, the album was selling OK and Dusty Springfield liked me. Bernie and I were writing song after song – we'd already started working on demos for the next album. Why lose the momentum by leaving now and going to America, where no one knew who I was?

The more I argued, the more adamant Dick became that we should go. But then I was handed a lifeline. After the Speakeasy show, Jeff Beck had invited me along to his rehearsal space in Chalk Farm to jam. Then his agent set up a meeting at DJM.

Jeff effectively wanted to use me, Dee and Nigel as his backing band for an American tour. I would get a solo spot during the set, where I could play my own songs. It seemed like an incredible offer. Jeff Beck was one of the greatest guitar players I'd ever seen. His last album, *Beck-Ola*, had been a huge hit. Admittedly, we were only to get 10 per cent of the nightly earnings, but 10 per cent of Jeff Beck's earnings was still a lot more than we were making now. And the important thing was the exposure. These would be big audiences, and I'd be playing my songs in front of them – not as a completely unknown artist, but as part of Jeff Beck's band; not as a support act that everyone could ignore, but in the middle of the main set.

I was ready to ask them where to sign when Dick told Beck's agent to stuff their 10 per cent. What was he doing? I tried to catch his eye, in order to wordlessly communicate that he should consider the wisdom of shutting up immediately. He didn't look at me. The agent said the deal was non-negotiable. Dick shrugged.

'I promise you now,' he said, 'that in six months' time, Elton John will be earning twice what Jeff Beck does.'

What? Dick, you fucking idiot. What did you have to say *that* for? It sounded remarkably like a statement that was going to follow me around for the rest of my career. I could see myself in five years' time, still slogging around the clubs, The Guy Who Was Going To Earn Twice What Jeff Beck Does. The agent swiftly disappeared – he was probably in a hurry to inform the rest of the music industry that Dick James had lost his marbles – but Dick was completely unrepentant. I didn't need Jeff Beck. I should go to America on my own. The songs on *Elton John* were great. The band was fantastic live. The US record label were behind us all the way. They were going to pull out all the stops to promote us. One day I'd thank him for this.

Back at Frome Court, I talked it over with Bernie. He suggested we should think of it as a holiday. We could visit places we had only seen on TV or in films – 77 Sunset Strip, the Beverly Hillbillies' mansion. We could go to Disneyland. We could go record shopping. Besides, the US record label were going to pull out all the stops. We'd probably be met at the airport by a limousine. Maybe a Cadillac. A Cadillac!

We stood blinking in the Los Angeles sunshine, a little cluster of us – me and Bernie, Dee and Nigel, Steve Brown and Ray Williams, who DJM had appointed my manager, our roadie Bob and David Larkham, who'd designed the covers for *Empty Sky* and *Elton John*. We were befuddled by jet lag and trying to work out why there was a bright red London bus parked outside LAX Airport. A bright red London bus with my name painted on the side of it: ELTON JOHN HAS ARRIVED. A bright red London bus that our excited American publicist, Norman Winter, was currently urging us to get on board. Bernie and I exchanged a dismayed glance: oh, for fuck's sake, this is our limo, isn't it?

You have no idea how slowly a London Routemaster bus goes until you've travelled on one from LAX to Sunset Boulevard. It took us two and a half hours, partly because the thing had a top speed of about forty miles an hour, and partly because we had to take the scenic route – they wouldn't allow a double-decker on the freeway. Out of the corner of my eye, I could see Bernie gradually sliding down in his seat, until he couldn't be seen from outside the window, presumably in case Bob Dylan or a member of The Band happened to drive past and laugh at him.

This really wasn't how I'd expected our arrival in California to pan out. Were it not for the fact that I could see palm trees out of the window and the bus was filled with Americans – the staff of Uni Records – I might as well have been on the 38 to Clapton Pond. It was my first experience of the difference between British record companies and US ones. In Britain, no matter how much your label loves you, no matter how passionate they are about working on your album, it's always tempered by a certain reserve, a national tendency to understatement and dry humour. That clearly wasn't the case in America: it was just non-stop enthusiasm, a completely different kind of energy. No one had ever talked to me the way Norman Winter was talking – 'this is gonna be huge, we've done this, we've done that, Odetta's coming to the show, Bread are coming to the show, The Beach Boys are coming to the show, it's gonna be incredible'. No one had ever talked to me as *much* as Norman Winter was talking: as far as I could tell, his mouth hadn't actually stopped moving since he'd introduced himself in the arrivals lounge. It was simultaneously startling and weirdly exhilarating.

And everything he said turned out to be completely true. Norman Winter and his promotions department *had* done this and done that: got LA record stores to stock the album and display posters, lined up interviews, invited umpteen stars to see the show. Someone had convinced my Uni labelmate Neil Diamond to get onstage and introduce me. I was headlining over David Ackles, which seemed completely ridiculous.

'But David Ackles is on *Elektra*,' protested Bernie weakly, remembering the hours we'd spent in Frome Court listening to his debut album and discussing the incomparable West Coast hipness of the label that had released it: Elektra, run by the great Jac Holzman, home to The Doors and Love, Tim Buckley and Delaney and Bonnie.

It was fantastic work from a passionate and committed team who had used every bit of their expertise in creating hype. They had miraculously turned a show by an unknown artist at a 300-capacity club into an event. And it certainly had a profound knock-on effect on me. Before, I'd been dubious about the idea of playing in America. Now, I was absolutely terrified. When everybody else went on a day trip to Palm Springs, arranged by Ray, I wisely elected to remain at the hotel alone, in order to concentrate on the pressing business of panicking about the gig. The more I panicked, the more furious I got. How dare they all go to Palm Springs and enjoy themselves, when they should have been back at the hotel with me, pointlessly worrying themselves sick? In the absence of anybody to shout at in person, I rang Dick James in London and shouted at him. I was coming back to England. Now. They could stick their gig and their star-studded guest list and their onstage introduction from Neil Diamond up their arses. It took all Dick's powers of avuncular persuasion to stop me packing my suitcase. I decided to stay, dividing my remaining time before the gig between record shopping and a little light sulking whenever anyone mentioned Palm Springs.

I can remember two things very clearly about the first show we played at the Troubadour. The first is that the applause as I walked onstage had a slightly odd quality to it: it was accompanied by a kind of surprised murmur, as if the audience were expecting someone else. In a way, I suppose they were. The cover of the *Elton John* album is dark and sombre. The musicians on the back are dressed down and hippyish – I'm wearing a black T-shirt and a crocheted waistcoat. And that's the guy they assumed they'd see: a brooding, introspective singer-songwriter. But when I'd gone shopping for new clothes a couple of weeks before I left for the States, I'd visited a clothes shop in Chelsea called Mr Freedom, about which there was a real buzz developing: the designer Tommy Roberts was letting his imagination run riot, making clothes that looked like a cartoonist had drawn them. The stuff in the window was so outrageous that I hung around on the pavement outside for ages, trying to pluck up the courage to go in. Once I did, Tommy Roberts was so friendly and enthusiastic that he talked me into buying a selection of clothes not even Tony King would have countenanced wearing in public. Wearing them, I felt different, like I was expressing a side of my personality that I'd kept hidden, a desire to be outrageous and over-the-top. I suppose it all went back to chancing on that photo of Elvis in the barber's in Pinner when I was a kid: I liked that sense of shock, of seeing a star who made you wonder what the hell was going on. The clothes from Mr Freedom weren't outrageous because they were sexy or threatening, they were outrageous because they were larger than life, more fun than the world around them. I loved them. Before I went onstage at the Troubadour, I put them all on at once. So instead of an introspective hippy singer-songwriter, the audience were greeted by the sight of a man in bright yellow dungarees, a long-sleeved T-shirt covered in stars and a pair of heavy workman's boots, also bright yellow, with a large set of blue wings sprouting from them. This was not the way sensitive singer-songwriters in America in 1970 looked. This was not the way anyone of sound mind in America in 1970 looked.

And the second thing I remember very clearly is peering out into the crowd while we were playing and realizing, with a nasty start, that Leon Russell was in the second row. I hadn't spotted any of the galaxy of stars that were supposed to be there, but you couldn't miss him. He looked incredible, a vast mane of silver hair and a long beard framing a mean, impassive face. I couldn't tear my eyes off him, even though looking at him made the bottom fall out of my stomach. The gig had been going well up to that point – Dee and Nigel sounded tight, we'd started to relax and stretch out the songs a little. Now I suddenly felt as nervous as I had at the hotel on the day of the Palm Springs trip. It was like one of those terrible nightmares where you're back at school, sitting a test, then realize that you're not wearing any trousers or underpants: you're playing the most important gig of your career, then see your idol in the audience, glaring at you, stony-faced.

I had to pull myself together. I had to do something to take my mind off the fact that Leon Russell was watching me. I jumped to my feet and kicked my piano stool away. I stood there, knees bent, pounding at the keys like Little Richard. I dropped to the floor, balancing on one hand and playing with the other, my head under the piano. Then I stood up, threw myself forward and did a handstand on the keyboard. Judging by the noise the audience made, they hadn't expected that either.

Afterwards, I stood, dazed, in the fug of the packed dressing room. It had gone amazingly well. Everyone from Britain was elated. Norman Winter was talking with a speed and intensity that suggested that on the journey from LAX he'd actually been at his most laid-back and laconic. People from Uni Records kept bringing other people over to shake my hand. Journalists. Celebrities. Quincy Jones. Quincy Jones's wife. Quincy Jones's children. He seemed to have turned up with his entire family. I couldn't take anything in.

Then I froze. Somewhere over the shoulder of one of Quincy Jones's umpteen relatives I could see Leon Russell in the doorway. He started pushing through the crowd towards me. His face was as impassive and mean as it had seemed from the stage: he didn't look much like a man who'd just enjoyed the night of his life. Shit. I've been found out. He's going to tell everyone what a fraud I am. He's going to tell me that I can't play piano.

He shook my hand and asked how I was doing. His voice was a soft Oklahoma drawl. Then he told me I'd just played a great gig, and asked if I wanted to go on tour with him.

The next few days passed like a strange, feverish dream. We played more shows at the Troubadour, all of them packed out, all of them fantastic. More celebrities came. Each night, I rummaged deeper in my bag of Mr Freedom clothes, pulling out stuff that was more and more outrageous, until I found myself facing an audience of rock stars and Los Angeles tastemakers wearing a pair of tight silver hot pants, bare legs and a T-shirt with ROCK AND ROLL emblazoned across it in sequins. Leon Russell appeared backstage again and told me his home-made recipe for a sore throat remedy, as if we were old friends. Uni Records took us all to Disneyland, and I bought armfuls of albums at Tower Records on Sunset Strip. The *LA Times* published a review by their music editor, Robert Hilburn. 'Rejoice,' it opened. 'Rock music, which has been going through a rather uneventful period recently, has a new star. He's Elton John, a 23-year-old Englishman, whose debut Tuesday night at the Troubadour was, in almost every way, magnificent.' Fucking hell. Bob Hilburn was a huge deal: I'd known he was at the gig, but I had no idea he was going to write that. Once it was published, Ray Williams was suddenly deluged with offers from American promoters. It was decided we'd extend our stay and play more shows, in San Francisco and New York. I did interview after interview. The *Elton John* album was all over FM radio. One station in Pasadena, KPPC, took out a full-page advert in the *Los Angeles Free Press* literally thanking me for coming to America.

As everyone knows, fame, especially sudden fame, is a hollow, shallow and dangerous thing, its dark, seductive powers no substitute for true love or real friendship. On the other hand, if you're a terribly shy person, desperately in need of a confidence boost – someone who spent a lot of their childhood trying to be as invisible as possible so you didn't provoke one of your mum's moods or your dad's rage – I can tell you for a fact that being hailed as the future of rock and roll in the *LA Times* and feted by a succession of your musical heroes will definitely do the trick. As evidence, I present to you the sight of Elton John, a twenty-three-year-old virgin, a man who's never chatted anyone up in his life, on the night of 31 August 1970. I am in San Francisco, where I'm due to play a gig in a few days' time. I am spending the evening at the Fillmore, watching the British folk-rock band Fairport Convention – fellow survivors of the sodden hell that was the

Krumlin Festival – and meeting the venue's owner, legendary promoter Bill Graham, who is keen for me to perform at his New York concert hall, the Fillmore East. But I'm not really concentrating on Fairport Convention or Bill Graham. Because I have decided that tonight is the night I'm going to seduce someone. Or allow myself to be seduced. Definitely one or the other; either will do.

I'd discovered that John Reid happened to be in San Francisco at the same time as me, attending Motown Records' tenth anniversary celebrations. Since meeting him through Tony King, I'd casually dropped in on him at EMI a couple of times. Whatever feeble signals I was attempting to give off – if indeed I actually *was* attempting to give any signals off – went completely unnoticed. He seemed to think I was only visiting in order to ransack the pile of soul singles in his office, or to give him copies of my own records. But that was then. Emboldened by the events of the last week, I managed to find out where he was staying and rang him up. I breathlessly told him about what had happened in LA, and then, as nonchalantly as possible, suggested we should meet up. I was staying at the Miyako, a nice little Japanese-themed hotel near the Fillmore. Perhaps he could come over for a drink one night?

The gig finished. I went backstage to say hello to Fairport, had a couple of drinks and a quick chat, then made my excuses and went back to the Miyako alone. I hadn't been in my room long when the phone rang: there's a Mr Reid to see you in reception. Oh God. This is it.

four

Things moved very quickly after that night in San Francisco. A week later, I was in Philadelphia, doing interviews, when I got a call from John, who'd gone back to England, telling me that he'd bumped into Tony King at the BBC. He'd told Tony what had happened, and what our plans were. Tony had gone from baffled – 'Reg? Reg is *gay*? You're moving in together, as in *moving in together*?' – to uproariously amused when he heard about my desire that the relationship stay low-key. 'What do you mean, Reg wants to keep it quiet? He's with you! Everyone who's set foot in a London gay club knows about *you*! He might as well hang a fucking neon sign out of the window with I AM GAY written on it.'

I wanted to keep it quiet because I wasn't sure how people would react if they knew. I needn't have worried. None of my friends or the people I worked with cared at all. Bernie, the band, Dick James and Steve Brown: I got the feeling they were just relieved that I'd finally had sex. And outside of those circles, no one seemed to entertain the faintest possibility that I might be anything other than straight. It seems insane now that no one even raised an eyebrow, when you consider what I was wearing and doing onstage, but it was a different world then. Homosexuality had only been

decriminalized in Britain for three years: the wider public's knowledge or understanding of the subject was pretty sketchy. When
we toured America, all the legendary groupies from that era – the
Plaster Casters and Sweet Connie from Little Rock – would turn
up backstage, to the evident delight of the band and road crew. I'd
think, 'Hang on, what are you doing here? Surely you're not here
for me? Surely someone's told you? And even if they haven't, I've
just been carried onstage by a bodybuilder, while wearing half the
world's supply of diamanté, sequins and marabou feathers – does
that not suggest *anything* to you?' Apparently not. I became quite
adept at slipping away and locking myself in the toilet to escape
their attentions.

If anyone I knew felt it was odd that I was setting up home
with John so soon, they didn't mention it. And as it turned out,
the speed with which my relationship with John progressed was
just the first indication of what I was like. I was the kind of
person who met someone, immediately fell head over heels and
started planning our life together. Incapable of telling a crush
from real love, I could see the white picket fence and an eternity
of connubial bliss before I'd even spoken to someone. Later,
when I was really famous, this became a terrible problem both
for me and the object of my affections. I'd insist they gave up
their own lives in order to follow me around on tour, with disastrous results every time.

But that was in the future. I really was in love with John – that
intense, guileless, naive kind of first love. And I'd just discovered
sex. It made sense to move in together. Under the circumstances,
my current living arrangements were hardly ideal. Straight or gay,
you're going to struggle to conduct a meaningful sexual relationship with someone if you're living in your mum's spare room and
your co-writer's trying to sleep in the bunk bed under yours.

When I got back from America we started looking for a flat
to rent together. We found one in a development called the Water

Gardens, near Edgware Road: one bedroom, a bathroom, a living room and a kitchen. Bernie temporarily moved in with Steve Brown. He'd fallen in love in California too, with a girl called Maxine, who'd been on the famous day trip to Palm Springs. No wonder he'd been so eager to go.

The last people I told were my mum and Derf. I waited until a few weeks after I'd moved out. I suppose I was psyching myself up. I finally decided the moment was right the night John and I were supposed to go and see Liberace at the London Palladium. We had tickets, but I told John to go on his own, I had to ring Mum that night. I was nervous, but the phone call went OK. I told Mum I was gay and she seemed totally unsurprised: 'Oh, we know. We've known that for a long time.' At the time I put her knowledge of my sexuality down to the intangible mystic power of a mother's intuition, although, with the benefit of hindsight, she and Derf probably got an inkling what was going on when they helped move my stuff into the Water Garden and realized that I was living in a one-bedroom flat with another man.

Mum wasn't exactly thrilled by the idea that I was gay – she said something about condemning myself to a life of loneliness, which didn't seem to make a huge amount of sense, given that I was in a relationship – but at least she hadn't disowned me, or refused to accept it. And bizarrely, when he got home, I noticed that John looked like he'd had a much more stressful evening than I had. It turned out that midway through the show, Liberace had unexpectedly announced that he had a very special guest in the audience, a wonderful new singer who was going to be a big star: '. . . and I know he's here tonight, and I'm going to make him stand up and wave to you all, because he's so fabulous . . . Elton John!' Assuming that my reluctance to make myself known was down to modesty, Liberace had become progressively more solicitous – 'Come on now, Elton, don't be shy, the audience want to meet you. Don't you wanna meet Elton John, ladies and gentlemen? I tell you, this guy's gonna be huge – let's give him a big hand and see if we can't get him to say hello' – while a huge spotlight vainly circled the stalls. In John's telling of the story, Liberace had carried on like this for about three weeks, during which time the audience had grown first restless, then audibly irritated at my churlish refusal to show myself. Meanwhile, the one person among them who actually knew Elton John's whereabouts had grown concerned he was going to become the first person in history to literally die of embarrassment. Eventually, Liberace had given up. According to John, he was still smiling, but something about the way he launched into Liszt's *Hungarian Rhapsody* suggested murderous fury.

Ruining a Liberace concert while coming out to my parents notwithstanding, life was heaven. I was finally able to be who I was, to have no fear about myself, to have no fear about sex. I mean it in the nicest possible way when I say John taught me how to be debauched. As Tony had noted, John really knew the gay scene, the clubs and the pubs. We'd go to the Vauxhall Tavern to see Lee Sutton, this great drag queen – 'The name is Lee Sutton, DSM, OBE – Dirty Sex Maniac, On the Bed with Everybody' – and to the Sombrero club on Kensington High Street. We would have dinner parties and other musicians would drop by. One night, after we went to see him play live, Neil Young came back home with us and, after a few drinks, elected to perform his forthcoming album in its entirety for us at 2 a.m. Already alerted to the fact that an impromptu party was going on by the nerve-jangling sound of my friend Kiki Dee drunkenly walking into a glass door while holding a tray containing every champagne glass we owned, the delight of the adjoining flats at Neil Young performing his forthcoming album was audible. So that's how I heard the classic 'Heart Of Gold' for the first time, presented in a unique arrangement of solo piano, voice and neighbour inter-mittently banging on the ceiling with a broom handle and loudly imploring Neil Young to shut up.

My career suddenly had real momentum. We weren't as big in Britain as we were in the US, but the band and I had come back from America with a new sense of purpose. We'd been validated, ratified by so many people over there that we knew we were on to something. Word of what had happened in Los Angeles had filtered back to Britain and the press were suddenly interested. A hippy magazine called *Friends* sent a journalist to interview me. I played him two tracks we'd already recorded for the next album, *Tumbleweed Connection*, and in the subsequent article he went as nuts as Robert Hilburn had done: 'I think that along with his lyricist he will possibly become the finest, and almost certainly the most popular songwriter in England, and eventually the world.' We played at the Royal Albert Hall, supporting Fotheringay, a band formed by Fairport Convention's former lead singer Sandy Denny. Like the audience at the Troubadour, they thought they were getting a sensitive singer-songwriter – the perfect complement to what they did, which was wistful folk rock – and instead they got rock 'n' roll and Mr Freedom clothes and handstands on the piano keyboard. They couldn't follow us: we had so much adrenalin and confidence. Of course, when the adrenalin wore off and I realized what we'd done, I felt terrible. Sandy Denny was one of my heroes, an amazing vocalist. It was meant to be their big showcase gig and I'd ruined it for them. I scuttled home, absolutely mortified, before they came onstage.

But it felt like the time was right. The sixties were over, The Beatles had split up and there was a new wave of artists that were all starting to make it at the same time: me, Rod Stewart, Marc Bolan, David Bowie. Musically we were all very different, but in some ways we were birds of a feather. We were all working-class Londoners, we'd all spent the sixties with our noses pressed against the glass, toiling away on the same club circuit, never really getting where we wanted to go. And we all knew each other. Our paths had crossed backstage in r'n'b clubs and at gigs at the Roundhouse. I was never great friends with Bowie. I loved his music, and we socialized a couple of times, visiting the Sombrero with Tony King and having dinner together in Covent Garden while he was rehearsing for the Ziggy Stardust tour, but there was always something distant and aloof about him, at least when I was around. I honestly don't know what the problem was, but there clearly was a problem. Years later, he'd always make snippy remarks about me in interviews: 'the token queen of rock and roll' was the most famous one, although in fairness, he was absolutely out of his mind on coke when he said it.

But I adored Marc and Rod. They couldn't have been more different. Marc seemed to have come from another planet: there was something otherworldly about him, as if he was just passing through Earth on his way to somewhere else. You could hear it in his music. 'Ride A White Swan' was never off the radio when we moved into the Water Garden, and it didn't sound like anything else, you couldn't work out where he was coming from. That's what he was like in person. He was larger than life – straight but very camp – and incredibly kind and gentle at the same time. He clearly had a big ego, but he also never seemed to take himself seriously at all. He somehow managed to be simultaneously completely charming and absolutely, brazenly full of shit. He'd say the most outrageous things with a straight face: 'Darling, I sold a million records this morning.' I'd think: Marc, *no one in the history of music* has ever sold a million records in a morning, let alone you. But something about him was so beguiling and endearing, you would never actually say that out loud. Instead, you'd find yourself agreeing with him: 'A million, Marc? Congratulations! How fabulous!'

I'd known about Rod for years, because of the connection with Long John Baldry, but I only really got to know him after he covered 'Country Comfort', one of the new songs that I'd played the journalist from *Friends*. He changed the lyrics, something I complained about at length in the press: 'He sounds like he made it up as he went along! He couldn't have got further from the original if he'd sung "The Camptown Races"!' That rather set the tone for our friendship. We've got a lot in common. We both love football and collecting art. We both grew up after the war in families that didn't have a lot, so neither of us has ever been coy about enjoying the fruits of our success, shall we say. But the thing we really share is our sense of humour. For a man with a well-documented lifelong obsession with leggy blondes, Rod's got a surprisingly camp sense of humour. He happily joined in when we started giving ourselves drag names back in the seventies. I was Sharon, John was Beryl, Tony was Joy and Rod was Phyllis. We've spent nearly fifty years constantly taking the piss out of, and trying to put one over, each other. When the press were speculating about my hair falling out, and whether or not I'd started wearing a hairpiece, Rod could be relied upon to send me a present: one of those old-fashioned, helmet-shaped hairdryers that old women used to sit under in salons. Keen to reciprocate his thoughtfulness, I sent him a Zimmer frame covered in fairy lights. Even today, if I notice he's got an album out that's selling better than mine, I know it's only a matter of time before I'm going to get an email: 'Hello, Sharon, just writing to say I'm so sorry that your record's not even in the Top 100, dear. What a pity when mine's doing so well, love, Phyllis.'

It reached a kind of peak in the early eighties, when Rod was playing Earls Court. They had advertised the gig by flying a blimp over the venue with his face on it. I was staying in London that weekend and I could see it from my hotel room window. It was too good an opportunity to miss. So I called my management and they hired someone to shoot it down: apparently it landed on top of a double-decker bus and was last seen heading towards Putney. About an hour later, the phone went. It was Rod, spluttering about the disappearance.

'Where's my fucking balloon gone? It was you, wasn't it? You cow! You bitch!'

A year later, I was playing Olympia and the promoters had hung a huge banner across the street. It was mysteriously cut down immediately after it was put up. The phone call that informed me of this sabotage came from Rod, who seemed curiously well informed about exactly what had happened.

'Such a shame about your banner, love. I heard it wasn't even up five minutes. I bet you didn't even get to see it.'

Not long after we moved into the Water Gardens, I was back in America for another tour. It's a huge country and most of it couldn't care less if the *LA Times* has called you the future of rock and roll. You have to get out there and show people what you can do. Besides, we had a new album to promote – *Tumbleweed Connection* was already finished: recorded in March 1970 and released in the UK in the October. That's just how it was then. You didn't take three years to make an album. You recorded quick, you got it out fast, you kept the momentum going, kept things fresh. It suited the way I worked. I hate wasting time in the studio. I suppose it's a legacy from my days as a session musician, or recording demos in the middle of the night at DJM: you were always working against the clock.

So we criss-crossed the States, usually playing as a support act, for Leon Russell, The Byrds, Poco, The Kinks and Eric Clapton's new band Derek And The Dominos. That was the idea of my booking agent, Howard Rose, and a really clever move: don't play top of the bill, play second, make people want to come back and see you again in your own right. Every artist we supported was incredibly kind and generous to us, but it was hard work. Each night, we'd go onstage with the intention of stealing the show. We'd go down great, and come off thinking we'd blown the headliners offstage, and every night, the headliners would come out and play better than us. People talk about Derek And The Dominos being a real disaster area, strung out on heroin and booze, but you would never have known that if you'd seen them live that autumn. They were phenomenal. From the side of the stage, I took mental notes about their performance. Eric Clapton was the star, but it was their keyboard player, Bobby Whitlock, that I watched like a hawk. He was from Memphis, learned his craft hanging around Stax Studios and played with that soulful, Deep Southern gospel feel. Touring with them or Leon was like being on the road with Patti LaBelle or Major Lance when I was in Bluesology: you watched and you learned, from people who had more experience than you.

If we still had a long way to go, it was clear on that tour that the word was spreading. In LA, we had dinner with Danny Hutton from Three Dog Night and he casually mentioned that Brian Wilson wanted to meet us. Really? I had idolized The Beach Boys in the sixties, but their career had tailed off, and Brian Wilson had turned into this mysterious, mythic figure – according to some lurid gossip he was supposed to have become a recluse, or gone insane, or both. Oh no, Danny assured us, he's a huge fan, he'd love you to visit.

So we drove up to his house in Bel Air, a Spanish-style mansion with an intercom at the gate. Danny buzzed it and announced he was here with Elton John. There was a deathly silence at the other end. Then there was a voice, unmistakably that of The Beach Boys' mastermind, singing the chorus of 'Your Song': 'I hope you don't mind, I hope you don't mind'. As we approached the front door, it opened to reveal Brian Wilson himself. He looked fine – a little chubbier than on the cover of *Pet Sounds*, perhaps, but nothing like the reclusive weirdo people gossiped about. We said hello. He stared at us and nodded. Then he sang the chorus of 'Your Song' again. He said we should come upstairs and meet his kids. It turned out that his kids were asleep in bed. He woke them up. 'This is Elton John!' he enthused. His daughters looked understandably baffled. He sang the chorus of 'Your Song' to them: 'I hope you don't mind, I hope you don't mind'. Then he sang the chorus of 'Your Song' to us again. By now, the novelty of hearing the chorus of 'Your Song' sung to me by one of pop history's true geniuses was beginning to wear a little thin. I was struck by the sinking feeling that we were in for quite a long and trying evening. I turned to Bernie and a certain look passed between us, that somehow managed to combine fear, confusion and the fact that we were both desperately trying not to laugh at the absolute preposterousness of the situation we found ourselves in, a look that said: *what the fuck is happening?*

It was a look that we grew increasingly accustomed to using during the last months of 1970. I was invited to a party at Mama Cass Elliot's house on Woodrow Wilson Drive in LA, famed as the leading hang-out for Laurel Canyon's musicians, the place where Crosby, Stills and Nash had formed, and David Crosby had shown off his new discovery, a singer-songwriter called Joni Mitchell, to his friends. When I arrived, they were *all* there. It was nuts, like the record sleeves in the bedroom at Frome Court had come to life: *what the fuck is happening?*

We passed Bob Dylan on the stairs at the Fillmore East, and he stopped, introduced himself, then told Bernie he loved the lyrics of a song from *Tumbleweed* called 'My Father's Gun': *what the fuck is happening?*

We were sitting backstage after a gig in Philadelphia when the dressing room door opened and five men walked in unannounced. You couldn't mistake The Band for anyone else: they looked like they'd just stepped off the cover of the album we'd played to death back in England. Robbie Robertson and Richard Manuel started telling us they'd flown in from Massachusetts by private plane just to see the show, while I tried to behave as if The Band flying in from Massachusetts to see me perform was a perfectly normal state of affairs, and occasionally stole a glance at Bernie, who was similarly engaged in a desperate attempt to play it cool. A year ago, we were dreaming of trying to write songs like them and now they're stood in front of us, asking us to play them our new album: *what the fuck is happening?*

It wasn't just The Band who wanted to meet us. It was their managers, Albert Grossman and Bennett Glotzer. They were legendary American music business figures, particularly Grossman, a renowned tough guy who'd managed Bob Dylan since the early sixties. He had reacted to another client, Janis Joplin, becoming addicted to heroin not by intervening but by taking a life insurance policy out on her. Word must have reached them that I was currently without a manager. Ray Williams was a lovely man, I owed him a great deal and he was incredibly loyal – he'd even named his daughter Amoreena, after another of the *Tumbleweed Connection* songs – but after the first American trip, I'd talked it over with the rest of the band, and no one thought he was the right person to look after us. But nor were Grossman and Glotzer, as I realized the moment I met them. They were like characters from a film, a film that had been panned for its hopelessly cartoonish depiction of two aggressive, motor-mouthed American showbiz managers. Nevertheless they were real people, and their collective efforts to win me over succeeded in scaring me witless. As long as there was a vacancy, they were not going to leave me alone.

'I'm going to follow you around until you sign for me,' Glotzer told me.

He wasn't joking. There seemed to be no way of getting rid of him short of applying for a restraining order. Once again, the allure of locking myself in the toilet became hard to resist.

It might have been while I was in hiding from Bennett Glotzer that I started thinking about getting John to manage me. The more I considered it, the more it made sense. John was young and ambitious and full of adrenalin. He'd grown up in working-class Paisley in the fifties and sixties, an experience which had left him tough enough to deal with anything the music business threw at him. We were already a couple, which meant he'd have my best interests at heart. He was a born hustler with the gift of the gab and he was brilliant at his job. He didn't just know music, he was smart about music. Earlier in the year, he'd personally convinced Motown to release a three-year-old album track by Smokey Robinson And The Miracles as a single, then watched as 'Tears Of A Clown' went to Number One on both sides of the Atlantic. It sold so many copies that Smokey Robinson had to put his plans to retire from music on hold.

Everyone agreed it was a good idea, including John. He quit EMI and Motown at the end of the year, got a desk in Dick James's office – initially, at least, he was effectively an employee of DJM, given a salary to act as a kind of liaison between me and the company – and that was that. To celebrate, we traded in my Ford Escort for an Aston Martin. It was the first really extravagant thing I ever bought, the first sign I was actually making good money from music. We got it off Maurice Gibb from The Bee Gees and it was a real pop star's car: a purple DB6, flashy and beautiful. And completely impractical, as we discovered when John had to meet Martha And The Vandellas off their flight at Heathrow Airport. It was one of his last jobs for Motown, and we proudly took the Aston Martin along. Martha And The Vandellas looked impressed until they realized they had to get into the back of it. The designers had clearly spent considerably more time on its sleek lines and poetic contours than they had worrying about whether the rear seats could house a legendary soul trio. Somehow they got in. Perhaps Motown's famous Charm School had given classes on contortionism. As I drove back down the A40, I looked in the rear-view mirror.

It was like a Tokyo tube train during rush hour back there. Hang on, Martha And The Vandellas were crammed into the back of my car, which was an Aston Martin. That would have seemed very strange twelve months ago, when I was driving a Ford Escort, its back seat noticeably devoid of Motown superstars. But after the year I'd had, strange was becoming a relative concept.

I didn't have too much time to ruminate on how my life had changed. I was working too hard. We spent 1971 touring: backwards and forwards between America and Britain, then down to Japan, New Zealand and Australia. We were headlining now, but we still followed Howard Rose's advice and played venues that were slightly smaller than we could fill, or one night in a city when we could have sold out two. We did the same thing in Britain – we kept playing the universities and rock clubs long after we could have filled theatres. It's a really smart thing to do: don't be greedy, build your career up gradually, and it was typical Howard. He was so bright and full of good advice: he's still my agent today. I was really lucky with the people I worked with when I was just starting out in America. Young British artists could easily fall in with a bunch of sharks over there, but I got people who went out of their way to make me feel part of a family: not just Howard, but my publisher David Rosner and his wife Margo.

If I wasn't onstage, I was in the studio. I released four albums in America in 1971: *Tumbleweed Connection* didn't come out there until January; the soundtrack to a movie called *Friends* in March – which was only a minor hit, but still did better than the film, a complete flop – a live album we'd recorded the previous year, *11-17-70*, in May; and *Madman Across the Water* in November. We recorded *Madman* in four days. It was supposed to be five, but we lost a day because of Paul Buckmaster. He stayed up the night before the sessions began to finish the arrangements – I suspect with a certain amount of chemical assistance – then managed to knock a bottle of ink all over the only score, ruining it. I was

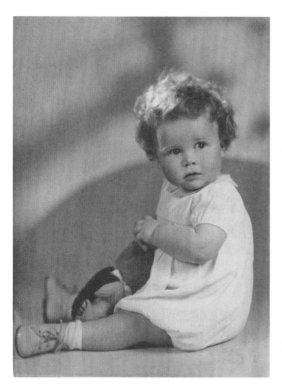

(*above left*) Aged one, in 1948.

(*above right*) With my mother, Sheila Dwight, in the back garden of my nan's house at 55 Pinner Hill Road.

(*right*) Outside Buckingham Palace with my mum and my grandad Fred Harris, June 1950.

If I heard a tune once, I could go to the piano and play it perfectly by ear.

(*left*) Me and my dad, in a rare moment when he wasn't complaining about the disastrous effects of Little Richard on my moral character; (*right*) Me, conspicuously ordinary, at Pinner County Grammar.

Bluesology in 1965. A photo used on the sheet music for our single 'Come Back Baby', printed in the demented belief that anyone other than Bluesology was going to sing it.

(*left*) The brother I'd never had. Bernie with my cousin Paul and my mercifully short-lived moustache. Mum, Auntie Win and Auntie Mavis are on the back row; (*right*) Frome Court, where Bernie and I lived with Mum and Derf in the upstairs flat.

April 1969, in front of my new Hillman Husky estate.

The genius arranger Paul Buckmaster demonstrating his striking approach
to style during the *Elton John* album sessions, 1970.

A promo shot of me and Bernie, taken in summer 1970, as a buzz
started building around the new album.

The Troubadour, 1970. If I'd had my way, I'd have gone home in a huff without actually playing there.

The night everything changed. Onstage at the Troubadour in my yellow dungarees and star-spangled T-shirt.

My hero. Me with Leon Russell in New York, 1970. Imagine that face glaring at you throughout the most important gig of your life.

Sharon and Beryl. Me and John Reid, young and in love, 1972.

I learned a lot about art from Bryan Forbes. Here I am, visibly embarking on another voyage of discovery in his Virginia Water bookshop.

Backstage at the Shaw Theatre with Princess Margaret and her husband Lord Snowdon. Princess Margaret invited me and the band to a memorable dinner party.

Dee, me, Davey and Nigel at the Château d'Hérouville in 1972. Note my idea of dressing down for a recording session.

furious. It was an expensive mistake to make, and we stopped working together for decades afterwards. But I was also quietly impressed when he wrote the whole score again, in twenty-four hours. Even when Paul screwed up, he screwed up in a way that reminded you he was a genius.

And I love *Madman Across the Water*. At the time, it was a much bigger hit in America than in Britain: Top Ten over there, but only number 41 at home. It's not particularly commercial; there were no huge smash singles, and the songs were much longer and more complex than I'd written before. Some of Bernie's lyrics were like a diary of the last year. One song, 'All The Nasties', was about me, wondering aloud what would happen if I came out publicly: 'If it came to pass that they should ask – what would I tell them? Would they criticize behind my back? Maybe I should let them'. Not a single person seemed to notice what I was singing about.

One other thing happened during the *Madman* sessions. Gus Dudgeon hired a guitarist called Davey Johnstone to play acoustic guitar and mandolin on a couple of tracks. I really liked him – he was Scottish, lanky and very forthright, and he had really good taste in music. I took Gus aside and asked what he thought about Davey joining the band. I'd been thinking about expanding the trio to include a guitarist for a while. Gus thought it was a bad idea. Davey was a wonderful guitarist, but he only played acoustic: as far as Gus knew, he'd never even played an electric guitar. He was in a band called Magna Carta, who specialized in bucolic folk, and there wasn't a lot of that in the Elton John repertoire.

It was a very persuasive argument. I ignored it and offered Davey the job anyway. If I'd learned anything over the last few years, it was that sometimes a gut feeling is the most important thing. You can work as hard as you like, and plan as carefully as you want, but there are moments when it's just about a hunch, about trusting your instincts, or about fate. What if I'd never responded to the Liberty advert? What if I'd passed the audition and they hadn't given me Bernie's lyrics? What if Steve Brown hadn't showed up at DJM? What if Dick hadn't been so certain I should go to America, when it seemed like such a stupid idea?

So when we went to France to record the next album at the Château d'Hérouville, Davey was with us. I'd changed things around a lot – it was the first time I'd tried to record an album with my touring band rather than crack session musicians; the first time that Davey had picked up an electric guitar; the first time we'd had the money to record abroad, in a residential studio – but I was in a really confident mood. Just before we left for France I'd legally changed my name to Elton John. Elton *Hercules* John. I'd always thought middle names were slightly ridiculous, so I did the most ridiculous thing I could think of and took mine from the rag and bone man's horse in the sitcom *Steptoe and Son*. Basically, I had got sick of the fuss in shops when the cashier recognized me but not the name on my chequebook. But it really seemed more symbolic than practical – like I was finally, conclusively, *legally* leaving Reg Dwight behind, fully becoming the person I was supposed to be. As it turned out, it wasn't quite as simple as that, but in that moment, it felt good.

I loved the idea of working at the Château, even though it came with a reputation attached. It was supposed to be haunted, and the locals had apparently become wary of the studio's clientele after The Grateful Dead had stayed there, offered to play a free concert for the villagers, then taken it upon themselves to expand the minds of rural France by spiking their audience's drinks with LSD. But it was a beautiful building, an eighteenth-century mansion – we ended up naming the album after it: *Honky Château* – and I was excited about the idea of having to write songs on the spot.

I'm not a musician who walks around with melodies in his head all the time. I don't rush to the piano in the middle of the night when inspiration strikes. I don't even think about songwriting when I'm not actually doing it. Bernie writes the words, gives them to me, I read them, play a chord and something else takes over, something comes through my fingers. The muse, God, luck: you can give it a name if you want, but I've no idea what it is. I just know straight away where the melody's going to go. Sometimes a song only takes as long to write as it does to listen to. 'Sad Songs (Say So Much)' was like that – I sat down, read the lyric and played it, pretty much the same as you hear on the record. Sometimes it takes a bit longer. If I don't like what I've done after about forty minutes, I give up and move on to something else. There are words that Bernie's written that I've never managed to come up with music for. He wrote a great lyric called 'The Day That Bobby Went Electric', about hearing Dylan sing 'Subterranean Homesick Blues' for the first time, and I just couldn't get a tune I thought was right; I tried four or five times. But I've never had writer's block, I've never sat down with one of Bernie's lyrics and nothing has come out. I don't know why. I can't explain it and I don't want to explain it. Actually, I love that I can't explain it. It's the spontaneity of it that's beautiful.

So Bernie brought his typewriter to the Château, and we set up some instruments in the dining room as well as the studio. Bernie would bash out his lyrics and leave them for me on the piano. I'd wake up early, go to the dining room, see what he'd come up with and write songs while I was having breakfast. The first morning we were there, I had three done by the time the band drifted downstairs looking for something to eat: 'Mona Lisas and Mad Hatters', 'Amy' and 'Rocket Man'.

Once Davey had been convinced that this wasn't an elaborate prank at the expense of the new boy, that I really had written three songs while he was having a lie-in, he picked up his guitar and asked me to play 'Rocket Man' again. He didn't add a solo or do anything that a regular lead guitar player might do. He used a slide and played odd, lonely notes that drifted around and away from the melody. It was great. Like I said, sometimes a gut feeling is the most important thing; sometimes you have to trust fate.

The rest of the band were so used to playing together that there was something almost telepathic between us: they just intuitively knew what to do with a song without being told. It felt fantastic, sitting together in the Château's dining room, hearing a song take shape around us, trying ideas and knowing straight away they were the right ideas. There's times in my life when music has been an escape, the only thing that worked when everything else seemed broken, but at that moment I had nothing to escape from. I was twenty-four, successful, settled and in love. What's more, tomorrow we had a day off and I was going to Paris, with every intention of absolutely *looting* the Yves Saint-Laurent store.

five

In 1972, John and I moved out of London to Virginia Water in Surrey, swapping the one-bedroom flat for something a little more grand: we bought a three-bedroom bungalow, with its own swimming pool, and a games room built in what had been the loft. I called it Hercules, to match my middle name. Bernie and Maxine, who had married in 1971, had a house nearby; Mum and Derf, who'd finally got married too, moved just down the road and kept an eye on the bungalow when we were away. They call that area of England the stockbroker belt, which makes it sound boring and suburban, but it wasn't at all. For one thing, Keith Moon lived ten minutes away from me, which obviously lent daily life a certain unpredictability. Keith was fabulous, but his diet of chemicals seemed to have left him without any understanding of the concept of time. He'd turn up unannounced at two thirty in the morning, completely out of his mind – usually with Ringo Starr, another local resident, in tow – and seem genuinely surprised that he'd got you out of bed. Or he'd materialize without warning in your driveway at 7 a.m. on Christmas Day, in a Rolls-Royce convertible with the top down and The Shadows' *Greatest Hits* playing at deafening volume. 'Dear boy! Look at the new car! Come for a spin! No, now! No need to change out of your dressing gown!'

But the most interesting person I knew in Virginia Water had nothing to do with the music business. I met Bryan Forbes when I walked into the bookshop he owned in the town, looking for something to read. He came over and introduced himself and said that he thought he recognized me. That didn't seem unlikely – by now, my onstage flamboyance had seeped into my everyday wardrobe, so my idea of dressing down for an afternoon's shopping in a Surrey commuter town involved wearing a bright orange fur coat and a pair of eight-inch platform boots. But it turned out that he didn't recognize me at all: as the conversation progressed, it became increasingly apparent that he thought I was one of The Bee Gees.

Once we'd established that I wasn't a Gibb brother, we got on very well. Bryan was fascinating. He'd been an actor, and was now a screenwriter, a novelist and a director, and he would go on to become a studio boss. He was married to the actress Nanette Newman and the two of them seemed to know everybody personally: Hollywood legends, writers, TV stars. If you were in America and expressed a long-held desire to meet David Niven or Groucho Marx, Bryan could arrange it, which is how I ended up with a Marx Brothers film poster signed 'to John Elton from Marx Groucho': he couldn't understand why my name was, as he put it, 'the wrong way round'. It's funny, I thought of Groucho years later at Buckingham Palace, when I got my knighthood, because that's how the Lord Chamberlain announced me to the Queen: 'Sir John Elton'.

One summer Sunday afternoon, John and I were sitting outside the bungalow having a snack, when we noticed a sixty-something lady who looked a little like Katharine Hepburn cycling up our drive. It was Katharine Hepburn: 'I'm staying with Bryan Forbes – he said it would be OK if I used your pool.' John and I just nodded, dumbstruck. Five minutes later, she reappeared in a swimsuit, complaining that there was a dead frog in the pool. When I dithered about how to get it out – I'm a bit squeamish about things like that – she just jumped in and grabbed it with her hand. I asked her how she could bear to touch it.

'Character, young man,' she nodded sternly.

If you were invited to the Forbes house for lunch you'd find yourself sitting between Peter Sellers and Dame Edith Evans, drinking in their stories, or you'd turn up to discover that the other guests included the Queen Mother. Bryan knew the Royal Family: he was president of the National Youth Theatre, and Princess Margaret was a patron. It turned out that Princess Margaret loved music and the company of musicians. She ended up inviting me and the band back to Kensington Palace for supper after a gig at the Royal Festival Hall, which turned out to be incredibly awkward. Not because of Princess Margaret – she was really sweet and friendly to everybody – but because of her husband, Lord Snowdon. Everyone knew the marriage was in trouble – there were always rumours in the press about one or the other having an affair – but even so, nothing could have prepared us for his arrival. He stormed in midway through the meal and literally snarled 'Where's my fucking dinner?' at her. They had a huge row, and she fled the room in tears. Me and the band were just sitting there, aghast, not really knowing what to do. You know, how bizarre can life in the Elton John Band get? Other musicians relax after a gig by smoking a joint or seducing groupies or trashing hotel rooms; we end up watching Princess Margaret and Lord Snowdon screaming at each other.

But it wasn't just who Bryan knew, it was what he knew, and the fact that he was a born teacher: patient and generous with his time, sophisticated in his tastes but completely unsnobbish, eager for others to love the things he loved. He taught me about art, and I started collecting under his influence. First it was art nouveau and art deco posters, which were very fashionable in the early seventies – Rod Stewart collected them too – then surrealist painters like Paul Wunderlich. I began buying Tiffany lamps and Bugatti furniture. Bryan got me interested in theatre, and recommended books to me. We became very close, and started going on holiday together: me and John, Bryan, Nanette and their daughters Emma and Sarah. We would hire a house in California for a month, and friends would come over and visit.

Nanette turned out to be a great accomplice when it came to shopping, something I'd become extremely fond of since I started making a bit of money. Actually, that's not strictly true. I've always loved shopping, since I was a kid. When I think of growing up in Pinner, I think of the shops: the different-coloured cotton reels in the wool shop where my gran used to get her knitting supplies; the smell of fresh peanuts as you walked into Woolworths; the sawdust on the floor of Sainsbury's, where Auntie Win worked on the butter counter. I don't know why, but something about those places fascinated me. I've always loved collecting things, and I've always loved buying people presents, more than I love receiving them. When I was a boy, my favourite thing about Christmas was working out what I was going to buy my family: some aftershave for my dad, a rain hat for my gran, maybe a little vase for my mum from the kiosk near Baker Street station that I used to pass on my way to the Royal Academy of Music.

Of course, becoming successful enabled me to pursue this passion on a slightly different scale. We'd come back from LA with so much stuff that the excess baggage charge would be as much as the ticket home. I'd hear that my auntie Win was feeling down in the dumps so I'd call a dealership and get them to send her a new car to cheer her up. Over the years, I've had therapists tell me that it's obsessive, addictive behaviour, or that I'm trying to buy people's affection by giving them gifts. With the greatest of respect to the members of the psychiatric profession who have said that sort of thing to me, I think that's a load of old shit. I'm not interested in buying people's affection. I just get a lot of pleasure out of making people feel included or letting them know I'm thinking about them. I love seeing people's faces when you treat them to something.

I don't need a psychiatrist to tell me that material possessions aren't a replacement for love or personal happiness. I've spent enough miserable, lonely nights in houses filled with beautiful things to have worked that out for myself a long time ago. And I really don't recommend going shopping in the depressing aftermath of a three-day cocaine binge, unless you want to wake up the next day confronted by bags and bags filled with absolute crap you don't actually remember buying. Or, in my case, you wake up the next morning to a phone call informing you that you've bought a tram. Not a model tram. An actual tram. A Melbourne W2 class drop-centre combination tram, that the voice at the end of the phone is now informing you has to be shipped from Australia to Britain, where it can only be delivered to your house by hanging it from two Chinook helicopters.

So I'd be the first person to admit that I've made some fairly rash decisions with a credit card in my hand. I probably could have struggled through life somehow without a tram in my garden, or indeed the full-scale fibreglass model of a *Tyrannosaurus rex* that I offered to take off Ringo Starr's hands at the end of a very long night. Ringo was trying to sell his house at the time, and the presence of a full-scale fibreglass *Tyrannosaurus rex* in the garden was apparently proving to be a bit of a sticking point with potential buyers. But for as long as I can remember, I've always found collecting things oddly comforting, and I've always enjoyed learning about things by collecting them, whether that's records or photographs or clothes or art. And that's never changed, regardless of what has been going on in my personal life. I've found it comforting and enjoyable when I've felt lonely and adrift, and I've found it comforting and enjoyable when I've felt loved and contented and settled. Lots of people feel that way: the world's full of model railway enthusiasts and stamp collectors and vinyl buffs. I'm just lucky enough to have the money to pursue my passions further than most people. I earned that money by working hard, and if people think the way I spend it is excessive or ridiculous, then I'm afraid that's their problem. I don't feel guilty about it at all. If it's an addiction, well, I've been addicted to far more damaging things over the years than buying tableware and photographs. It makes me happy. You know, I've got 1,000 candles in a closet in my home in Atlanta, and I suppose that is excessive. But I'll tell you what: it's the best-smelling closet you've ever been in in your life.

My shopping habit wasn't the only thing that was ramped up a notch. Everything seemed to be getting bigger, louder, more excessive. Bernie and I hadn't intended 'Rocket Man' to be a huge hit single – we saw ourselves as album artists – but that's what it turned into: it was Number Two in Britain, much higher than any of our singles had reached before, and went triple-platinum in the States. We'd stumbled onto a different kind of commerciality, and its success changed our audience. Screaming girls started appearing in the front rows and outside the stage door, tearfully clinging on to the car as we tried to get away. It felt really peculiar, as if they'd gone to see The Osmonds or David Cassidy but taken a wrong turn and somehow ended up at our gig instead.

I worked really hard, maybe too hard, but it felt like there was an unstoppable momentum behind me that carried me on no matter how exhausted I was, that drove me through any kind of setback. I contracted glandular fever just before we went into the studio to record *Don't Shoot Me, I'm Only the Piano Player* in the summer of 1972. I should have cancelled the sessions in order to recuperate, but I just went to the Château d'Hérouville and ploughed through them, running on adrenalin. You would never have known I was ill from listening to the album: the guy singing 'Daniel' and 'Crocodile Rock' doesn't sound unwell. A few weeks after we finished, I was back on tour again. I kept pushing the live show, trying to make it more over-the-top and outrageous. I started employing professional costume designers – first Annie Reavey, then Bill Whitten and Bob Mackie – and egging them on to do whatever they wanted, no matter how insane: more feathers, more sequins, brighter colours, bigger platforms. You've designed an outfit covered in multicoloured balls attached to pieces of elastic that glow in the dark? How many balls? Why don't you add some more? I won't be able to play the piano in it? Let me worry about that.

Then I got the idea of bringing 'Legs' Larry Smith, who'd been in The Bonzo Dog Doo-Dah Band, on tour with us. Legs was a drummer, but his other big talent was tap dancing. When we were making *Honky Château*, we had got him to come to the studio and tap-dance on a song called 'I Think I'm Going To Kill Myself', and now I got him to tap-dance onstage as well. His routine got more and more elaborate as the tour went on. Legs came onstage in a crash helmet and the vast train of a wedding dress. Then he started coming onstage accompanied by two dwarfs dressed as US Marines, while confetti rained from the ceiling. Then he came up with a routine where he and I would mime to 'Singing In The Rain', complete with dialogue. Larry would lean on my piano and sigh at me: 'Gee, Elton, I wish I could play like you. I'll bet you get all the boys.' As usual, no one even raised an eyebrow.

I even invited Larry along when I was asked to do the Royal Variety Performance, which caused a huge row. Bernard Delfont, who organized the show, mystifyingly didn't want a man in a wedding train and a crash helmet tap-dancing in front of the Queen Mother. I told him to fuck off, that I wouldn't play unless Larry came on, and he eventually relented. I thought that it was the best thing about the whole evening, apart from the fact that I got to share a dressing room with Liberace. He'd clearly forgotten about, or forgiven me for, my failure to appear at his London Palladium performance a couple of years before and was just divine, like a living embodiment of showbiz. He turned up with trunk after trunk of clothes. I thought I looked pretty outrageous myself – I was dressed in multicoloured lurex pinstripes with matching platform shoes and top hat – but, by comparison with his side of the dressing room, mine looked like a particularly dowdy corner of Marks and Spencer. He had a suit covered in tiny bulbs that lit up when he sat at the piano. He signed an autograph for me – his signature was in the shape of a piano – then spent the after-noon reeling off one fantastic story after another in an impossibly camp accent. The month before, he said, the hydraulic platform that raised him up through the stage had broken midway through his grand entrance; nothing if not a trouper, he'd performed for forty minutes with only his head visible to the audience.

I had become increasingly obsessed with making a big entrance onstage myself, because it was the one time that I was really mobile, when I wasn't stuck behind the piano. It reached a peak when we played the Hollywood Bowl in 1973. The stage was hung with a huge painting of me in top hat and tails, surrounded by dancing girls. First Tony King came onstage and introduced Linda Lovelace, who was the biggest porn star in the world at the time. Then a succession of lookalikes walked down an illuminated staircase flanked with palm trees at the back of the stage: the Queen, Batman and Robin, Frankenstein's Monster, the Pope. Finally I appeared, to the sound of the Twentieth-Century Fox theme, dressed in what I called the Incredible Cheese Straw Outfit: it was completely covered in white marabou feathers – the trousers as well as the jacket – and came with a matching hat. As I descended, the lids of five grand pianos sprang open, spelling out ELTON.

For the benefit of anyone who felt this was too subtle and understated, 400 white doves were meant to fly out of the grand pianos. I don't know whether they were asleep or too frightened to come out, but none appeared. As I jumped on top of my own piano, I found myself unexpectedly joined onstage by John Reid – who, judging by his furious expression, seemed to have taken the doves' non-appearance as a personal insult, as if they'd done it deliberately to challenge his managerial authority – and a more sheepish-looking Bernie, running from one piano to the next, frantically grabbing doves and throwing them into the air.

Dance routines, marabou feathers, doves flying – or not, as the case may be – out of grand pianos with my name on their lids: the band didn't like this kind of thing much, and nor did Bernie. He thought it was distracting attention from the music. I thought I was forging myself into a personality that was like nobody else in rock. And, besides, I was having fun. We would have these preposterous disagreements about it. The biggest song-writing partnership of the era, locked in a dispute backstage at the Santa Monica Civic, not about money or musical direction, but about whether it was a good idea for me to go onstage with an illuminated model of Father Christmas hanging in front of my willy. Sometimes Bernie had a point. The costumes literally did affect the music. I had a pair of glasses made in the shape of the word ELTON, with lights all over them. The combined weight of the glasses and the battery pack that powered the lights squashed my nostrils, so that it sounded like I was singing while holding my nose. In fairness, that probably did undercut the emotional impact of his lovingly crafted lyrics.

The Hollywood Bowl show was a huge event, a kind of launch for my next album, *Goodbye Yellow Brick Road*. By my standards at least, its making had been slightly torturous. We had decamped to Dynamic Sounds Studios in Kingston, Jamaica: it was considered very hip in those days to go and make your album somewhere more exotic than Europe. Dynamic Sounds had seemed like an obvious destination. Bob Marley had recorded there. So had Cat Stevens. It was where The Rolling Stones had made *Goats Head*

Soup. But we arrived to find there was a record-pressing plant attached to the studio, and the pressing plant workers were on strike. When you arrived, they would pull open the windows of the minibus that brought us from our hotel, and spit crushed fibreglass at everyone inside with blowpipes, which brought you out in a rash. Once you got into the studio itself, nothing worked. You would ask for a different microphone and someone would nod slowly and say, 'We can get one in maybe . . . three days?' It was hopeless. I've no idea how The Rolling Stones made an album there. Maybe Keith was so stoned that three days' wait for a working microphone felt like twenty minutes.

Eventually we gave up, went back to the hotel, and called to book recording sessions at the Château d'Hérouville. While we were waiting for a plane out of there, the band sat by the pool, occupying themselves with what appeared to be some kind of determined world record attempt involving the consumption of marijuana. By the time we got to the Château, we had so many songs that *Goodbye Yellow Brick Road* ended up a double album. When it came out, it took off in a way that none of us expected. It's quite a dark record in a lot of ways. Songs about sadness and disillusion, songs about alcoholics and prostitutes and murders, a song about a sixteen-year-old lesbian who ends up dead in a subway. But it just kept selling and selling and selling until I couldn't work out who was still buying it. I don't mean that flippantly: I really *didn't* know who was buying it. The American record company kept pushing me to release 'Bennie And The Jets' as a single and I fought them tooth and nail: it's a really odd song, it doesn't sound like anything else I've done, it's five minutes long; why don't you just put out 'Candle In The Wind', like we've done in Britain? Then they told me it was being played all over black radio stations in Detroit. When they released it, it shot up the Billboard Soul Chart: an unreal thing, seeing my name in among the singles by Eddie Kendricks and

Gladys Knight and Barry White. I may not have been the first white artist to do that, but I can say with some certainty I was the first artist from Pinner.

I was now so successful that I toured America using the Starship, an old Boeing 720 passenger plane that had been converted into an opulent flying tour bus for the exclusive use of the seventies' rock and roll elite. There were lurid tales about the parties Led Zeppelin had thrown on it. I was less bothered about what they'd done inside it than by what they'd done to the outside of it. The thing was painted purple and gold. It looked like a giant box of Milk Tray with wings. No problem: we could have it repainted to our specification. It was redone in red and blue with white stars. Much more tasteful.

Inside, the Starship had a bar decorated in orange and gold foil, with a long mirror behind it, an organ, dining tables, sofas and a TV with a video recorder, on which my mother insisted on watching *Deep Throat* – 'Everyone's talking about it, aren't they? What's it about, then?' – while she was eating her lunch. Whatever foul deeds Led Zeppelin had got up to on board, I'm pretty sure they never kept themselves amused for an hour watching a middle-aged lady shriek with horror while Linda Lovelace did her thing: 'Oh gawd, no, what's happening now? Oh! I can't look! How's she doing that?'

There was a bedroom at the back with shower, a fake fireplace and bedside tables made of plexiglass. You could hide yourself away in there and have sex. Or sulk, which is what I was doing one night when my American publicist, Sharon Lawrence, started knocking on the door and pleading with me to come out: 'Come back to the bar, we've got a surprise for you.' I told her to fuck off. She kept coming back. I kept telling her to fuck off. Eventually she burst into tears – 'You have to come to the bar! You have to! You have to!' – so I angrily opened the door and did as she asked, with a lot of huffing and eye-rolling and 'for fuck's sake, can't you leave me alone'-ing en route. When I got to the bar, Stevie Wonder was sitting at the organ, ready to play for me. He launched into 'Happy Birthday'. Had I not been cruising at 40,000 feet, I'd have prayed for the ground to open and swallow me.

From the outside, everything looked perfect: the tours were getting bigger and more spectacular, the records were selling so much that journalists had started to say I was the biggest pop artist in the world. John had taken over my management completely: the contract he had signed with DJM in 1971 had run out, and he had moved out of his offices and started his own management company. We had also started our own record company with Bernie and Gus Dudgeon called Rocket: not to release my records, but to find talent and give them a break. Sometimes we were better at spotting talent than developing it – we couldn't make a success of a band called Longdancer, despite the fact that their guitarist, a teenager called Dave Stewart, clearly had something about him, as was proven years later when he formed Eurythmics. But we had successes, too. We signed Kiki Dee, who John and I had known for years: she had been the only white British artist signed to Motown when John worked for them. She had been putting out singles since the early sixties, but never had a hit until we released her version of 'Amoureuse', a song by a French singer called Véronique Sanson that had flopped in the UK, but that Tony King had noticed and suggested to Kiki.

But beneath the surface, things were starting to go wrong. We spent the first weeks of 1974 recording at the Caribou Ranch, a studio up in the Rocky Mountains that gave its name to our new album: *Caribou*. It could be hard to sing at such a high altitude, which is how I ended up throwing a tantrum while we were recording 'Don't Let The Sun Go Down On Me'. After announcing that I hated the song so much we were going to stop recording it immediately and send it to Engelbert Humperdinck – 'and if he doesn't want it, tell him to send it to Lulu! She can put it on a B-side!' – I was coaxed back to the vocal booth and completed the take. Then I yelled at Gus Dudgeon that I hated it even more now it was finished and was going to kill him with my bare hands if he put it on the album. Apart from that, it was great up at Caribou. The studio was much plusher than the Château. You stayed in beautiful log cabins, filled with antiques – the bed I slept in was supposed to have belonged to Grover Cleveland, a nineteenth-century president of the United States. There was a screening room for movies, and musicians passing through Denver or Boulder would drop by to visit. Having obviously forgiven me for the incident on the Starship, Stevie Wonder turned up one day and took out a snowmobile, insisting on driving it himself. To pre-empt your question: no, I have absolutely no idea how Stevie Wonder successfully piloted a snowmobile through the Rocky Mountains of Colorado without killing himself, or indeed anyone else, in the process, but he did.

One night we were finishing up, when I wandered into a room at the back of the studio and spotted John fiddling with something on a table. He had a straw and some white powder. I asked what it was, and he told me it was cocaine. I asked what it did and he said, 'Oh, it just makes you feel good.' So I asked if I could have some, and he said yes. The first line I snorted made me retch. I hated the feeling in the back of my throat, that weird combination of numbness brought on by the drug itself and a sort of powdery dryness from whatever crap the coke had been cut with. I couldn't get rid of it, no matter how often I swallowed. I went out to the toilet and threw up. And then I immediately went back into the room where John was and asked for another line.

What the hell was I doing? I tried it, I hated it, it made me puke – hello? Talk about God's way of telling you to leave it at that. It's hard to see how I could have been given a clearer warning that this was a bad idea unless it had started raining brimstone and I'd been visited by a plague of boils. So why didn't

I leave it at that? Partly because throwing up didn't stop the coke affecting me, and I liked how it made me feel. That jolt of confidence and euphoria, the sense that I could suddenly open up, that I didn't feel shy or intimidated, that I could talk to anybody. That was all bullshit, of course. I was full of energy, I was inquisitive, I had a sense of humour and a thirst for knowledge: I didn't need a drug to make me talk to people. If anything, cocaine gave me too much confidence for my own good. If I hadn't been coked out of my head when The Rolling Stones turned up in Colorado and asked me to come onstage with them, I might have just performed 'Honky Tonk Women', waved to the crowd and made my exit. Instead, I decided it was going so well, I'd stay on and jam along to the rest of their set, without first taking the precaution of asking the Stones if they wanted an auxiliary keyboard player. For a while, I thought Keith Richards kept staring at me because he was awestruck by the brilliance of my improvised contributions to their oeuvre. After a few songs, it finally penetrated my brain that the expression on his face wasn't really suggestive of profound musical appreciation. Actually, he looked remarkably like someone who was about to inflict appalling violence on a musician who'd outstayed his welcome. I quickly scuttled off, noting as I went that Keith was still staring at me in a manner that suggested we'd be discussing this later, and decided it might be best if I didn't hang around for the aftershow party.

But there was something more to cocaine than the way it made me feel. Cocaine had a certain cachet about it. It was fashionable and exclusive. Doing it was like becoming a member of an elite little clique, that secretly indulged in something edgy, dangerous and illicit. Pathetically enough, that really appealed to me. I'd become successful and popular, but I never felt cool. Even back in Bluesology, I was the nerdy one, the one who didn't look like a pop star, who never quite carried off the hip clothes, who spent all his time in record shops while the rest of the band were out getting laid and taking drugs. And cocaine felt cool: the subtly coded conversations to work out who had some, or who wanted some – who was part of the clique and who wasn't – the secretive visits to the bathrooms of clubs and bars. Of course, that was all bullshit, too. I already was part of a club. Ever since my solo career had begun, I'd been shown nothing but kindness and love by other artists. From the minute I turned up in LA, musicians I adored and worshipped – people who'd once just been mythic names on album sleeves and record labels – had fallen over themselves to offer friendship and support. But when it finally arrived, my success had happened so fast that, despite the warm welcome, I couldn't help but still feel slightly out of place, as if I didn't quite belong.

As it turned out, doing a line of coke then immediately going back for another one was very me. I was never the kind of drug addict who couldn't get out of bed without a line, or who needed to take it every day. But once I started, I couldn't stop, until I was absolutely certain there was no cocaine anywhere in the vicinity. I realized quite quickly that I had to get someone else – a PA or a roadie – to look after my coke for me: not because I was too grand or too scared to be the stash holder, but because if you left me in charge of that evening's supply of cocaine there would be none of it left by teatime. My appetite for the stuff was unbelievable – enough to attract comment in the circles I was moving in. Given that I was a rock star spending a lot of time in seventies LA, this was a not inconsiderable feat. Once again, you might think this would have given me pause for thought, but I'm afraid the next sixteen years were full of incidents that would have given any rational human being pause concerning their drug consumption, as we shall discover. That was the problem. Because I was doing coke, I wasn't a rational human being anymore. You might tell yourself you're fine, using as evidence the fact that your drug use isn't affecting your career. But you can't take that amount of coke and think in a sane and proper way. You become unreasonable and irresponsible, self-obsessed, a law unto yourself. It's your way or the highway. It's a horrible fucking drug.

I'd made the worst decision of my life, but I didn't realize it then. By contrast, the problems in my relationship with John were staring me in the face. I said before that I was incredibly naive about gay relationships. One thing I didn't know was that John thought it was perfectly acceptable to have sex with other people, behind my back. Open relationships are a lot more common among gay men than straight couples, but that's not what I wanted. I was in love. When he realized that, it didn't stop him being promiscuous, it just made him dishonest about it. That led to some really humiliating scenes. John vanished during a party at the director John Schlesinger's house in LA. I went looking for him and found him upstairs, in bed with someone. My mum rang me up on tour to tell me that she'd popped round to the house in Virginia Water and discovered John was hosting a sex party in my absence. I'd confront him, there would be a huge row, things would calm down and then he'd go out and do exactly the same thing again. Or, worse, he'd come up with some new variant on sleeping around that seemed designed to send me even more hysterical. I found out he'd gone to a film premiere, picked up a famous TV actress and started an affair with her. *Her.* So now he was fucking women as well. What was I supposed to do about that particular twist in our relationship?

It went on and on and on, and it was miserable. I seemed to spend half my life in tears over his behaviour, but it made absolutely no difference. So why didn't I leave him? Partly it was out of love. I'd fallen head over heels for John, and when you're like that with someone who cheats, you'll make any excuse for them, over and over again, kid yourself that this time they really mean it and from now on it's going to be OK. And, in his own way, John really did love me. He was just completely incapable of keeping his dick in his pants if left to his own devices.

I also stayed because I was scared of him. John had a temper that could easily spill over into violence, especially if he'd been drinking or doing coke. Sometimes his rages were unwittingly funny. I'd ring the offices of Rocket and ask to speak to him: 'Oh, he's not here. He lost his temper and tried to throw an electric typewriter down the stairs. But it was still plugged in, so that didn't really work. Which made him even more angry, so he fired the entire staff and stormed out. We're just wondering whether we should go home or not.' But most of the time, they weren't funny at all. I watched John threaten someone with a broken glass at a party hosted by Billy Gaff, Rod Stewart's manager. He hit a doorman outside a hotel in San Francisco after an argument about parking a car. He punched a sound engineer in front of a room full of American journalists at the launch of *Goodbye Yellow Brick Road*. When we were touring in New Zealand in 1974, he threw a glass of wine in the face of the local record label promotions guy when the party they'd thrown for me ran out of whisky. When a female reporter from a local paper tried to intervene, he punched her in the face. Later the same night, at a different party, I got into an argument with another local journalist over the earlier incident, which I hadn't actually seen happen. John came flying across the room, knocked him to the floor and started kicking him.

The next morning, we were both arrested and charged with assault. I was acquitted, charged $50 costs, paid up and got out of New Zealand as quickly as possible. I left without John, who had his appeal for bail turned down and was eventually sentenced to twenty-eight days in Mount Eden prison. I flew home without him. His behaviour was completely indefensible, but it was an era in which the line between tough-guy rock manager and thug was frequently blurred – look at Peter Grant and Led Zeppelin – and as I waited in on a Saturday night for his weekly call from prison, I somehow managed to construct a version of events in my head where he was the injured party, acting nobly in my defence, aided by his claim that the female journalist had called him a poof before he hit her, as if that justified it.

It wasn't until John hit *me* that I came to my senses. It happened the night we threw a fancy dress party at Hercules. I can't even remember what the argument was about, probably the latest episode in John's catalogue of cheating, but it started before the guests even got there and became more and more heated. There was shouting, doors were slammed, and a beautiful art deco mirror that Charlie Watts from The Rolling Stones had given us got smashed. Then John dragged me into the bathroom and punched me in the face, hard. I reeled backwards. I was so shocked, I didn't retaliate. He stormed out and I looked in the bathroom mirror. My nose was bleeding and my face was cut. I cleaned myself up and the party went ahead as if nothing had happened. Everyone had a great time – Derf turned up in drag, Tony King arrived completely covered in gold paint, like Shirley Eaton in *Goldfinger*. But something had happened and, to me, it felt like a switch had finally been flicked off. I couldn't make excuses for John's behaviour any longer. I couldn't stay with someone who hit me.

I really don't think John expected me to tell him it was over. Even after he moved out, to a house on Montpelier Square in Knightsbridge, and I asked my mum and Derf to help me find a place to live on my own – I literally didn't have time to go house-hunting myself – I think he was still in love with me. I got the sense that if I'd asked him to come back, he would have been there like a shot. But I didn't want him back. I wanted him to stay as my manager, but everything else about our relationship changed. The balance of power shifted: until then, he'd been the dominant personality, but after we broke up as a couple, I became more confident and assertive. He took on other acts as a manager – not

just musicians, comedians like Billy Connolly and Barry Humphries
– but our business relationship still worked, because I knew how
astute he was, and how great his ear was for music. One morning,
at the offices in South Audley Street, he said he wanted to play
me something by one of his new clients that was going to be a
huge hit all over the world. We listened to the song and I shook
my head, incredulous.

'You're not actually going to release that, are you?'

He frowned. 'What's wrong with it?'

'Well, for one thing, it's about three hours long. For another,
it's the campest thing I've ever heard in my life. And the title's
absolutely ridiculous as well.'

John was completely unfazed. 'I'm telling you now,' he said,
lifting the test pressing of 'Bohemian Rhapsody' off the turntable,
'that is going to be one of the biggest records of all time.'

But if Queen's most famous song sailed over my head at first, I
got Freddie Mercury straight away. From the minute I met him, I
loved him. As was tradition, he got given a drag name: Melina, after
Melina Mercouri, the Greek actress. He was just magnificent.
Incredibly smart and adventurous. Kind and generous and thoughtful,
but outrageously funny. Oh God, if you went out clubbing with
him and Tony King – they were great friends – you'd spend the
whole night howling. No one was spared, not even the other
members of Queen: 'Have you seen the guitarist, darling? Mrs
May? Have you seen what she wears onstage? Clogs! Fucking clogs!
How did I end up onstage with a guitarist who wears fucking
clogs?'

And not Michael Jackson, who Freddie called Mahalia, a name
I don't think Michael found anywhere near as hilarious as Freddie
did. He had incurred Freddie's wrath by trying to interest him in
his menagerie of animals, and Freddie had turned retelling the
story into a tour-de-force performance that rivalled anything he
did onstage. 'Oh, darling! That dreadful llama! All the way to

California to see Mrs Jackson and she leads me out into the garden and there's the llama. Then she asks me to help get it back into its pen! I was wearing a white suit and I got covered in mud, and eventually I had to shout at her: "For fuck's sake, Mahalia, get your fucking llama away from me!" Oh,' he would add, shuddering for comic effect, 'it was a nightmare, darling.'

six

I first met John Lennon through Tony King, who had moved to LA to become Apple Records' general manager in the US. In fact, the first time I met John Lennon, he was dancing with Tony King. Nothing unusual in that, other than the fact that they weren't in a nightclub, there was no music playing and Tony was in full drag as Queen Elizabeth II. They were at Capitol Records in Hollywood, where Tony's new office was, shooting a TV advert for John's forthcoming album *Mind Games*, and, for reasons best known to John, this was the big concept.

I took to him straight away. It wasn't just that he was a Beatle and therefore one of my idols. He was a Beatle who thought it was a good idea to promote his new album by dancing around with a man dragged up as the Queen, for fuck's sake. I thought: We're going to get on like a house on fire. And I was right. As soon as we started talking, it felt like I'd known him my entire life.

We began spending a lot of time together, whenever I was in America. He'd separated from Yoko and was living in Los Angeles with May Pang. I know that period in his life is supposed to have been really troubled and unpleasant and dark, but I've got to be honest, I never saw that in him at all. I heard stories occasionally – about some sessions he'd done with Phil Spector that went completely out of control, about him going crazy one night and smashing up the record producer Lou Adler's house. I could see a darkness in some of the people he was hanging out with: Harry Nilsson was a sweet guy, an incredibly talented singer and songwriter, but one drink too many and he'd turn into someone else, someone you really had to watch yourself around. And John and I certainly took a lot of drugs together and had some berserk nights out, as poor old Dr John would tell you. We went to see him at the Troubadour and he invited John onstage to jam. John was so pissed he ended up playing the organ with his elbows. It somehow fell to me to get him offstage.

In fact, you didn't even need to go out to have a berserk night in John's company. One evening in New York, we were holed up in my suite at the Sherry-Netherland hotel, determinedly making our way through a pile of coke, when someone knocked at the door. My first thought was that it was the police: if you've taken a lot of cocaine and someone unexpectedly knocks at the door, your immediate thought is *always* that it's the police. John gestured at me to see who it was. I looked through the spyhole. My reaction was a peculiar combination of relief and incredulity. 'John,' I whispered. 'It's Andy Warhol.'

John shook his head frantically and drew his finger across his throat. 'No fucking way. Don't answer it,' he hissed.

'What?' I whispered back. 'What do you mean don't answer it? It's *Andy Warhol.*'

There was more knocking. John rolled his eyes. 'Has he got that fucking camera with him?' he asked.

I looked again through the spyhole and nodded. Andy took his Polaroid camera everywhere.

'Right,' said John. 'And do you want him coming in here taking photos when you've got *icicles* of coke hanging out of your nose?'

I had to concede that I did not. 'Then don't fucking answer it,' whispered John, and we crept back to doing whatever we were doing, trying to ignore the continued knocking of the world's most famous pop artist.

But I genuinely never encountered that nasty, intimidating, destructive aspect of John that people talk about, the biting, acerbic wit. I'm not trying to paint some saintly posthumous portrait at all; I obviously knew that side of him existed, I just never saw it first-hand. All I ever saw from him was kindness and gentleness and fun, so much so that I took my mum and Derf to meet him. We went out to dinner, and when John went to the toilet, Derf thought it would be a great joke to take his false teeth out and put them in John's drink: there was something infectious about John's sense of humour that made people do things like that. Jesus, he was so funny. Whenever I was with him – or even better, him and Ringo – I just laughed and laughed and laughed.

We became so close that when his ex-wife Cynthia brought their son Julian to New York to see him, he asked me and Tony to chaperone them on their voyage over. We travelled to America on the SS *France*, this gorgeous old ship, on its last voyage from Southampton to New York. Most of my band and their partners came too. The other passengers were quite snooty towards us – these rich, enormous American women saying things like, 'He's supposed to be famous, but I've never heard of him,' whenever I walked past them – but in fairness, I had dyed my hair bright green and brought suitcases filled with suits by the designer Tommy Nutter that were so loud they could permanently damage your hearing. I could hardly complain about attracting attention, adverse or otherwise. They liked me even less when I won the bingo one afternoon, not least because I got overexcited and screamed 'BINGO!' at the top of my voice. I subsequently discovered that the correct way to signify that you'd won on board the SS *France* was to graciously and demurely murmur the word 'house'. Well, that's not how they teach you to play bingo in Pinner, baby.

I didn't care. I was having a blast: playing squash, going to the terrible cabaret shows, which for some reason always ended with a rousing singalong of 'Hava Nagila'. Midway through the journey, I got a ship-to-shore call telling me that my latest album, *Caribou*, which had been released in June 1974, had gone platinum. And I was writing its follow-up. Bernie had come up with a set of songs about our early years together: they were all in sequence and they kind of told our story. They were beautiful lyrics. Songs about trying to write songs. Songs about no one wanting our songs. A song about my stupid failed suicide attempt in Furlong Road and a song about the weird relationship we had developed. The latter was called 'We All Fall In Love Sometimes'. It made me well up because it was true. I wasn't in love with Bernie physically, but I loved him like a brother; he was the best friend I'd ever had.

The lyrics were even easier than usual to write music for, which was just as well, because they'd only let me use the music room for a couple of hours a day during lunch. The rest of the time it was occupied by the ship's classical pianist. When I turned up, she would leave with a great display of weary altruism, then head to a room directly above it and immediately strike up again. Sometimes she'd have an opera singer with her, who was the star turn at the aforementioned terrible cabaret. So I'd spend two hours trying to drown them out. That was how *Captain Fantastic and the Brown Dirt Cowboy* was written. I'd write a song – or sometimes two – every day during lunch break, to the accompaniment of an aggrieved pianist hammering away through the ceiling. And I'd have to remember them. I didn't have a tape recorder with me.

In New York, we stayed at the Pierre hotel on Fifth Avenue. John Lennon was in the suite above mine, and called down. He wanted to play us the rough mixes of his new album. Moreover, he wanted me to play on two of the songs, 'Surprise Surprise' and 'Whatever Gets You Thru The Night'. The second track sounded like a hit, even more so a couple of nights later when we went to the Record Plant East studio, just off Times Square. The overdub engineer was Jimmy Iovine, who ended up becoming one of the biggest music moguls in the world, but John produced it himself and he worked really quickly. Everyone thinks of John as someone who spent ages in the studio experimenting, because of *Sergeant Pepper* and 'Strawberry Fields', but he was fast, and he got bored easily, which was right up my street. By the time we were finished, I was convinced it was going to be Number One. John wasn't: Paul had had number one solo singles, George had had number one solo singles, Ringo had had number one solo singles, but he never had. So I said we'd have a bet – if it got to Number One, he had to come onstage with me. I just wanted to see him play live, which he'd hardly done at all since The Beatles split up; a couple of appearances at benefit gigs and that was it.

To his credit, he didn't try to shirk the bet when 'Whatever Gets You Thru The Night' did make Number One, not even after he travelled up to a show in Boston with Tony to see what he was getting himself into. I came onstage for the encore wearing something that basically resembled a little heart-shaped chocolate box with a tunic attached to it, and John turned to Tony, looking a bit aghast, and said, 'Fucking hell, is this what rock and roll's all about nowadays, then?'

But he still played with us at Madison Square Garden on Thanksgiving 1974, on the condition that we made sure Yoko didn't come: they were still estranged. Of course, Yoko turned up anyway – which I have to say is *very* Yoko – but Tony made sure her tickets were out of the sightline of the stage. Before the show, she sent John a gardenia, which he wore in his buttonhole onstage. I'm not sure whether that was what made him so nervous beforehand, or if it was just because he didn't know what to expect when he walked out. But either way, he was suddenly terrified. He threw up before the show. He even tried to get Bernie to come onstage with him, but to no avail: Bernie always hated the limelight, and not even a desperate Beatle could convince him to change his mind.

In my whole career, I've honestly never heard a crowd make a noise like the one they made when I introduced him. It just went on and on and on. But I knew how they felt. I was as giddy about it as they were, so were the rest of the band. It was probably the highlight of our careers to that point, to have someone like that share a stage with you. The three songs flew by, and he was off. He came back for the encore, this time with Bernie in tow, both of them playing tambourines on 'The Bitch Is Back'. It was fabulous.

After the show, Yoko came backstage. We all ended up back at the Pierre hotel – me, John, Yoko, Tony and John Reid. We were sat in a booth having a drink and – as if the whole situation wasn't peculiar enough – Uri Geller suddenly materialized out of nowhere, came over to our table and started bending all the spoons and forks on it. Then he began doing his mind-reading act. It had been a bizarre day. But ultimately it led to John reuniting with Yoko, having Sean – my godson – and retreating into a life of domestic contentment in the Dakota Building. I was happy for him, even if I could think of better places to retreat into domestic contentment in than the Dakota. There was something really sinister about that building, the architecture of it. Just looking at it gave me the creeps. You know, Roman Polanski chose to film *Rosemary's Baby* there for a reason.

Recording *Captain Fantastic* had turned out to be as easy as writing it. The sessions were a breeze: we had gone back to Caribou in the summer of 1974 and taped the songs in the order they appear on the album, as though we were telling the story as we went along. We had knocked out a couple of singles, too, a cover of 'Lucy In The Sky With Diamonds' that John played guitar and sang backing vocals on, and 'Philadelphia Freedom', which is one of the few songs I ever commissioned Bernie to write. Normally,

I just let him write lyrics about whatever he wanted – we'd learned we couldn't really write to order back in the days when we kept trying to write singles for Tom Jones or Cilla Black and failing miserably – but Billie Jean King had asked me to write a theme song for her tennis team, the Philadelphia Freedoms. I couldn't refuse; I adored Billie Jean. We'd met at a party in LA a year before, and she'd become one of my best friends. It seems a strange comparison, but she and John Lennon reminded me of each other. They were both really driven, they were both kind, they both loved to laugh, they both felt really strongly that they could use their fame to change things. John was politically engaged, Billie was a huge pioneer for feminism, for gay rights, for women's rights in sport, not just tennis. All today's huge female tennis stars should get on their knees and thank her, because she was the one who had the guts to turn round when she won the US Open and say, 'You have to give women the same prize money as men, or I'm not playing next year'. I just love her to death.

Perhaps understandably, Bernie wasn't hugely enamoured with the idea of writing about tennis – it's not exactly the ideal topic for a pop song – so instead, he wrote about the city of Philadelphia. That worked perfectly, because the song's sound was influenced by the music that was coming out of the city at the time: The O'Jays, MFSB, Harold Melvin And The Blue Notes. That was the music I heard when I went out to gay clubs in New York: Crisco Disco, Le Jardin and 12 West. I loved them, even though Crisco Disco once refused to let me in. I was with Divine, too, the legendary drag queen. I know, I know: Elton John and Divine getting turned away from a gay club. But he was wearing a kaftan, I had on a brightly coloured jacket and they said we were over-dressed: 'Whaddaya think this is? Fuckin' Halloween?'

You didn't go to those places to pick up guys, or at least I didn't. I just went there to dance, and if there was someone there at the end of the night, then great. No drugs, except maybe poppers.

You didn't need them. The music was enough: 'Honey Bee' by Gloria Gaynor, 'I'll Always Love My Mama' by The Intruders. Fabulous records, really inspiring, brave music. We got Gene Page, who arranged all Barry White's records, to do the strings on 'Philadelphia Freedom' and we got the sound and style right. We must have done – a few months after it came out, MFSB covered it and named an album after it.

'Philadelphia Freedom' went platinum in America, then a few months later, *Captain Fantastic* became the first album in history to go straight into the US charts at Number One. I was everywhere in 1975. Not just on the radio: *everywhere*. I was in amusement arcades – Bally made a Captain Fantastic pinball machine. I was on black TV: one of the first white artists ever to be invited to appear on *Soul Train*. I was interviewed by the exceptionally laid-back Don Cornelius, who took a shine to yet another Tommy Nutter creation I was wearing, this time with huge lapels and brown and gold pinstripes: 'Hey, brother, where did you get that *suit*?'

But I was still keen to keep moving. I decided to change the band and let Dee and Nigel go. I rang them myself. They took the news quite well – Dee was more upset than Nigel, but there wasn't a huge row or a feeling of bad blood from either of them. I feel worse about it now than I did at the time. It must have been devastating for them – they'd been integral for years and we were at the peak of our careers. Back then, I was always looking forward, and I felt in my gut that I needed to revamp our sound: make it funkier and harder-driving. I brought in Caleb Quaye on guitar and Roger Pope on drums, who'd played on *Empty Sky* and *Tumbleweed Connection*, and two American session musicians, James Newton Howard and Kenny Passarelli, on keyboards and bass.

I auditioned another American guitarist as well, but it wasn't a success. For one thing, it didn't gel musically, and for another he freaked out everyone else in the band by telling us that he liked fucking chickens up the arse, then cutting their heads off. Apparently when you do that their sphincters contract and it makes you come. I couldn't work out whether he had an absolutely horrendous sense of humour or an absolutely horrendous sex life. There aren't many rules in rock and roll, but there are some: follow your gut musical instincts, make sure you read the small print before you sign and, if at all possible, try not to form a band with someone who fucks chickens up the arse and decapitates them. Or even talks about it. Whichever it is, it's going to wear on your nerves after a while if you have to share a hotel room with them.

There was one other complication. Bernie's marriage to Maxine had broken up, and she'd started having an affair with Kenny Passarelli. So my new bass player was sleeping with my songwriting partner's wife. It was obviously really hurtful for Bernie, but I had enough going on in my own life without getting embroiled in other people's relationships.

I took the new band to Amsterdam to rehearse. The rehearsals were fantastic – we were an absolutely shit-hot band – but the days off were bedlam: it turned out we were absolutely shit-hot at taking drugs, too. Tony King turned up with Ringo Starr and we all went on a boat trip along the canals, which swiftly degenerated into a mammoth drug fest. It was completely debauched. I'm afraid the aesthetic loveliness of the Grachtengordel went entirely unnoticed that day. Everybody was too busy doing coke and blowing spliff smoke into each other's mouths. Ringo got so stoned that, at one point, he asked if he could join the band. At least, that's what people told me afterwards – I didn't hear him. If he did, he probably forgot he said it about ninety seconds after the words came out of his mouth.

One of the reasons I was taking so many drugs was because I was heartbroken. I'd fallen in love with someone who was straight and didn't love me. I spent so much time in my hotel room weeping and listening to 10CC's 'I'm Not In Love' that Tony eventually had a gold disc made up and presented me with it: to Elton John for a million plays of 'I'm Not In Love'.

In fact, since I had broken up with John, my personal life had been, more or less, a disaster. I'd fall in love with straight men all the time, chase after the thing I couldn't have. Sometimes it went on for months and months, this madness of thinking that today was the day you'd get a phone call from them saying 'oh, by the way, I love you', despite the fact that they'd told you it was never going to happen.

Or I'd see someone I liked the look of in a gay bar and before I'd actually spoken to them, I'd be hopelessly in love, convinced this was the man I was fated to share the rest of my life with and mentally sketching out a wonderful future. It was always the same type of guy. Blond, blue eyes, good-looking and younger than me, so I could smother them with a kind of fatherly love – the sort of love I suppose I thought I'd missed out on myself as a kid. I didn't pick them up so much as take them hostage. 'Right, you have to give up what you're doing, come on the road, fly round the world with me.' I'd buy them the watch and the shirt and the cars, but eventually these boys had no reason to be, except to be with me, and I was busy, so they'd be left on the sidelines. I didn't realize it at the time, but I was taking their existence away from them. And after three or four months they'd end up resenting it, I'd end up getting bored with them, and it would end in tears. And then I'd get someone else to get rid of them for me and start again. It was absolutely dreadful behaviour: I'd have one leaving at the airport at the same time as the new one was flying in.

It was a decadent era, and plenty of other pop stars were behaving in a similar way – Rod Stewart occasionally let girls know he'd finished with them by just leaving a plane ticket on their bed, so he wasn't going to win any awards for chivalry either. But somewhere in the back of my mind, I knew *this can't be right*.

I had to have some arm-candy, though, someone to talk to. I

couldn't stand being on my own. There was no solitude, no reflec-
tion. I had to be with people. I was incredibly immature. I was
still the little boy from Pinner Hill Road underneath it all. The
events, the shows, the records, the success were all great, but when
I was away from that, I wasn't an adult, I was a teenager. I had
been completely wrong when I thought that changing my name
meant I'd changed as a person. I wasn't Elton, I was Reg. And
Reg was still the same as he'd been fifteen years ago, hiding in
his bedroom while his parents fought: insecure and body-conscious
and self-loathing. I didn't want to go home to him at night. If I
did, the misery could be all-consuming.

One night, while I was recording with the new band up at
Caribou studios, I took an overdose of Valium before I went to
bed. Twelve tablets. I can't remember what exactly prompted me
to do that, although it was probably some catastrophic love affair
gone wrong. When I woke up the next day, I panicked, rushed
downstairs and called Connie Pappas, who worked with John Reid,
and told her what I'd done. While I was talking to her, I blacked
out. James Newton Howard heard me collapse and carried me
back upstairs to my room. They called a doctor, who prescribed
me pills for my nerves. With the benefit of hindsight, that seems
quite an odd thing to do to someone who's just tried to finish
himself off with a load of pills for his nerves, but they must have
helped, at least in the short term – the sessions got finished.

The new band's first show was at London's Wembley Stadium
on 21 June 1975. It was more like a one-day festival than a
gig, called Midsummer Music. I'd picked the bill myself: a band
signed to our label, Rocket, called Stackridge, Rufus with Chaka
Khan, Joe Walsh, The Eagles and The Beach Boys. They were all
great. The audience loved them. For my headlining set, I played
Captain Fantastic and the Brown Dirt Cowboy in its entirety, all ten

songs, from start to finish. It was the biggest show I'd ever played. Everything was perfect – the sound, the support acts, even the weather. And it was an unmitigated disaster.

Here's something I learned. If you've elected to come onstage immediately after The Beach Boys – whose set has consisted of virtually every hit from one of the most incredible and best-loved catalogues of hits in the history of pop music – it's a really, really bad idea to play ten new songs in a row that no one in the audience is particularly familiar with, because the album they come from was only released a couple of weeks ago. Unfortunately, I learned this vital lesson about three or four songs into the Wembley performance, when I sensed a restlessness in the crowd, the way schoolkids get restless during a particularly long assembly. We ploughed on. We sounded wonderful – like I said, we were a shit-hot band. People started to leave. I was terrified. It was years since I'd lost an audience. The feeling I used to get onstage in the clubs when Long John Baldry insisted on playing 'The Threshing Machine' or doing his Della Reese impersonation came flooding back.

The obvious thing to do would be to turn it around and start playing the hits. But I couldn't. For one thing, it was a matter of artistic integrity. And for another, I'd made a big speech when we came onstage about performing the album in full. I couldn't just suddenly strike up with 'Crocodile Rock' halfway through. Fuck. I'd have to stick with it. I could already imagine what the reviews were going to be like, and I was only half an hour into the show. We kept going. The songs still sounded wonderful. More people left. I started thinking about the big celebratory post-gig party that was planned. It was going to be filled with stars who were supposed to have been dazzled by my performance: Billie Jean, Paul McCartney, Ringo Starr. Great. This is just fucking wonderful. I'm screwing up in front of 82,000 people *and half The Beatles*.

We eventually got round to the hits, but it was too little, too late, as the reviews quite rightly pointed out. We went back to America, having been taught both a lesson in the perils of artistic integrity and that you're never too successful to fall flat on your arse.

I was spending more and more time over in the States, so much that it made sense to rent a house in LA. I found one at the top of Tower Grove Drive, which I eventually bought. It was a Spanish Colonial-style house that had been built for the silent movie star John Gilbert. He'd lived there while he was having an affair with Greta Garbo. There was a hut in the garden by a waterfall, and that was allegedly where Garbo slept when she wanted to be alone.

It was a nice neighbourhood, although a house nearby did burn down shortly after I moved there. The fire allegedly started because the owner was freebasing cocaine, something I very much frowned on. Cooking up drugs meant that you were a druggie, which – with the help of some remarkably convoluted internal logic – I had worked out that I definitely wasn't, despite some pretty compelling evidence to the contrary. I would stay up all night on coke, then not touch it for six months. So I wasn't an addict. I was fine.

It was a beautiful house, and I employed a housekeeper called Alice to look after the place and nurse me through my hangovers. I filled it with all the stuff I was collecting – art nouveau, art deco, Bugatti furniture, Gallé lamps, Lalique, incredible posters – but I only really lived in three rooms: my bedroom, the TV room and the snooker room. Actually, I mostly used the snooker room to seduce guys. Strip snooker! It usually seemed to do the trick, especially after a couple of lines of coke.

That was another reason I took a lot of coke: I found it was an aphrodisiac, which is strange, because for most people it kills the erection side of things completely. Never a problem for me, I'm afraid. Quite the opposite. If I took enough coke I could stay hard for days. And I liked the fantasy of it: I did things on coke that I would never have had the courage to do or try if I hadn't been. It takes all the inhibitions out of people. Even straight guys sometimes. You gave them a couple of lines and they'd do stuff they wouldn't ordinarily do in a million years. Then regret it in the morning, I suppose – or occasionally come back for more.

But I was never actually into fucking that much. I was an observer, a voyeur. I'd kind of set up my perversion, have two or three guys doing things for me to watch. That was where my sexual pleasure came from, getting a bunch of people who wouldn't normally have sex with each other, to have sex with each other. But I didn't really participate. I just watched, took Polaroids, organized things. The only problem was that I was incredibly houseproud, so they'd end up having sex on the snooker table with me shouting, 'Make sure you don't come on the baize!' which tended to puncture the atmosphere a bit. Not being that interested in having sex myself is the reason I never got HIV. If I had been, I'd almost certainly be dead.

Tower Grove Drive turned into a big party house, the place everyone came back to after a night out. LA was the centre of the music industry in the mid-seventies. Plus, LA had amazing gay clubs: the After Dark and Studio One. The first was a disco, quite underground; the second had cabaret. It was where I saw Eartha Kitt, who I'd loved when I was a kid, although strictly speaking I didn't actually see Eartha Kitt perform. I went backstage to meet her before the show and her opening words to me were: 'Elton John. I never liked anything you did.' Oh, really? Well, thanks for your frank and honest appraisal. I think I'll go home.

If Dusty Springfield was around, we'd go to the roller derby to see the LA Thunderbirds. It was so camp and fabulous, all scripted, like wrestling, but lesbians loved it – it was basically a load of dykes whizzing round on skates and fighting each other. And we'd have fantastic lunch and dinner parties. Franco Zeffirelli came for lunch and revealed that his close friends called him Irene. Simon and Garfunkel had dinner one night, then played charades. At least, they tried to play charades. They were terrible at it. The best thing I can say about them is that they were better than Bob Dylan. He couldn't get the hang of the 'how many syllables?' thing at all. He couldn't do 'sounds like' either, come to think of it. One of the best lyricists in the world, the greatest man of letters in the history of rock music, and he can't seem to tell you whether a word's got one syllable or two syllables or what it rhymes with! He was so hopeless, I started throwing oranges at him. Or so I was informed the next morning, by a cackling Tony King. That's not really a phone call you want to receive when you're struggling with a hangover. 'Morning, darling – do you remember throwing oranges at Bob Dylan last night?' Oh God.

There was a strange, dark undercurrent to LA, too. The Manson murders still hung over the place six years on. They'd left this weird sense that you were never really safe there, even in a big house in Beverly Hills. These days, everyone has security guards and CCTV, but no one did then, not even the former Beatles, which is why I woke up one morning to find a girl sitting on the end of my bed, staring at me. I couldn't get up, because I never wore anything when I slept. All I could do was sit there screaming at her to get the fuck out. She didn't say anything back, she just kept staring, which was somehow worse than if she'd spoken. Eventually the housekeeper came down and got her out of there. It scared the shit out of me – we couldn't work out how the hell she'd got in.

But you didn't need a stalker to alert you to LA's dark side. One night, I went to see the Average White Band play at the Troubadour. They were so fantastic that I got onstage and jammed with them, dragging Cher and Martha Reeves up with me. After the gig, I took the band out to a place called Le Restaurant, which served great food and didn't frown on outré behaviour: the management hadn't even blanched at John Reid's birthday party, which was extremely tolerant of them, given that a friend had brought the horse he bought John as a present into the restaurant and it had immediately shat on the floor. We stayed out until 6 a.m. There was something lovely about spending time with them, a young British band just on the verge of becoming huge, playing a residency at the Troubadour and boggling at the prospect of making it in America: they reminded me of me five years before. But two days later, I got a phone call from John Reid, telling me the Average White Band's drummer, Robbie, was dead. They'd gone to another party the following night, up in the Hollywood Hills, and taken heroin some creep had given them, thinking it was cocaine. He died in his hotel room a few hours later.

I suppose it could have happened anywhere, but his death seemed to sum up LA. It could feel like a place where the tired old line about dreams coming true wasn't a tired old line but a statement of fact. It was the city where, more or less, I'd become a star; where I'd been feted by my idols; where I'd somehow ended up taking tea with Mae West (to my delight, she swanned in with a lascivious smile and the words, 'Ah, my favourite sight – a room full of men', which, given that the men present were me, John Reid and Tony King, suggested she was in for an evening of disappointment). But if you didn't keep your wits about you – if you took a wrong turn or kept the wrong company – LA could just as easily swallow you up.

The mayor of Los Angeles, Tom Watson, declared the 20–26 October 1975 Elton John Week. Among other things, I was to have a star unveiled on the Hollywood Walk of Fame, right outside Grauman's Chinese Theatre. There were two gigs booked at Dodger Stadium, an audience of 55,000 at each. I'd played to larger crowds than that – there were 82,000 people at Wembley

Stadium, or at least there had been before they decided they'd had enough and started storming the exits – but the Dodger gigs still seemed like a zenith. I was the first artist who'd been allowed to play there since The Beatles in 1966, when the promoter hadn't booked enough security staff. There had been a kind of mini riot at the end of The Beatles' set, and the stadium's owners had subsequently banned rock gigs. And there was a peculiar sense of homecoming about them, given that my career had really taken off at the Troubadour five years previously.

So I chartered a Boeing 707 plane through Pan Am and flew my mum and Derf, my grandma and a load of my friends over from England, along with the staff of Rocket, journalists and media and a TV documentary crew fronted by the chat show host Russell Harty. I met them on the runway with Tony King and a fleet of Rolls-Royces and Cadillacs: the kind of welcome I'd been expecting the first time I got to America, instead of that fucking double-decker bus. I suppose it was quite an outrageous thing to do, but I wanted my family to see it; I wanted them to have the time of their lives; I wanted them to be proud of me.

Elton John Week passed in a blur. My family went on trips to Disneyland and Universal Studios. There was a party on John Reid's yacht, *Madman*, to celebrate the release of *Rock of the Westies*. The grand unveiling of the star on the Hollywood Walk of Fame turned out to be a bit naff. I was wearing a lime-green Bob Mackie suit, covered in the names of other Walk of Fame stars, and matching bowler hat. I had to travel there on a gold-painted golf cart with an enormous pair of illuminated glasses and a bow tie stuck to the front of it. I'm aware that I was hardly the model of shy understatement onstage, but there were limits. There's footage of it on YouTube, and if you look at the expression on my face, it's pretty clear what a wonderful idea I thought that was. I don't know if you've ever been driven very slowly through a crowd of screaming fans, in full view of the world's media, on a gold-painted golf cart with a pair of enormous illuminated glasses and a bow tie on the front, but if you haven't, I can tell you that it's a pretty excruciating experience.

I felt incredibly awkward and tried to defuse the situation by pulling faces during the speeches and making jokes when my turn came to speak – 'I now declare this supermarket open!' – but I couldn't wait for it to be over and done with. Afterwards, they told me that it was the first time in the history of the Walk of Fame that so many fans had turned up to an unveiling, they had to close Hollywood Boulevard completely.

The next day, I invited my family over to lunch at Tower Grove Drive. Like *Captain Fantastic, Rock of the Westies* went straight into the US album charts at Number One. No one had ever done that before – not Elvis, not The Beatles – and now I'd done it twice, in the space of six months. I was twenty-eight years old and I was, for the moment, the biggest pop star in the world. I was about to play the most prestigious gigs of my career. My family and friends were there, happily sharing in my success. And that was when I decided to try and commit suicide again.

Again, I can't remember exactly what provoked me to do it, but as my family were eating I got up from the table by the swimming pool, went upstairs and swallowed a load of Valium. Then I came back down in my dressing gown and announced that I'd taken a bunch of tablets and that I was going to die. And then I threw myself in the pool.

I can't remember exactly how many tablets I swallowed, but it was fewer than I'd taken that night at Caribou studios – a sign that, deep down, I had absolutely no intention of actually killing myself. This fact was brought very sharply into focus when I felt the dressing gown start to weigh me down. For someone who was supposed to be in the process of trying to end it all – who was apparently convinced that life had nothing more to offer him and was filled with a longing for death's merciful release – I suddenly became surprisingly keen not to drown. I started frantically swimming to the side of the pool. Someone helped me get out. The thing I remember most clearly is hearing my grandmother's voice pipe up. 'Oh,' she said. And then, in a noticeably aggrieved tone – unmistakably the voice of an elderly working-class lady from Pinner who's realized her wonderful holiday in California is suddenly in danger of being cut short – she added: 'We might as well bleedin' go home, then.'

I couldn't stop myself laughing. That might have been exactly the response I needed. I was looking for 'oh, you poor thing', but instead I got 'why are you behaving like such a twat?'

It was a good question: why *was* I behaving like such a twat? I suppose I was doing something dramatic to try and get attention. I realize that, on one level, it sounds nuts, given that I was living in a city that had declared it was Elton John Week, I was about to play in front of 110,000 people, and there was an ITV camera crew in the process of making a documentary about me. How much more attention can a man need? But I was looking for a different kind of attention from that. I was trying to make my family understand that there was something wrong, however well my career was going: it might seem that it's all great, it might seem that my life is perfect, but it's not. I couldn't say to them, 'I think I'm taking too many drugs', because they would never understand; they didn't know what cocaine was. I hadn't got the guts to tell them, 'Look, I'm really not feeling very good, I need a bit of love', because I didn't want them to see any cracks in the facade at all. I was too strong-willed – and too afraid of her reaction – to just take my mum aside and say, 'Listen, Mum, I really need to talk to you – I'm not doing very well here, I need a bit of help, what do you think?' Instead of doing that, I bottled it up and bottled it up and then eventually I went off like Vesuvius and staged this ridiculous suicide bid. That's who I am: it's all or nothing. It wasn't my family's fault at all, it was mine. I was too proud to admit that my life wasn't perfect. It was pathetic.

They called a doctor. I refused to go to hospital and have my stomach pumped, so he gave me this hideous liquid that made me vomit. And as soon as I threw up, I felt all right: 'OK, I'm better now. So, anyway, I've got these two gigs to do.' It sounds ridiculous – it *was* ridiculous – but I bounced back very quickly from my deathbed: right, I've tried to commit suicide, done that, what's next? If anyone around me thought that was strange, they kept it to themselves. And twenty-four hours later I was onstage at Dodger Stadium.

The shows were a complete triumph. That's the thing about playing live, for me at least. Even now, whatever turmoil I might be going through just gets pushed aside. Back then, when I was onstage I just felt different from when I was offstage. It was the only time I really felt in control of what I did.

They were huge events. Cary Grant was backstage, looking incredibly beautiful. I had gospel singers, James Cleveland's Southern California Community Choir, performing with me. I had Billie Jean King come out and sing backing vocals on 'Philadelphia Freedom'. I had the security guards dressed in ridiculous lilac one-piece jumpsuits with frills. I had California's most famous used-car dealer, a man called Cal Worthington, come on with a lion – Christ knows why, but I suppose it all added to the general gaiety. Even Bernie put in an appearance in front of the audience, which was almost unheard of.

I wore a sequinned Dodgers uniform and cap, designed by Bob Mackie. I climbed on top of the piano and swung a baseball bat around. I hammered at the piano keys until my fingers split and bled. We played for three hours and I loved it. I know how to pull off a show because of all those years I spent in clubs, backing Major Lance or playing with Bluesology to twenty people; I've got the experience, so my gigs are never really below a certain standard. But sometimes, something else happens onstage: from the minute you start playing you just know you can do no wrong. It's as if your hands are moving independently of your brain; you don't even have to concentrate, you just feel as free as a bird, you can do anything you want. Those are the gigs you live for, and Dodger Stadium was like that, on both days. The sound was perfect, so was the weather. I can remember standing onstage, feeling the adrenalin coursing through me.

It was a pinnacle, and I was smart enough to know that it couldn't last, at least not at that pitch. Success on that level never does; it doesn't matter who you are, or how great you are, your records aren't going to enter the charts at Number One forever. I knew someone or something else was going to come along. I was waiting for that moment to happen, and the thought of it didn't scare me at all. It was almost a relief when the second single from *Rock of the Westies*, 'Grow Some Funk Of Your Own', wasn't a huge hit. For one thing, I was exhausted: exhausted from touring, exhausted from giving interviews, exhausted by the ongoing catastrophe that was my personal life. And for another, I'd never really set out to have hit singles. I was an album artist, who made records like *Tumbleweed Connection* and *Madman Across the Water*, and I'd inadvertently become this huge singles machine, having smash after smash after smash, none of which had been intentionally written to be hit singles.

In fact, one of the few times I ever sat down and tried to write a hit single was at the end of 1975. I was on holiday in Barbados with a big group of friends: Bernie was there, Tony King, Kiki Dee, lots of people. I thought we should write a duet for Kiki and me to sing. Bernie and I came up with two. One was called 'I'm Always On The Bonk': 'I don't know who I'm fucking, I don't know who I'm sucking, but I'm always on the bonk'. The other was 'Don't Go Breaking My Heart'. I wrote the melody on the piano, came up with the title and then Bernie finished it off. He hated the end result, and I can't really blame him – Bernie was not, and is not, a fan of anything he thinks is shallow pop music. But even he had to admit it had substantially more commercial potential than 'I'm Always On The Bonk'.

seven

I only agreed to do an interview with *Rolling Stone* because I was bored out of my mind. The 1976 Elton John world tour was supposed to be a journalist-free zone. I didn't need to do any press to promote it, because every date had sold out instantly. But I'd been stuck in a suite at the Sherry-Netherland in New York for two weeks – we were playing a run of shows at Madison Square Garden – and I'd completely run out of things to do when I wasn't onstage.

It was hard to get out of the hotel. It was August, and Manhattan was unbearably hot, but there was a crowd of fans permanently stationed outside the entrance. If I managed to get past them, wherever I went, there was chaos. I'd literally seen little old ladies get knocked over and trampled by people who were trying to get a look at me, not a sight designed to make you feel good about your celebrity. Still, I'd tried to keep myself occupied. I'd been to see, or been visited by, everyone I knew that was in town. I'd been out clubbing to 12 West and visited a radio station called WNEW. They'd given me champagne, an act of generosity they swiftly came to regret when I went on air immediately afterwards and offered listeners my full and frank appraisal of a rock critic called John Rockwell, who'd given me a bad live review: 'I bet he's got smelly feet. I bet he's got bogeys up his nose.' I went shopping, although I realized I might have exhausted the possibilities of retail therapy when I found myself buying a cuckoo clock that, instead of a cuckoo, had a large wooden penis that popped in and out of it every hour. I gave it to John Lennon when I went to visit him. I thought it was a good present for a man who had everything. John and Yoko were as bad as me when it came to shopping. The various apartments they owned in the Dakota were so full of priceless artworks, antiques and clothes that I once sent them a card, rewriting the lyrics to 'Imagine': 'Imagine six apartments, it isn't hard to do, one is full of fur coats, another's full of shoes'. They owned herds of cows, for God's sake – prize Holstein cattle. Years later, I asked what had happened to them. Yoko shrugged and said: 'Oh, I got rid of them. All that *mooing*.'

But, having delivered a penis-themed cuckoo clock to John Lennon, I had nothing else to do, or at least nothing that I wanted to do enough to see a little old lady get hospitalized in the process. I just mooched around the hotel. The band certainly weren't in the mood to hang out with me, because I'd fired them all the night before last, just before we went onstage.

It had been a weird tour. Commercially, it had been a huge success, and, on one level, it had been fun. Kiki Dee had come along with us to sing 'Don't Go Breaking My Heart', which, despite Bernie's profound misgivings, went to Number One on both sides of the Atlantic that summer. In Britain, we'd travelled around by car, visiting the tourist sites between shows, stopping off for ice creams and ducking into pubs for lunch. In America, the shows had been massive events – Hollywood stars backstage; a big performance in Massachusetts for the American Bicentennial on 4 July, where I dressed up as the Statue of Liberty; a guest appearance from Divine, who shimmied away around the band despite the fact that one of his high heels broke off the minute he got onstage.

And I met Elvis Presley, backstage at the Capital Centre in Landover, Maryland, a couple of nights before I played there myself. I took Bernie with me, and my mum. It seemed to make sense: Mum had introduced me to Elvis's music; now I was going to introduce her to Elvis himself. We were ushered into a dressing room full of people: I was used to rock stars who went everywhere mob-handed, but I'd never seen anything like Elvis's entourage. He was surrounded by cousins, old buddies from back home in Memphis, people who seemed to be employed specifically to hand him drinks and towels. When I squeezed past them to shake his hand, my heart broke. There was something desperately, visibly wrong with him. He was overweight, grey and sweating. There were expressionless black holes where his eyes should have been. He moved like a man coming round from a general anaesthetic, weird and sluggish. There was a trickle of black hair dye running down his forehead. He was completely gone, barely coherent.

Our meeting was short and painfully stilted. I was simultaneously starstruck and horrified, which is hardly a recipe for sparkling conversation. And Elvis . . . well, I couldn't work out whether Elvis just had no idea who I was – there seemed every chance he had no idea who *anyone* was – or whether he knew perfectly well and wasn't very pleased to see me. Everyone knew that Elvis wasn't keen on competition – there was a crazy rumour going around that when he visited Richard Nixon in the White House, he had literally complained to the US president about The Beatles – and, a couple of years before, I'd been contacted by his ex-wife Priscilla, saying that their daughter Lisa Marie was a huge fan, and asking if I would meet her as a birthday treat. We had tea together at my house in LA. Maybe he was angry about that.

I asked him if he was going to play 'Heartbreak Hotel' and he grunted in a way that strongly implied he wasn't. I asked for his autograph and saw his hands shaking as he picked up the pen.

The signature was just about legible. Then we went to watch the show. Occasionally, you would see something spark, a flash of the incredible artist he had been. It would last for a couple of lines of a song and vanish again. My main memory is of him handing out scarves to women in the audience. In the past he'd been famous for giving away silk scarves onstage, a grand gesture befitting the King of Rock and Roll. But times had clearly changed, and these scarves were cheap, nylon things: they didn't look like they would last long. Nor did Elvis, as Mum pointed out.

'He'll be dead next year,' she said, as we left. She was right.

But for weeks afterwards, I couldn't stop turning over our meeting in my mind. It wasn't just that he was in such a bad way, although that was incredible in itself – the last thing I'd expected to feel when I finally met Elvis was pity. It was that I could understand a little too easily how he ended up like that, closeted away from the outside world. Maybe he'd just spent too much time trapped in expensive hotels with nothing to do. Maybe he'd just seen one little old lady too many stretchered away and decided the outside world wasn't worth the bother.

For all its success, the tour had felt very familiar: the stadiums, the Starship, the celebrities, even the set we played. We had a new album recorded, a double called *Blue Moves*, but it wasn't due out until the autumn, and I'd learned my lesson about inflicting new material on an unsuspecting audience at Wembley the year before. Especially if the material was like the stuff on *Blue Moves*. I'm very proud of it, but the music was complex and hard to play, quite experimental and jazz-influenced. And its mood was very sombre and reflective: Bernie pouring his heart out about his divorce from Maxine and me writing music to match. I even wrote some lyrics myself, the opening lines of 'Sorry Seems To Be The Hardest Word', the fallout from another disastrous infatuation with a straight guy: 'What can I do to make you love me? What can I do to make you care?' It's a great album, but it's not exactly the work of two people who are cartwheeling down the street, over-flowing with the joys of life.

And that was the real problem with the tour. The holiday in Barbados had been great, but it seemed like a distant memory. I was back in exactly the same place emotionally as I had been when I threw myself into the swimming pool in LA. My mum and Derf had found me a new home, called Woodside. It certainly sounded nice – a huge mock-Georgian house in Old Windsor, with thirty-seven acres of land – but I couldn't tell you for sure how nice it was, because I had hardly been there since I moved in. I'd had enough time to ask Derf to build some shelves for my record collection, and to install a small menagerie of pets: a rabbit called Clarence, a cockatoo called Ollie and Roger, a mynah bird that someone had taught to say 'piss off', a phrase he later disgraced himself by using in front of Princess Margaret when I invited her for lunch. But no sooner had Roger arrived and told everyone present to piss off than I took his advice: there were always recording sessions to do, tours to go on.

I still loved playing live, but I was physically spent. I'd started having seizures, almost like epileptic fits; not often, but often enough to scare me. I'd had a brain scan, but the neurologist I saw couldn't find anything wrong with me, although I'm sure if I'd told him what was going up my nose on a regular basis, he could have made an accurate diagnosis on the spot. Bernie didn't look in much better shape than me. Since his divorce, the only time you saw him without a beer in his hand was when he put it down to do a line of coke. I started suggesting to him that he try writing with other people as well as me – not that there was anything wrong with our relationship, either profes-sionally or personally, but maybe a change of scenery would do us both good.

Everything came to a head on the penultimate night of the Madison Square Garden residency. Backstage, I told the band that

I couldn't do it anymore. They could have another year's wages as severance pay, but there would be no more tours for the foreseeable future. Towards the end of the show, I mumbled something non-committal about going away for a while. The minute I said it, I couldn't work out whether I really meant it or not. On the one hand, I clearly couldn't carry on like this, schlepping around the world. I'd convinced myself it was the root of all my problems. It was why I was so knackered, it was why my relationships never worked out, it was why I was unhappy. On the other, I still loved playing live. And I had been on the road since I was eighteen. It was my job. I didn't really know adult life without it. What was I going to do all day? Watch Derf put shelves up and listen to a mynah bird telling me to piss off every ten minutes?

So I was in a thoughtful mood when the journalist from *Rolling Stone* arrived at my hotel. He was called Cliff Jahr and he'd been pestering for an interview for weeks. I had no idea that Cliff was an out-and-proud gay man who'd turned up determined to find out the truth about my sexuality. I don't think he saw it as a political thing – outing people wasn't really viewed as striking a blow against a repressive society back then. I think he was just a hungry freelancer after a scoop.

I later learned that Cliff had an elaborate plan to wheedle the information out of me. It involved a secret code word that he was going to drop into the conversation as a signal for the photographer to leave the room, at which point he would deploy his journalist's guile to get me to confess my darkest secret to him. Bless him, he didn't get the chance to put his meticulous plan into action. I brought the subject up before he did. He asked me if I was in love with anyone, which was very much the wrong question to ask me in those days, unless you had a few hours to spare and a burning desire to fill them listening to me moaning about the terrible state of my personal life. I started telling him how desperate I was to find someone to love. I despairingly wondered aloud if relationships with women might not be longer-lasting than the relationships I'd had with men. He looked a little taken aback and – to his immense credit – asked if I wanted him to turn his tape recorder off and speak off the record. I said no. Fuck it. It honestly didn't seem like that big an issue. Everyone around me had accepted I was gay years before. Everyone in the music business knew about my relationship with John Reid. And it really can't have been that much of a shock for Cliff Jahr, given that I'd previously told him the story of Divine and me being turned away from Crisco Disco. Let's look at the circumstantial evidence: I'd been trying to get into a gay club, named after a famous anal lubricant, with the world's most famous drag queen. The news that I wasn't heterosexual could hardly have come as a bolt from the blue.

He asked me if I was bisexual and I said yes. You can see that as fudging the issue if you want, but in fairness I'd had a relation-ship with a woman before, and I had a relationship with a woman afterwards. He asked if Bernie and I were ever a couple and I told him we weren't. John Reid's name came up and I fibbed and said I'd never had a serious affair with anyone. It certainly wasn't my business to start outing anyone in *Rolling Stone*. I told him I thought everyone should be able to go to bed with whoever they wanted. 'But they should draw the line at goats,' I added.

At that moment, John Reid suddenly stuck his head round the door and asked if everything was all right. I don't know whether it was just perfect timing, or whether he'd been listening at the door in a state of mounting panic and finally, when I started making jokes about bestiality, couldn't stand it any longer. Perhaps he drew the line at goats, too. I told John everything was fine. And I meant it. I didn't feel relieved, or nervous, or proud, or any of the things you might expect to feel when you publicly come out. I didn't feel anything really. I'd done all the fretting I had to do about my sexu-ality and what people might think about it years ago. I didn't care.

This was not an attitude that was shared by those around me. Not that anyone said anything directly to me. Respectful of the amount of money I was earning everyone, and wary of encouraging our old friend the Dwight Family Temper to put in one of its show-stopping guest appearances, they wouldn't have dared. But around the time the feature came out, I got the feeling that John Reid and my American record company were in a state of anxiety, waiting to see what disastrous impact its revelations were going to have on my career.

Eventually, the dust settled and the full, staggering extent of the damage I had caused became clear. There wasn't any. A couple of nutcases wrote into *Rolling Stone* and said they were praying that my perverted soul be spared God's wrath and eternal damnation. A few radio stations in the US announced they weren't going to play my records anymore, but that didn't bother me in the slightest: at the risk of sounding arrogant, I strongly suspected my career would limp on somehow without their help. People have said the *Rolling Stone* piece caused a dip in my record sales in the States, but my album sales had started to dip long before then. *Rock of the Westies* may have got to Number One, but it had sold far less than *Captain Fantastic*.

In Britain, meanwhile, the *Sun* cancelled a competition to win copies of *Blue Moves*, on the grounds that its cover – a beautiful Patrick Procktor painting I owned of people sitting in a park – didn't feature any women, and thus, presumably, constituted terrifying homosexual propaganda from which the public must be protected. Their logic seemed to be that if a *Sun* reader saw a painting of some men sitting in a park, they might immediately rip off their wedding ring, abandon their wife and children and race to the nearest gay bar singing 'I Am What I Am' as they went. But that was about it as far as adverse reactions went.

★

Actually, the British press seemed less interested in what was happening in my sex life than what was happening on top of my head. In one sense, I couldn't blame them: I'd been pretty gripped by what was going on up there myself for the last year or so. My hair had started thinning a little in the early seventies, but a bad dye job in New York had suddenly caused the stuff to stage a mass walkout. Impressed by the way the fashion designer Zandra Rhodes seemed to change her hair colour to match her outfits, I had been getting mine dyed every shade imaginable at a salon in London for years with no apparent ill-effects. I've no idea what the New York hairdresser had put on it but, not long afterwards, it started coming out in chunks. By the time of the 1976 tour, there was virtually nothing left on top.

I hated how I looked. Some people are blessed with the kind of face that looks good with a bald head. I am not one of those people. Without hair, I bear a disturbing resemblance to the cartoon character Shrek. But salvation was apparently at hand. I was directed to a man called Pierre Putot in Paris, who was supposedly a great pioneer in the art of hair transplants. At that point in history, hair transplants were so new that any doctor who could be bothered to do them counted as a great pioneer, but I was assured he was the best. Undergo a simple procedure, I was told, and I would leave his Paris clinic a changed man, to cries of *incroyable!* and *sacre bleu!* from onlookers dazzled by my new, leonine coiffure.

It didn't quite work out like that. For one thing, it wasn't a simple procedure at all. It went on for five hours. I had it done twice, and both times it hurt like hell. The technique they used had the unappetizing name of 'strip harvesting': they took strips of hair from the back of my head with a scalpel and attached them to the crown. The sound of the hair being removed was disconcertingly like a rabbit gnawing its way through a carrot. I left the clinic after the first procedure reeling in agony, lost my footing as I tried to get into the back of a waiting car and hit the top of my head on the door frame. It was at that moment I discovered that however much a hair transplant hurt, it was a mere pinprick compared to the sensation of hitting your head on a car door immediately after having a hair transplant. Frantically dabbing my now-bleeding scalp with a tissue, I did the one thing I could think of that might take my mind off the pain I was in. I told the driver to take me shopping.

To make matters worse, the hair transplant just didn't work. I'm not sure why, but it didn't take. It wasn't the doctor's fault. Perhaps it had something to do with the amount of drugs I was taking. Perhaps it had something to do with the fact that the one thing they told me I must not do in the weeks after the procedure was wear a hat, advice I chose to completely ignore on the grounds that, without a hat, I now looked like something that turns up towards the end of a horror film and starts strip-harvesting teenage campers with an axe. My head was covered in scabs and weird craters. I suppose I could have split the difference and worn something lighter than a hat, like a bandana, but appearing in public dressed as a gypsy fortune teller seemed a look too far, even for me.

When news of recent events at Monsieur Putot's clinic reached the press, they went crazy. Nothing I'd done in my career to date seemed to fascinate them in quite the way that having a hair transplant did. The paparazzi became obsessed with getting a photo of me without a hat on. You would have thought I was hiding the secret of eternal life and happiness under there rather than a bit of thinning hair. The paparazzi were out of luck – I kept a hat on in public more or less permanently for the next decade or so. In the late eighties, just before I got sober, I decided I'd had enough, dyed what was left of my hair platinum blond, and appeared that way on the cover of my album *Sleeping with the Past*. After I got sober, I had a weave done, where they take what's left of your hair and attach more hair to it. I debuted my new look at the Freddie Mercury Tribute Concert. A writer noted that I looked like I had a dead squirrel on my head. He was mean, but, I was forced to concede, he also had a point.

Eventually I gave up and got a hairpiece, made by the same people who make wigs for Hollywood movies. It's the strangest thing. People were absolutely obsessed with my hair, or lack of it, for years. Then I started wearing a wig and virtually no one's mentioned it since. That said, a wig is not without drawbacks of its own. A few years back, I was sleeping at my home in Atlanta, when I woke up to the sound of voices in the apartment. I was convinced we were being burgled. I pulled on my dressing gown and started creeping out to see what was happening. I was halfway down the corridor when I realized I didn't have my hairpiece on. I rushed back to the bedroom, reasoning that if I was going to be bludgeoned to death by intruders, at least I wouldn't be bald when it happened. Wig on, I went into the kitchen to find two workmen, who had been sent up to fix a leak. They apologized profusely for waking me up, but despite my relief, I couldn't help noticing they were staring at me. Perhaps they were starstruck, I thought, as I headed back to bed. Stopping off in the bathroom, I realized that the workmen weren't bedazzled by the sight of the legendary Elton John appearing before them. They were bedazzled by the sight of the legendary Elton John appearing before them with his wig on back to front. I looked completely ridiculous, like Frankie Howerd after a heavy night in a strong wind. I took the thing off and went back to sleep.

If the world at large seemed to take the news about my sexuality very well, I did start to wonder if I could perhaps have timed the announcement a little better. One piece of advice I would give anyone planning on publicly coming out is this. Try and make sure you don't do it immediately after being appointed chairman of a British football club, unless you want to spend your Saturday afternoons listening to thousands of away supporters singing – to the tune of 'My Old Man Said Follow The Van' – 'Don't sit down when Elton's around, or you'll get a penis up your arse'. I suppose I should deliver a lecture here decrying the homophobia of football fans in the mid-seventies, but I have to be honest: I thought it was funny. Mortifying, but funny. I didn't feel threatened or frightened by it, it was obviously good-humoured, you had to take it on the chin. They'd sing it and I'd just smile and wave at them.

In fact, when it came to Watford FC, I had far bigger problems to deal with than whatever the opposition supporters were singing. It was a Watford-supporting journalist who came to interview me back in 1974 who first mentioned that the club was in trouble, and not just on the pitch. I still followed them avidly, still went and watched them whenever I could, still stood on The Bend, the same place on the terrace at Vicarage Road where I'd stood with my dad as a kid. Standing there wasn't the only thing about watching them that brought back childhood memories. Watford were still just as hopeless a team as they had been in the fifties, permanently stuck at the bottom of the football league. Supporting them sometimes made me think of being a member of Bluesology: I loved them to bits, but I knew we were going absolutely nowhere.

Thanks to the journalist, I now learned that the club was in financial trouble, too. They had no money, because no one was interested in coming to watch them lose every week. They were desperately looking for ways to make some. I rang them up and suggested I could play a benefit gig at the ground. They agreed, and in return, offered me the chance to buy shares in the club and become vice-chairman. For the gig, I dressed up in a bee outfit – the closest thing I could find to the club's mascot, a cartoon hornet called Harry – and brought Rod Stewart along to perform with me. If nothing else, this provided Rod with an afternoon of unceasing hilarity at the awfulness of Watford's ground – which admittedly was a crumbling dump, still with a greyhound track running around the pitch – the abysmal nature of the team's results in contrast to his beloved Celtic and, especially, my new role as vice-chairman.

'What the fuck do you know about football, Sharon?' he asked. 'If you knew anything, you wouldn't support this lot.'

I told him to fuck off. The rest of the board couldn't have been more welcoming. If they were bothered about having the only vice-chairman in the football league who turned up to meetings with green and orange hair, towering over everyone else because of his platform soles, they never mentioned it. But my presence didn't seem to be making much difference to Watford itself: the team was still hopeless, and the club was still broke. A thought kept playing on my mind. If supporting Watford was as frustrating as being in Bluesology, then maybe, as in Bluesology, it was down to me to do something about it.

So when the chairman, a local businessman called Jim Bonser, offered to sell me the club outright in the spring of 1976, I said yes. John Reid was furious, going on and on about what a drain on my finances owning a football club was going to be. I told him to fuck off, too. I really wanted to do this. I've always had a competitive streak, whether it was squash or table tennis or Monopoly. Even today, if I play tennis, I don't want to just knock a ball about and get some exercise. I want to play a game, and I want to win. So taking on the chairman's job appealed to that aspect of my character. I liked the challenge. What's more, I was sick of having my weekends ruined because Watford had lost.

And I loved the club. Supporting Watford was something that ran through my whole life, while everything else had changed beyond recognition. Vicarage Road was five or six miles from where I was born. It connected me to my roots, reminded me that no matter how successful I was, or how famous, or how much money I made, I was still a working-class boy from a council house in Pinner.

But there was something else, too. I loved being around the club, because everything about it was different from the music world I usually inhabited. There was no glamour, no luxury, no limousines, no Starship. You got on the train to Grimsby with the players, you watched the game, listened to the opposition supporters sing about your allegedly insatiable desire to stick your penis up the arse of anyone nearby, and then you got the train home, carrying a box of local fish the Grimsby directors had presented you with as a gift at the end of the match.

There was no bullshit. Once you reach a certain level of success in the music business, you realize that a lot of people around you have started telling you what they think you want to hear, rather than what they actually think. No one wants to upset you, no one wants to rock the boat. But at Watford, it wasn't like that. The staff and players were friendly, they were respectful, but they weren't interested in massaging my ego. They would happily tell me if they didn't think much of my new album – 'Why don't you do a song like "Daniel" again? I liked that one' – or if they thought the coat I was wearing looked ridiculous. That I wasn't getting any kid glove treatment because I was Elton John was brought home quite forcefully whenever I elected to join in a five-a-side game with them. I'd get the ball, see a Watford player on the opposite team coming in to tackle me and the next thing I knew, they'd have possession and I'd be flying through the air at high speed, backwards, as a prelude to landing flat on my arse.

And there was no bad behaviour, no diva tantrums from me. I had to learn to be a good loser, to shake the hands of the opposition's directors when they beat us. I couldn't lose my temper, or sulk, nor could I get drunk or take drugs, because I wasn't there as a huge star whose every whim had to be catered for, I was there as a representative of Watford Football Club. I broke the rules once. I turned up at a Boxing Day game hungover after a mammoth coke bender and started helping myself to the boardroom Scotch. The following day, I was given a real dressing down, the kind of telling-off no one ordinarily had the balls to deliver to me.

'What the fuck do you think you're doing? You're letting yourself down and you're letting the club down.'

The man delivering the talking-to was Graham Taylor, the new manager I'd personally convinced to join Watford in April 1977. He was thirty-two years old when I met him – young for a football manager – and he reminded me of Bernie. Like Bernie, he came from Lincolnshire. Like Bernie, he took a chance on me. Graham was paid very well for a manager of a team as lowly as Watford, but taking the job was definitely a step down for him. He had already taken his last team, Lincoln City, out of the fourth division and was supposed to move on to somewhere much bigger, not go back to the bottom. But, like Bernie, I clicked with him immediately, and like Bernie, I didn't interfere with what he did, I just let him get on with doing his job.

And, like Bernie, when things took off for us, they took off in a way beyond anything we could have imagined. Graham was an incredible manager. He assembled a fantastic back-room team around him. Bertie Mee came from Arsenal to be his assistant, a veteran who'd been a player in the thirties and knew the game inside out. Eddie Plumley arrived from Coventry as chief executive. Graham bought new players and encouraged amazing young talent. He signed John Barnes, aged sixteen: one of the greatest players England's ever seen, and Graham got him for the price of a new football kit. He turned club apprentices like Luther Blissett and Nigel Callaghan into star players. He made them all train harder than they'd ever trained before, and he got them to play exciting football – two big centre-forwards, two fast wingers, a great attack, lots of goals, which meant that people wanted to come and watch us. He got rid of the greyhound track and built new stands and a family enclosure, a place specifically designed for parents to bring their kids to watch the game in safety. Every team has one now, but Watford were the first.

All of this cost money, which meant more moaning from John Reid. I didn't care. I wasn't a businessman, pouring cash into the club as a financial investment. Watford were in my blood. I was obsessed to the point that I became superstitious – if we were on a winning streak, I wouldn't change my clothes or empty my pockets – and so insanely enthusiastic, I could literally talk people into becoming Watford fans. I converted my old friend Muff Winwood from a West Brom supporter to a member of the Watford board. I went to local council meetings and tried in vain to convince them to let us build a new stadium on the outskirts of the town. After matches, I'd go to the Supporters' Club, a little building up on the main stand, meet with Watford fans and listen to what they had to say. I wanted them to know that I really cared about the club, that we weren't taking them for granted, that without the supporters Watford was nothing. I threw huge parties for the players and staff and their families at Woodside, with five-a-side games and egg and spoon races. I bought an Aston Martin, had it painted in Watford's colours – yellow, with a red and black stripe down the middle – and drove to away games in it; I called it the Chairman's Car. I didn't realize how much attention it had attracted until I was introduced to Prince Philip. We were making polite conversation, when he suddenly changed the subject.

'You live near Windsor Castle, don't you?' he asked. 'Have you seen the bloody idiot who drives around that area in his ghastly car? It's bright yellow with a ridiculous stripe on it. Do you know him?'

'Yes, Your Highness. It's actually me.'

'Really?' He didn't appear particularly taken aback by this news at all. In fact, he seemed quite pleased to have found the idiot in question, so that he could give him the benefit of his advice. 'What the hell are you thinking? Ridiculous. Makes you look like a bloody fool. Get rid of it.'

If the Chairman's Car couldn't get me to the game on time, I'd charter a helicopter. If I couldn't make it because I was abroad, I would phone the club and they would plug my call into the local hospital radio broadcast of the match: backstage somewhere in America, the band would listen to me in my dressing room, alone, screaming my head off because we'd beaten Southampton in a cup tie. If it was the middle of the night in New Zealand, I'd get up to listen. If it clashed with the start of a gig, I'd delay the start of the gig. I loved it: the excitement of the games, the feeling of camaraderie, of being part of a team where it felt like everyone was working towards the same end, from the players to the tea ladies. I couldn't have bought the personal happiness that Watford brought me at any price.

Besides, I wasn't throwing money into a bottomless pit. I could see the results of my spending. Watford started winning and kept winning. After one season, we were into the Third Division. After two, we were in the Second. In 1981, Watford were promoted to the First Division for the first time in their history. The next year we were runners-up, the second most successful football team in Britain. It meant we would be playing in the UEFA Cup, against the biggest teams in Europe: Real Madrid, Bayern Munich, Inter Milan. That was what I'd told Graham I'd wanted the club to achieve at our first meeting. He had looked at me like I was out of my mind and started telling me how we'd be lucky to stay in the Fourth Division with the team we had – 'you've got a fucking giraffe for a centre-forward' – before realizing I was deadly serious and prepared to put my money where my mouth was. We decided it would probably take ten years. Watford had done it in five.

And then, in 1984, we made the FA Cup Final. It's the oldest and most prestigious football competition in Britain: Wembley stadium, 100,000 fans. I was used to Watford doing well by now – it's funny how easily you become accustomed to success after decades of failure – but just before the match started, it suddenly hit me how far we had come, from a hopeless little club that no one went to watch, that people laughed at, to this. The brass band struck up with 'Abide With Me', the traditional FA Cup hymn, and that was it: I burst into tears in full view of the BBC's cameras. As it turned out, that was the highlight of the day. We were beaten 2–0 by Everton. It should have been a much closer game – one of their goals should have been disallowed – but ultimately they played better than we did. I was distraught, but we still threw a party for the team: it was a fantastic achievement.

Looking out at the crowd at Wembley before the game began, I'd felt like I had onstage at Dodger Stadium. And, like the Dodger Stadium gigs, I think I knew that this was a sort of pinnacle, that it didn't get any better than this. I was right. A couple of years later, Graham left to become manager at Aston Villa. I appointed a manager called Dave Bassett as his replacement, but it didn't work out; the chemistry wasn't right, he didn't gel with the team. I started thinking that I should have left Watford when Graham did. I still loved the club, but there had been a serendipity, a magic, about the two of us together, and I couldn't conjure up that same magic without him.

Eventually I sold Watford to Jack Petchey, a multimillionaire who'd made his money in cars. Seven years later, I bought back a load of shares in the club and became chairman again – a businessman rather than someone who put his heart into the club, I felt Jack was making a terrible mess of things, and Watford had slipped back into the Second Division. I only did it because Graham agreed to come back as manager. The team did well, but it wasn't the same as the first time around; there wasn't that incredible challenge of rising from the bottom. Finally, Graham left again, and this time, so did I. I resigned as chairman for good in 2002.

In a weird way, our partnership quietly continued. Right up until he died in 2017, I still rang Graham all the time to talk about the team: how they were playing, what we thought of the latest manager. Whatever else Graham Taylor achieved in football, nothing took his heart away from Watford.

I'm incredibly proud of what we achieved together, but I owe Watford far more than Watford owe me. I was chairman throughout the worst period of my life: years of addiction and unhappiness, failed relationships, bad business deals, court cases, unending turmoil. Through all of that, Watford were a constant source of happiness to me. When I didn't feel I had any love in my personal life, I knew I had love from the club and the supporters. It gave me something else to concentrate on, a passion that could take my mind away from everything that was going wrong. For obvious reasons, there are chunks of the eighties I have no recollection of – I struggled to remember what had happened the next day, let alone thirty years later – but every Watford game I saw is permanently etched on my memory. The night we knocked Manchester United out of the League Cup at Old Trafford, when we were still a Third Division side: two goals by Blissett, both headers, the newspapers that never normally bothered writing about Watford calling them Elton John's Rocket Men the next morning. The night in November 1982 when we were away to Nottingham Forest in the Milk Cup. They beat us 7–3, but I thought it was one of the greatest games of football I'd ever seen in my life and Forest's legendary manager Brian Clough agreed with me, before turning to Graham and telling him he would never allow *his* chairman to sit on the bloody touchline the way I did. If I hadn't had the football club then God knows what would have happened to me. I'm not exaggerating when I say I think Watford might have saved my life.

eight

Back at home in the autumn of 1976, and theoretically retired from live performance, I set about getting Woodside renovated. There has been a house on the same site in Old Windsor since the eleventh century – it was originally built for William the Conqueror's physician – but it kept burning down; the latest version was built in 1947 for Michael Sobell, who made a fortune manufacturing radios and televisions. It was built in a mock-Georgian style, but when doing it up, I decided to eschew Regency or Palladian decoration in favour of a style known among interior design specialists as Mid-70s Pop Star On Drugs Goes Berserk. There were pinball machines, jukeboxes, brass palm trees, memorabilia everywhere. There were Tiffany lamps next to the pair of four-foot-high Doc Marten boots I'd worn while singing 'Pinball Wizard' in The Who's film *Tommy*. On the walls, Rembrandt etchings jostled for space with gold discs and stuff fans had sent me. I had a five-a-side football pitch installed in the grounds and a fully equipped disco built just off the living room, complete with lights, mirrorball and DJ booth, and a pair of enormous speakers. One room housed a replica of Tutankhamun's state throne. I had speakers rigged up outside the house, linked to the stereo in my bedroom. When I woke up, I'd play a fanfare through the speakers, to let everyone in the house know I was coming. I thought this was hilarious, a camp joke, but for some reason, visitors who weren't prepared for the fanfare tended to react to it with a thoughtful expression, as if considering the possibility that success might have gone to my head.

In the grounds there was an orangery that had been converted into a separate flat with its own garden, which I moved my grandmother into. Her second husband Horace had died and I didn't like the thought of her living on her own in her seventies. She spent the rest of her life there until she passed away in 1995. I thought there was a beautiful circularity about that. I was born in her house, she died in mine, although her life there was very self-contained. She was always an independent woman, and I didn't want to take that away from her. She was behind the gates of Woodside, so I knew she was safe, but she lived her own life, had her own friends. I could drop in to see her whenever I wanted, but I could also keep the madness of my life away from her, protect her from all the excess and stupidity. And she seemed really happy there, pottering around in the garden. She was weeding her borders when the Queen Mother came to Woodside for lunch – we'd got on well when I met her at Bryan Forbes's house, and I'd been invited to the Royal Lodge in Windsor for dinner. She was really good fun. After the meal, she'd insisted that we dance to her favourite record, which turned out to be an old Irish drinking song called 'Slattery's Mounted Fut': I think Val Doonican recorded a version of it.

So, having enjoyed the surreal experience of dancing with the Queen Mum to an Irish drinking song, there seemed no harm in inviting her to lunch. She told me she had been friends with the family who had lived at Woodside before the war, and I thought she might want to see the house again. When she accepted, I decided it would be hilarious not to tell my grandmother in advance who was coming. I just called her over: 'Come here, Gran, there's someone who wants to meet you.' Unfortunately, my grandmother didn't see the funny side of it. All hell broke loose when the Queen Mother left.

'How could you do that to me? Standing there talking to the Queen Mum in my bleedin' wellies and gardening gloves! I've never been so embarrassed in my life! Don't ever do that to me again!'

I employed some staff to look after Woodside. A guy called Bob Halley was my chauffeur at first, and his wife Pearl was the house-keeper: a lovely woman, but, as it turned out, useless at cooking. There were a couple of cleaners and a PA called Andy Hill. He was the son of the landlord of the Northwood Hills, the pub where I'd played the piano as a kid, and I'd employed him largely because I had a crush on him; when that wore off, I realized he wasn't right for the job. There was a lesson in there somewhere. Eventually I gave Bob Halley the PA role.

I got my mum to come and manage the house, which turned out to be a dreadful mistake. She was very good at the accounts, but she ruled the place with a rod of iron. I'd noticed a change in the way she was behaving. She was still happy with Derf, but somehow seemed to be slipping back into the way she had been before she met him: moody and difficult and argumentative, nothing ever good enough. I thought getting her to work with me might bring us closer together again, like we had been in Frome Court when Bernie and I were starting out. But no. It was as if the pleasure she had taken in my early success had worn off. She seemed to hate everything I did. There was a constant drizzle of pissy criticism from her – about what I wore, about my friends, about the music I made. And there were a lot of arguments about money. I suppose she'd lived through the war and rationing and had that frugal, waste-not-want-not outlook ingrained in her. But, as I think we've established quite thoroughly by now, that's not really my attitude to spending. I got sick of having my every purchase queried, having to have a row with her every time I bought someone else a gift. It felt like there was no escape from her, no privacy. You get up in the morning after you've slept with someone, and the first person you and your latest conquest bump into is your mum, angrily waving a receipt under your nose and demanding: 'Why have you spent this much on a dress for Kiki Dee?' It's just weird. It really takes the shine off the atmosphere of post-coital bliss. Worse, she had a habit of being absolutely foul to the rest of the staff at the house, treating them like shit, like she was the lady of the manor and they were her servants. I was always having to patch things up after she'd lost her temper and screamed at someone. Eventually the situation just became too claustrophobic and tense. She and Derf moved down to the south coast, which frankly came as a relief.

I was in bed alone at Woodside one Sunday morning, half watching television, when a guy with bright orange hair suddenly appeared on the screen and called Rod Stewart a useless old fucker. I hadn't really been paying attention, but now I was suddenly riveted: someone slagging Rod off was clearly too good to miss. His name was Johnny Rotten, he was wearing the most amazing clothes and I thought he was hilarious – like a cross between an angry young man and a bitchy old queen, really acidic and witty. He was being interviewed about the burgeoning punk scene in London by a woman called Janet Street-Porter. I liked her, too; she was gobby and bold. In absolute fairness to Rod, Johnny Rotten appeared to hate everything – I was fairly certain he thought I too was a useless old fucker. Nevertheless, I made a mental note to ring Rod later, just to make sure he knew all about it. 'Hello, Phyllis, did you see the TV this morning? This new band were on called the Sex Pistols and, you'll never believe this, they said you were a useless old fucker. Those were their exact words: Rod Stewart is a useless old fucker. Isn't that terrible? You're only thirty-two. How awful for you.'

I didn't really care what they thought of me. I loved punk. I loved its energy, attitude and style, and I loved that my old friend Marc Bolan immediately claimed he'd invented it twenty years ago; that was just the most Marc response imaginable. I didn't feel shocked by punk – I'd lived through the scandal and social upheaval that rock 'n' roll provoked in the fifties, so I was virtually immune to the idea of music causing outrage – and I didn't feel threatened or rendered obsolete by it either. I couldn't really imagine Elton John fans burning their copies of *Captain Fantastic* in order to go to the Vortex and spit at The Lurkers. And even if they did, that was out of my hands: it wasn't a musical trend I was interested in chasing. But I thought The Clash and Buzzcocks and Siouxsie And The Banshees were fantastic. I thought Janet Street-Porter was fantastic too. The day after the show I got hold of her on the phone and invited her to lunch, and that was that: we've been lifelong friends ever since.

Even if punk didn't affect me directly, it felt like a sign that things were changing. *Another* sign that things were changing. There were a lot of them around. I'd stopped working with Dick James and DJM. My contract with them ran out just after *Rock of the Westies* was released. They were entitled to put out a live album called *Here and There*, which I hated – it wasn't that the music on it was bad, but it was made up of old recordings from 1972 and 1974, and it seemed to exist only in order to make money. And that was it. I declined to sign another contract with them and moved to my own label, Rocket. John Reid was muttering darkly that Dick had been ripping us off for years. He thought the contracts Bernie and I had signed with Dick in the sixties were unfair; that the royalty rates we received were too low; that there was something fishy about the way our foreign royalties were worked out. By the time DJM, its administrators and foreign subsidiaries had taken their cut, Bernie and I were only getting fifteen quid each from every £100 we earned. It was just the standard music business practices of the day, but the standard music business practices of the day were wrong. It all ended up in a court case in the mid-eighties, which we won. I hated every minute of it, because I loved Dick; I never had a bad word to say about him personally. And yet I felt I had to: the industry had to change the way it treated artists. Dick had a fatal heart attack not long afterwards, and his son Steve blamed me for his death. It was really ugly, really sad. That wasn't how the story of Dick and I was supposed to end at all.

In addition to leaving DJM, Bernie and I had agreed to take a break from working together. There was no huge row, no big falling-out. It just seemed like the right thing to do. We had been tied to each other for ten years, and it was good to stop before our partnership felt like a rut we were stuck in. I didn't want us to end up like Bacharach and David, who worked together until they couldn't stand the sight of each other. The only thing Bernie had really done without me was make a solo album – he'd read some of his poetry over a musical backing provided by Caleb Quaye and Davey Johnstone. Dick James released it, then called a completely ludicrous meeting at which he kept insisting I should use Bernie as a support act on a forthcoming American tour: 'He can read his poems! People will love it!' I couldn't imagine why Dick thought this was a good idea, unless he'd secretly taken out a life insurance policy on Bernie and was hoping to make a swift financial return by getting him killed onstage. American rock audiences in the early seventies were many things, but prepared to listen to a man read poems about his Lincolnshire boyhood for forty-five minutes wasn't one of them, however wonderful said poems were. I pointed out that it was hard enough to get Bernie to come onstage and take a bow at the end of a show, let alone perform an experimental spoken-word support set, and the idea was mercifully dropped.

Now, however, Bernie had really struck out on his own. He'd

made an album with Alice Cooper, a big concept work about Alice's alcoholism and recent stay in rehab. He got our old bass player Dee Murray involved, and Davey Johnstone on guitar. It was a good album. I was impressed. So why did I feel so odd when I looked at the songwriting credits and saw Alice Cooper's name next to Bernie's instead of mine? Actually, there was nothing odd about how I felt. It was very straightforward. I hated admitting it to myself, but I felt jealous.

I put it out of my mind. After all, I had a new writing partner, Gary Osborne, who I'd first met when he wrote the English lyrics for 'Amoureuse', the French song that had finally given Kiki Dee a hit. It was the opposite of working with Bernie – Gary wanted me to write the music before he started the lyrics – but we came up with some really good songs together: 'Blue Eyes', 'Little Jeannie', a ballad called 'Chloe'. And we became very close friends. So close that it was Gary and his wife Jenny that I called on Christmas Day in tears, when my then boyfriend mysteriously failed to fly in from LA as arranged. A catastrophic choice of partner even by my standards, this one had decided he wasn't gay after all and had run off with an air stewardess who worked on the Starship. Not that he told me any of this. He just vanished. His plane arrived at Heathrow, he wasn't on it, and I literally never heard from him again. Perhaps I should have seen it coming but, in fairness, he didn't seem very straight when he was in bed with me. I was in a terrible state, sitting at home alone with only a load of unopened presents and an uncooked turkey for company: anticipating a quiet romantic Christmas, I'd given everyone who worked at Woodside the week off. Gary and Jenny changed their plans and drove down from London to stay with me. They were a lovely couple.

And there were definitely other advantages to not working with Bernie. I could experiment with music in ways I never had before. I flew to Seattle to record a few songs for an EP with producer

Thom Bell, the man who had made the Philadelphia soul records that had inspired 'Philadelphia Freedom'. He made me sing lower than I previously had and wrapped the songs in luxurious strings. Twenty-seven years later, one of the tracks we recorded, 'Are You Ready For Love', went to Number One in Britain, which tells you something about how timeless Thom Bell's sound is. After that I wrote some great songs with the new wave singer Tom Robinson. One was called 'Sartorial Eloquence', a title that my US record company decided Americans were too stupid to understand: they insisted on renaming it 'Don't Ya Wanna Play This Game No More', which really didn't have the same poetic quality to it. Another of Tom's tracks, 'Elton's Song', was very different from anything Bernie would have done, a melancholy depiction of a gay schoolboy with a crush on one of his friends. I wrote with Tim Rice, who had spent the seventies breaking records and winning awards with *Jesus Christ Superstar* and *Evita*, musicals he had written with Andrew Lloyd Webber. Only one song we wrote was released at the time – 'Legal Boys', which came out in 1982 on my album *Jump Up!* – but decades later, it ended up being one of the most important musical partnerships of my career.

And, just occasionally, I wrote completely alone for the first time. One Sunday at Woodside, gloomy and hungover, I wrote an instrumental that fitted my mood, and kept singing one line of lyrics over the top: 'Life isn't everything'. The next morning I found out that a boy called Guy Burchett who worked for Rocket had died in a motorbike crash at virtually the same time I was writing the song, so I called it 'Song For Guy'. It was like nothing I'd ever done before, and my American record label refused to release it as a single – I was furious – but it became a colossal hit in Europe. Years later, when I first met Gianni Versace, he told me it was his favourite song of mine. He kept saying how wonderfully brave he thought it was. I thought that was a bit over-the-top; it was certainly different, but I wouldn't have described it as brave.

After a while it became apparent that Gianni thought it was wonderfully brave because he'd misheard the title and was under the impression I'd called it 'Song For A Gay'.

Some of my experiments, however, should probably have stayed in the laboratory. Pop videos were still a new thing in early 1978, and I decided to jump in feet first. Of course I did: I was going to make the most incredible, expensive, lavish pop video of all time, for a song called 'Ego'. We spent a fortune on it, hiring the director Michael Lindsay-Hogg. It was shot like a movie. There were dozens of actors involved, stage sets, flaming torches, murder scenes, flashbacks shot in sepia. Such was my commitment to the project, I even agreed to take my hat off onscreen at one point. We hired a West End cinema for a premiere, overlooking the fact that if people turn out for a film premiere they expect the film to last longer than three and a half minutes. As it ended, there was some hesitant applause and an unmistakable air of 'is that it?' filled the room, as if I'd invited the audience to a black-tie dinner and then given them a Twix. So I made them show the whole thing twice, which succeeded in changing the atmosphere quite dramatically: 'is that it?' was swiftly replaced by the equally unmistakable air of 'not this again'. Better yet, no one would show the bloody thing – this was years before MTV started, and there weren't really the outlets for a video on TV shows – so the single flopped. If nothing else, this gave John Reid the opportunity to go on one of his celebrated rampages through the office personnel, firing people for their incompetence, then having to hire them again shortly afterwards. I've hated making videos ever since.

And then there was the disco album, an idea I think was partly inspired by the amount of time I was spending at Studio 54. I went there every time I visited New York. It was astonishing, different from any club I'd been to before. The guy who ran it, Steve Rubell, was blessed with the ability to create an amazing environment, full of gorgeous waiters in tiny shorts and other extraordinary characters.

I don't mean the celebrities, although there were plenty of them. I mean people like Disco Sally, who looked about seventy and always seemed to be having a whale of a time, and Rollereena, a guy who dressed up like Miss Havisham from *Great Expectations* and went around the dance floor on roller skates. More impressive still, Steve Rubell could create this incredible environment while seemingly permanently out of his mind on Quaaludes. You got the feeling that Studio 54 was a magical space in which anything could happen and sometimes did. Rocket once threw a party there, and at one point, I spotted Lou Reed and Lou's transgender lover Rachel locked in conversation with, of all people, Cliff Richard. While it was nice to see people with what you might tactfully describe as having differing outlooks on life getting along so famously, the mind did boggle a little at what on earth they were actually talking about.

There was a basement downstairs where celebrities could go and snort coke off a pinball machine. It was certainly an experience going down there – one night I was interrupted by a visibly zonked Liza Minnelli, who wanted to know if I would marry her – but the thing that really attracted me to the club was the thing that no one ever mentions about Studio 54: the music. Well, the music and the waiters, but the waiters were a dead loss. I'd try and chat them up, but they didn't get off work until 7 a.m. Of course, I'd happily hang around until 7 a.m., but by that point, the evening's excesses had usually taken their toll on me and nothing would come of it. It's hard to conjure up a seductive mood when your eyeballs are pointing in different directions and it takes you three attempts to successfully navigate your way through the exit.

So the lure really was the music. I loved disco as much as I had when I first heard it in LA's gay clubs. That was the whole reason I'd had a disco built at Woodside: so I could DJ when people came to stay, impress them with my extensive collection of 12-inch singles. But, I was forced to admit, the DJs at Studio 54 had a better collection than me, and a sound system at their disposal that made the speakers I'd had brought in specially from Trident Studios in London sound like a transistor radio with its battery running out. They could make anyone dance, even Rod Stewart, which was quite a feat – for some reason, Rod used to carry on as if dancing was against his religion. He always needed a little encouragement to actually get on the floor, which is where the bottles of amyl nitrate I used to bring along came in handy. Poppers had become a big thing in gay clubs in the seventies: you sniffed it and it gave you a brief, legal, euphoric high. The brand I had was called, I regret to inform you, Cum, and it seemed to have a particularly transformative effect on Rod. I offered some to him, and suddenly – after hours of refusing to budge from his seat – he was up and dancing for the rest of the night. The only time he stopped was when he was after another sniff: ''Ere, you got any more of that Cum, Sharon?'

One of disco's big producers was Pete Bellotte, who I'd known back in the sixties: Bluesology had played alongside his band The Sinners at the Top Ten Club in Hamburg. It was good to see him again, and the album we made might have worked, had I not decided that I wasn't going to write any songs for it – I'd just sing whatever Pete and his staff writers came up with. I suspect the thinking behind this idea was influenced by the fact that I only owed my American label, Uni, a couple more albums. I was still furious about them refusing to release 'Song For Guy' and had decided that I wanted to get out of my contract as quickly as possible, with the minimum of effort. Not everything on *Victim of Love* was terrible – if the title track had come on at Studio 54, I'd have danced to it – but making an album in bad faith like that is never a good idea. No matter what you do, it somehow gets into the music: you can just tell it's not coming from an honest place. Furthermore, it was released at the end of 1979, just as a huge backlash against disco started in the States, with particular venom reserved for rock artists who had dared to dabble in the genre. *Victim of Love* sank like a stone on both sides of the Atlantic. Once more, the offices of Rocket rang to the screams of John Reid firing everybody, then sheepishly having to hire them again.

As I suspected the moment I'd announced it onstage at Madison Square Garden, retiring from live performance wasn't a plan I could stick to. Or at least, sometimes I couldn't. I was unable to decide whether it was the smartest move I'd ever made, or the stupidest. My opinion changed all the time, depending on my mood, with predictably demented results. One day, I would be perfectly happy at home, telling anyone who'd listen about how wonderful it was not being shackled to the old cycle of touring, delighting in the free time that allowed me to concentrate on being chairman of Watford FC. The next, I'd be on the phone to Stiff Records, a small independent label that was home to Ian Dury and Elvis Costello, offering my services as a keyboard player on their upcoming package tour, which they accepted. My sudden urge to get in front of an audience again was bolstered by the fact that I had a crush on one of their artists, Wreckless Eric – sadly, he was nowhere near wreckless enough to get involved with me.

Then I assembled a fresh set of backing musicians, based around China, the band Davey Johnstone had formed when I said I wouldn't tour anymore. We spent three weeks frantically rehearsing for a fundraising concert at Wembley that I had committed to because I was involved with the charity behind it, Goaldiggers. During the rehearsals, I started making vague noises about going back on the road with them. Then I decided on the night that the whole idea was a terrible mistake and announced my retirement onstage again, this time without telling anyone first. John Reid was furious. The full and frank discussion between us that took place backstage after the gig could apparently be heard not just throughout Wembley but most of north London.

Eventually, I realized that if I was going to play live again, it had to be different, a challenge. I decided to tour with Ray Cooper, who I'd known since before I was famous. He'd played in a band called Blue Mink, who were part of the scene around DJM – their singer Roger Cook was also a songwriter signed to Dick James's publishing company, and virtually every member of Blue Mink had ended up helping out on my early albums. Ray had been the percussionist in my band on and off for years; but these shows would be just me and him, playing theatres rather than stadiums. We had done a few shows like that before, a couple of charity concerts at the Rainbow in London, the first of which had been enlivened by the presence of the Queen's cousin, Princess Alexandra. She had sat politely through the performance, then come backstage, and got the conversation off to a flying start by smiling sweetly and asking, 'How do you have so much energy onstage? Do you take a lot of cocaine?'

It was one of those moments where time appears to stand still while your brain tries to work out what the hell's going on. Was she incredibly naive, and didn't really understand what she'd just said? Or, worse, did she realize exactly what she'd just said? Jesus, did she *know*? Had news of my gargantuan appetite for coke – already quite the hot topic around the music business – actually reached Buckingham Palace? Were they all discussing it over dinner? 'I hear you had lunch at Elton John's house and met his nan, Mother – have you heard he's an absolute fiend for the old blow?' I managed to collect myself enough to mumble a shaky denial.

Still, the Rainbow shows had been really exhilarating, unexpected enquiries from members of the Royal Family about my drug habits notwithstanding. They were terrifying in the best possible way – if it's only you and a percussionist onstage, you can't switch off for a moment and let the band take the strain. You have to concentrate every second, and your playing has to be razor-sharp. And when we went on tour, it really worked. The gigs got fabulous reviews and, every night, I felt that perfect cocktail of apprehension and excitement, exactly how a performer should feel before they go onstage. It was freeing and challenging and fulfilling, because it was completely different from anything I'd done before: the songs we performed, the way it was presented, even the places we played. I was keen to go to countries I hadn't previously visited, even if I wasn't that well known there: Spain, Switzerland, Ireland, Israel. And that's how I ended up flying out of Heathrow, flat on my back with my legs in the air, heading for Moscow.

I was flat on my back with my legs in the air because we were flying Aeroflot, and the moment we took off, it became apparent that the Russian state airline didn't stretch to actually bolting the seats to the floor of the plane. Nor, I couldn't help noticing, did there seem to be any oxygen masks in case of an emergency. What the plane did have in abundance was a very distinctive smell: antiseptic and sharp, it reminded me a bit of the carbolic soap my grandma used to wash me with when I was a kid. I never found out exactly what it was, but it was the smell of Russia in 1979 – every hotel had it too.

I'd suggested playing in Russia to the promoter Harvey Goldsmith almost as a joke. I never thought it would happen. Western rock music was more or less forbidden under communism – tapes of albums got passed around like contraband goods – and homosexuality was illegal, so the chances of them agreeing to be entertained by an openly gay rock star seemed almost non-existent. But Moscow was scheduled to host the Olympic Games in 1980, and I think they were looking for some positive advance publicity. They didn't want the Soviet Union to be seen as a monolithic, grey state where fun was banned. Harvey made a request via the

Foreign Office and the Russians sent an official from the state music promoter to see a gig Ray and I played in Oxford. Having established that we weren't the Sex Pistols, and deeming us no great threat to the morals of communist youth, they gave the green light to the tour. I took my mum and Derf, a handful of British and American journalists and a film crew, fronted by the writers Dick Clement and Ian La Frenais, to make a documentary. It felt hugely exciting, a genuine journey into the unknown, albeit one that could end at any moment with death by suffocation if the plane lost pressure.

We were met at Moscow Airport by a group of dignitaries, two girls who were going to act as our translators and an ex-army guy called Sasha. I was told he was going to be my bodyguard. Everyone else in our party automatically assumed he was spying on us for the KGB. I decided he could spy on me to his heart's content – he was extremely good-looking, if disappointingly keen on telling me about his wife and children. We boarded a sleeper train bound for Leningrad. It was hot – I'd dressed for winter in the Siberian steppes, only to find Moscow in the grip of a sweltering heatwave – and it was uncomfortable, but that wasn't the Russians' fault. It was down to the fact that, through the thin wall, I could very clearly hear John Reid, in the next sleeper cabin, apparently doing his persistent best to seduce a reporter from the *Daily Mail*.

The hotel in Leningrad didn't look terribly promising. The food was indescribable: fifty-seven varieties of beetroot soup and potatoes. If this was what they were serving in the best hotels, what the hell were ordinary people eating? Every floor was guarded by a stern-faced old woman, a proper Russian babushka, on the lookout for any kind of Western impropriety. But it turned out to be quite the swinging spot. The first morning we were there, the road crew turned up for breakfast looking dazed and delighted. They had learned that being from the West and having any connection to rock and roll, even carrying the speakers, made you sexually irresistible to the chambermaids. They would turn up in the room, start running a bath in order to distract the ears of the ever-vigilant babushkas, then take all their clothes off and jump on you. The hotel bar seemed to be a non-stop party, filled with people who'd travelled from Finland with the specific intention of getting as pissed as possible on cheap Russian vodka. The stuff was lethal. At one point, someone sidled up to me and, to my disbelief, handed me a joint. Here, in the middle of repressive, communist Russia, the road crew had somehow managed to source some pot. They seemed to be having all the luck. Perhaps it was rubbing off – not long afterwards, Sasha showed up and suggested we go up to my room. I was so taken aback, I brought up the subject of his wife and children unprompted. No, he said, it was fine: 'In the army, all the men have sex with each other, because we don't see our wives.' So I ended the evening drunk, stoned and having sex with a soldier. I don't know exactly what I'd been expecting from my first forty-eight hours in Russia, but this def-initely wasn't it.

I still would have fallen in love with Russia even if one of its citizens hadn't taken me to bed. The people were impossibly kind and generous. Weirdly, they reminded me of Americans: they had that same sense of instant warmth and hospitality. We were shown the Hermitage and the Summer Palace; Peter the Great's log cabin and the Kremlin. We saw collections of Impressionist art and Fabergé eggs extraordinary enough to take your mind off what you'd be having for lunch. Everywhere we went, people tried to give us presents: bars of chocolate, soft toys, things that they must have had to save up to buy. They would press them into your hands in the street or push them through the windows of your train as it pulled out of the station. It made my mum cry: 'These people have got absolutely nothing, and they're giving things to you.'

The gigs were in Leningrad and Moscow, and they turned out

to be fantastic. I say turned out, because they always started badly. All the best seats were given to high-ranking Communist Party officials, to ensure that the reaction was nothing more exciting than polite applause. The people who actually wanted to see me were crammed at the back. But they had reckoned without Ray Cooper. Ray is a fabulous musician, who plays the most inconspicuous instruments in the most conspicuous way imaginable. He's like the Jimi Hendrix of the tambourine, a born frontman trapped in a percussionist's body. And in Russia, he played as if every other wildly flamboyant performance he'd given over the years was merely a warm-up. He would goad the audience into clapping along, or run to the front of the stage and scream at them to get on their feet. It worked. The kids at the back ran down the aisles to the front. They threw flowers and asked for autographs in between songs. I'd been told not to sing 'Back In The USSR', so of course I did. If the KGB had been spying on me, they clearly hadn't been spying closely enough to learn that one of the quickest ways to get me to do something is to tell me not to do it.

After the Moscow show, there were thousands of people crowded around the venue, chanting my name – far more than could possibly have been at the show. From the window of the dressing room, I threw the flowers I'd been given back to them. My mum looked on. 'You'd be better off throwing them a tomato,' she said, the memory of our most recent feast of beetroot soup and potatoes still fresh in her mind. 'They've probably never bleedin' seen one.'

As a PR exercise for the Soviet Union, my visit was a waste of time. Six months later, they invaded Afghanistan, and whatever international goodwill they'd built up by letting me sing 'Bennie And The Jets' didn't count for much after that. But for me, it was the beginning of a lifelong love affair with Russia and with Russians. I've never stopped going back there, even when people have said

I shouldn't. If anything, things are worse for gay Russians under Vladimir Putin than they were in 1979, but what would I achieve by boycotting the place? I'm in a very privileged position in Russia. I've always been accepted and welcomed, despite the fact they know I'm gay, so I'm not afraid to speak out while I'm there. I can make statements that get reported; I can meet with gay people and people from the Health Ministry and promote the work that the Elton John AIDS Foundation does over there. I never saw Sasha again, but I later learned he was one of the first people to die of AIDS in Russia. Today it has one of the fastest-growing HIV/AIDS epidemics in the world. That isn't going to change without negotiation, without sitting down and talking. And the debate has to start somewhere. So I keep going back, and every time I do, I say something onstage about homophobia or gay rights. Sometimes a few people walk out, but the vast majority applaud. I owe it to the Russian people to keep doing that. I owe it to myself.

If the shows with Ray Cooper taught me anything, it was that I belonged onstage. My private life was still the usual chaos of different boyfriends and drugs – at one point I was rushed from Woodside to hospital with what was reported as a heart problem, but in reality had nothing to do with my heart and everything to do with electing to play tennis against Billie Jean King in the immediate aftermath of yet another coke binge. *Victim of Love* aside, my albums were selling OK – its follow-up, *21 at 33*, went gold in America in 1980 – but they clearly weren't selling like they used to, even though I'd started working with Bernie again, albeit tentatively, just a couple of songs each time. Sometimes the lyrics he gave me seemed quite pointed. You didn't have to be a genius to work out what he was driving at when he sent me a song called 'White Lady White Powder', a portrait of a hopeless cocaine addict. I had the brass balls to sing it as if it was about someone else.

But onstage, everything else melted away for a couple of hours. After *21 at 33* was released, I headed out on a world tour. I had re-formed the original Elton John Band – me, Dee and Nigel – and augmented them with a couple of stellar session guitarists, Richie Zito and Tim Renwick, and James Newton Howard on keyboards. For the shows with Ray, I had dressed down, leaving the theatrics to him, but now, I decided to go to town again. I contacted my old costumier Bob Mackie and a designer called Bruce Halperin and told them both to do their worst: the flares and platforms were obviously gone, in keeping with changing fashions, but Bruce came up with something that resembled a military general's uniform covered in red and yellow thunderflashes and arrows, with lapels that looked like a piano keyboard and a peaked cap to match.

The gigs were bigger than ever. In September 1980, I played in front of half a million people in Central Park, the largest crowd I'd ever performed to. For the encore, Bob had made me a Donald Duck costume. It was a fantastic idea in theory, but the practicalities of it left a little to be desired. First of all, I couldn't get the bloody thing on properly. I was backstage, with one arm through the leg hole and my leg through the arm, crying with laughter while everyone around urged me to get a move on: 'There's 500,000 people out there and they'll think there's no encore! They'll think the gig's over and go home!' When I eventually got onstage it struck me that I should probably have had some kind of dress rehearsal to see how the outfit might work. Had I done that I might have discovered that there were two minor problems. First, I couldn't walk in it – it had huge duck feet, like divers' flippers. And secondly, I couldn't sit down in it either – it had an enormous padded bum that meant the best I could manage was perching gingerly on the piano stool. I attempted to play 'Your Song', but I couldn't stop laughing. Every time I caught Dee's eye – wearing an expression of weary resignation, the look of a man who had turned up again after five years to discover that things were as ridiculous as ever – I had a fit of the giggles. Once again, Bernie's tender ballad of blossoming young love was decimated by my choice of stage wear.

But the duck costume aside, it was a fantastic show: perfect New York autumn weather, audience members climbing the trees to get a better view. I played 'Imagine', and dedicated it to John Lennon. I hadn't seen him for a few years. He'd really gone to ground after Sean was born – probably the last thing he wanted to be reminded of was the boozy madness of 1974 and 1975. But after the gig there was a big party on the *Peking*, a ship that had been converted into a floating museum on the East River, and he and Yoko showed up, completely out of the blue. He was as hilarious as ever, full of excitement about making a new album, but I was too exhausted to stay long. We said we'd meet up again next time I was in New York.

The tour moved on, crossing America, then heading down to Australia. Our plane had just landed in Melbourne when a stewardess's voice came over the tannoy, saying that the Elton John party couldn't disembark; we had to stay onboard. It's strange, the moment they said it, my heart sank; I just knew it meant someone was dead. My first thought was that it was my grandmother. Every time I went away and popped into the Orangery to say goodbye to her, I wondered if she'd still be there when I came back. John Reid went to the cockpit to find out what was going on, and came back in tears, looking completely bewildered. He told me John Lennon had been murdered.

I couldn't believe it. It wasn't just the fact of his death, it was the brutality of how it happened. Other friends of mine had died young: first Marc Bolan in 1977 and then Keith Moon in 1978. But they hadn't died the way John died. Marc had been killed in a car crash and Keith had basically died from an incurable case of being Keith Moon. They hadn't been murdered, by a complete stranger, outside their home, for no reason whatsoever. It was inexplicable. It was inconceivable.

I didn't know what to do. What could you do? Rather than flowers, I sent Yoko a huge chocolate cake. She always loved chocolate. There was no funeral to go to, and we were still in Melbourne when the memorial Yoko had asked for took place on the Sunday after his death. So we hired the city cathedral and held our own service at exactly the same time people gathered in Central Park. We sang the 23rd Psalm, 'The Lord is My Shepherd', everyone crying: the band, the road crew, everyone. Later, Bernie and I wrote a song for him, 'Empty Garden'. It was a great lyric. Not mawkish or sentimental – Bernie knew John too, and knew he would have hated anything like that – just angry and uncomprehending and sad. It's one of my favourite songs, but I hardly ever play it live. It's too hard to perform, too emotional. Decades after John died, we put 'Empty Garden' in one of my Las Vegas shows and used beautiful images of him given to us by Yoko on the screens. I still used to tear up every time I sang it. I really loved John, and when you love someone that much, I don't think you ever quite get over their death.

A couple of years after John died, I got a phone call from Yoko. She said she needed to see me, it was urgent, I had to come to New York right away. So I got on a plane. I had no idea what it was about, but she sounded desperate. When I arrived at the Dakota, she told me she'd found a load of tapes with unfinished songs John had been working on just before he died. She asked me if I would complete them, so they could be released. It was very flattering, but I absolutely didn't want to. I thought it was too soon; the time wasn't right. Actually, I didn't think the time would ever be right. Just the thought of it freaked me out. Trying to work out how to finish songs John Lennon had started writing – I wouldn't be so presumptuous. And the idea of putting my voice on the same record as his – I thought it was horrible. Yoko was insistent, but so was I.

So it was a very uncomfortable meeting. I felt terrible after I left. Yoko thought she was honouring John's legacy, trying to fulfil his wishes, and I was refusing to help. I knew I was right, but that didn't make it any less depressing. (In the end, she put the songs out as they were, on an album called *Milk and Honey*.) In search of something to take my mind off it, I went to the cinema and watched Monty Python's *The Meaning of Life*. I ended up laughing my head off at Mr Creosote, the disgusting man who eats until he explodes. Then I thought how funny John would have found it. It was exactly his sense of humour: surreal and biting and satirical. I could almost hear his laugh, that infectious cackle that always used to set me off. That was how I wanted to remember him. And that's how I do remember him.

nine

I was awoken by the sound of someone hammering on the door of my hotel suite. I couldn't think who it was, because I couldn't think at all. The moment I opened my eyes, I realized I had the kind of hangover that makes you think it's not a hangover: you can't possibly feel this ill just through overindulgence – there has to be something more serious wrong with you. It wasn't just my head. My whole body hurt. Especially my hands. Since when did hangovers make your hands hurt? And why wouldn't the person knocking at the door just fuck off, despite my repeated instructions to do so?

Instead, the hammering continued, accompanied by a voice calling my name. It was Bob Halley. I got out of bed. God, this hangover was *astonishing*. I felt worse than I did after Ringo Starr's 1974 New Year's Eve party, and that had started at 8 p.m. and ended around three thirty the following afternoon. I felt worse than I had in Paris a couple of years before, when I'd hired an apartment overlooking the Seine, ostensibly to do some recording, then taken delivery of some pharmaceutical-grade cocaine and refused to go to the studio at all. John Reid had turned up one morning with the intention of dragging me to a session, only to discover I was still awake from the night before and so wasted I was cheerfully hallucinating that the furniture in the kitchen was dancing with me. It might have been on that same trip to Paris that I decided to have a shave while completely out of my mind and – in my altered state – became so overenthusiastic about the very idea of shaving that I removed not just my stubble but one of my eyebrows, too. These events tend to blur into one.

I opened the door, and Bob gave me a searching look, like he was expecting me to say something. When I didn't, he said, 'I think you should come and see this.'

I followed him into his own room. He opened the door to reveal a scene of total devastation. There wasn't a single piece of furniture left intact, except the bed. Everything else was on its side, or upside down, or in pieces. Sitting among the splinters was a cowboy hat that Bob liked to wear. It was completely flat, like Yosemite Sam's after Bugs Bunny drops an anvil on his head.

'Fucking hell,' I said. 'What happened?'

There was a long pause. 'Elton,' he said eventually. 'You happened.'

What did he mean, I happened? What was he talking about? I couldn't see how this had anything to do with me. The last thing I remembered, I was having an absolutely marvellous time. So why would I smash anything up?

'I was in the bar,' I said indignantly. 'With Duran Duran.'

Bob gave me another look, one that suggested he was trying to work out whether I was being serious or not. Then he sighed. 'Yes, you were,' he said. 'At first.'

It had all been going so well. It was June 1983, and we were in Cannes, shooting a video for 'I'm Still Standing', which was planned as the first single off my forthcoming album *Too Low for Zero*. Ever since the 'Ego' debacle, I had tried to have the minimum level of involvement in the making of videos, but this time I'd decided to push the boat out. That was partly because the director was Russell Mulcahy, who I'd worked with before, and really liked. Russell was the go-to man in the early eighties if you wanted your video glossy, exotic and expensive-looking – he was the guy who flew Duran Duran to Antigua and filmed them singing 'Rio' on a yacht. But it was also because I wanted 'I'm Still Standing' and *Too Low for Zero* to be commercial successes. Bernie and I were back writing together full-time. We had come up with some good songs during our trial separation, but we realized that we needed to make a whole album together for the partnership to really click. I'd enjoyed the gigs I'd played with Dee and Nigel, so got my old band back together in the studio, with Davey on guitar and Ray Cooper on percussion. My friend from the Royal Academy of Music Skaila Kanga came and played harp, just as she had on *Elton John* and *Tumbleweed Connection*.

We flew to George Martin's studio in Montserrat to record, where the producer Chris Thomas had assembled a really good team of engineers and tape operators: Bill Price, Peggy McCreary, who arrived fresh from working with Prince, and a German girl called Renate Blauel. I'd taped some of my previous album, *Jump Up!*, there in 1981, but this was different. Bernie was there and it was the first album to properly reunite the old Elton John Band since *Captain Fantastic* in 1975. It was like a well-oiled machine coming back to life, but the results didn't sound like the albums we had made in the 1970s, they sounded really fresh. I'd been experimenting more with playing a synthesizer as well as piano. The songs sparkled: 'I Guess That's Why They Call It The Blues', 'Kiss The Bride', 'Cold As Christmas'. And 'I'm Still Standing' sounded like the whole album's calling-card. The lyric was about one of Bernie's exes, but I also thought it worked as a message to my new American record company, who were, quite frankly, turning out to be a terrible pain in the arse.

Geffen Records was a relatively new label – it had been founded in 1980 – but it opened its account by signing the biggest stars it could: not just me, but Donna Summer, Neil Young, Joni Mitchell and John Lennon. All of us had been lured by David Geffen's reputation – he had steered The Eagles and Jackson Browne to success in the seventies – and by the promise of complete artistic freedom. But my first album for them, 1981's *The Fox*, hadn't done great. *Jump Up!* had been an improvement sales-wise, but the only one of their big signings who thus far had had a big hit for them was John, and that was because he was murdered. Before his death his album with Yoko, *Double Fantasy*, had received bad reviews and sales had been slow. That seemed a pretty drastic way to get a hit. So Geffen panicked and started doing ridiculous things. They fired Donna Summer's producer, Giorgio Moroder, who had master-minded literally every hit single she had made. They put Joni Mitchell in the studio with a synthesizer whizzkid called Thomas Dolby, which was about as appropriate for Joni's music as putting her in the studio with an Alpine yodelling choir. They eventually tried to sue Neil Young for being unpredictable, which if you knew anything at all about his career, was like suing Neil Young for being Neil Young. I didn't like the look of any of it, and thought 'I'm Still Standing' sounded like a warning shot across their bows. It was a big, swaggering, confident fuck-you of a song.

It needed a big, swaggering, confident video to match, and Russell provided it, a huge production involving aerial shots from helicopters and legions of dancers wearing body paint and costumes. My convertible Bentley was brought to Nice for me to cruise along the Croisette in. There was choreography, in which I was expected to take part, at least initially. Visibly stunned by my demonstration of the moves I'd honed on the dance floors of Crisco Disco and Studio 54, the choreographer Arlene Phillips went pale and suddenly scaled down my involvement in that side of things, until all I really had to do was click my fingers and walk along the seafront in time to the music. Perhaps she was afraid I was going to upstage the professionals, and the thing she later said about me being the worst dancer she'd ever worked with was a brilliant double-bluff, designed to spare their blushes.

Filming started at 4 a.m. and went on all day. As the sun went down, a break was called and I went back to my hotel, the Negresco, to freshen up before the night shoot. I was in the lobby when I bumped into Simon Le Bon. He was in town with Duran Duran, and they were just heading to the bar. Did I want to come along? I didn't know him that well, but I thought a quick drink might liven me up. I was dithering over what to order, when Simon asked if I'd ever had a vodka martini. I had not. Perhaps I should try one.

Reports vary about precisely what happened next. I'm afraid I can't confirm or deny them because I don't really remember anything beyond thinking Duran Duran were enormously jolly company and noticing that the vodka martini had slipped down remarkably easily. Depending on who you believe, I had either six or eight more of them in the space of an hour, and a couple of lines of coke. I then apparently returned to the video set, demanded they begin running the cameras, took all my clothes off and started rolling around on the floor naked. John Reid was there, performing as an extra in the video, dressed as a clown. He remonstrated with me, an intervention I took very badly. So badly, in fact, that I punched him in the face. Some observers said it looked like I'd broken his nose. That explained why my hands hurt, but I was quite shocked. I had never hit anyone in my adult life before, and I never have since. I hate physical violence to the point that I can't even watch a rugby match. Then again, if I was going to break the habit of a lifetime and punch someone in the face, it might as well be John Reid; he could take it as payback for thumping me when we were a couple.

John stormed off set, grabbing the keys to the Bentley, and sped away into the night. The next anybody heard of him was the following day, when he rang Rocket's office, screaming at them to call the AA. He had driven through the night to Calais, jumped on the ferry to Dover, then promptly broken down. When the breakdown truck arrived, they were understandably disconcerted to find themselves attending a convertible Bentley driven by a man in a clown suit and make-up, covered in blood.

After John Reid's departure, someone else managed to get my clothes back on – this, I was told, took several attempts – and Bob Halley hustled me upstairs. I expressed my displeasure about his intervention by smashing up his hotel room. As a finale, I'd stamped on his hat, then staggered back to my own room and passed out.

Bob and I sat on the bed in hysterics. There was nothing to do other than howl with laughter at the awfulness of it all, and then make some apologetic phone calls. It was a day that should have made me think long and hard about how I was behaving. But, and you might be ahead of me here, it didn't work out that way at all. The main impact the events in Nice had on my life was that – wait for it – I decided to drink more vodka martinis. From now on, that's how an evening out would begin: four or five vodka martinis, then out to a restaurant – perhaps L'Orangerie if I was in Los Angeles – a bottle and a half of wine over dinner, then all back to mine to start on the coke and the spliffs. They became my drink of choice partly because they came with an added bonus – they made me black out, so I couldn't remember how appallingly I'd behaved the night before. Occasionally someone would feel impelled to ring up and remind me and I would say sorry. I recall one livid phone call from Bernie after a night at Le Dome, an LA restaurant I had a financial stake in, where I got drunk and made what I thought was a hilarious speech, during which I managed to insult John Reid's mother. But there was something comforting about not knowing first-hand. It meant I could kid myself that it probably wasn't as bad as people had said, or that it was just an isolated incident. After all, most of the time no one dared say anything, because of who I was. That's the thing about success. It gives you a licence to misbehave, a licence that doesn't get revoked until your success dries up completely, or you man up and decide to hand it in yourself. And, for the time being, there was no danger of either of those things happening to me.

I spent the rest of 1983 travelling. I went on holiday with Rod Stewart, which was becoming a regular event. We'd previously gone to Rio de Janeiro for the carnival, which was hilarious. Trying to ensure we could identify each other in the crowds, we had bought sailor suits from a fancy dress shop. We put them on and left the hotel to discover that a huge naval ship had just docked in the port and that the streets were thronged with sailors in uniform: it was like a Royal Navy conference out there. This time, we went on safari to Africa. We thought that everyone there was going to assume we were boorish, scruffy rock stars, so insisted on dressing for dinner every night in full white tie, despite the sweltering heat. Far from being reassured, our fellow safari-goers – dressed in a way more befitting the climate – kept passing troubled glances our way, as if the safari party had been joined by a couple of maniacs.

Next, I went to China with the Watford team, who were flying out on a post-season tour, the first British football club to be invited to visit. It was strange, and not unappealing, to be in a country where literally no one, other than the people I was with, had any idea who I was. And China was fascinating. It was before the country had really opened up to the West. I went back there with Watford a couple of years later, and you could see a Western influence creeping in. There were people cycling around with microwave ovens strapped to their backs and Madonna records were played in bars. But, for the moment, it was still like visiting another world. For reasons known only to the Communist Party of China, no one was allowed to cheer during football games, so the matches took place in eerie silence. We went to visit Mao's tomb, and had a look at him in his crystal coffin, which was a bizarre experience. I'd seen Lenin's body in Russia, and he looked fine, but there was definitely something not right about Mao or, rather, what had been done to Mao in order to preserve his corpse. He was the same shade of bright pink as those foam-like shrimp sweets kids used to eat. I don't want to cast aspersions on the embalmers who'd worked on him, but Mao looked suspiciously like he might be going off.

And then, in October, I flew to South Africa and played Sun City, a spectacularly stupid idea. The campaign against it hadn't really picked up steam – that only happened after Queen performed there in 1984 – but there was still enough controversy around playing in South Africa at all to fuel my doubts. John Reid assured me it was going to be fine. Black artists had played at Sun City: Ray Charles, Tina Turner, Dionne Warwick, even Curtis Mayfield. How bad could it be if the great poet of the civil rights movement had agreed to play there? It wasn't technically in South Africa, it was in Bophuthatswana. The audiences weren't racially segregated.

Of course, it wasn't fine at all. The audience might as well have been racially segregated – the ticket prices meant black South Africans couldn't afford to go even if they wanted to. If I'd bothered to look into it more closely I'd have found out that when Ray Charles played there, black South Africans were so enraged that they stoned his tour bus, and his concerts in Soweto had to be cancelled. But I didn't. I just blundered into it. It wasn't like going to Russia in the face of opposition. In South Africa, the people who were suffering as a result of apartheid really did want artists to boycott the country. You couldn't achieve anything positive by going there. So there's no point trying to justify it. Sometimes you fuck up, and you have to hold your hand up and admit it. Every one of those black artists I mentioned bitterly regretted their decision later, and so did I. When I got back I signed a public pledge put together by anti-apartheid campaigners, saying I would never go there again.

Back in England, my father was seriously ill. One of my half-brothers had come backstage at a gig in Manchester and told me he had a heart problem and needed a quadruple bypass operation. I'd kept my distance over the years, but I phoned him at home and offered to pay for him to have the operation done privately. He flatly refused. It was a shame, as much for his other kids and my stepmother as anything else: he loved them and they loved him, and it would have been good for them to try and get his health problems sorted as quickly as possible. But he didn't want my help. I suggested we should meet up in Liverpool, when Watford played there. It wouldn't be too far for him to travel. He agreed. Football was the only thing we had in common. I don't recall him ever coming to see me play live, or talking about music with him. What I was doing clearly wasn't really his thing.

Before the match, I took him to lunch at the Adelphi Hotel. It was fine. We stuck to cordial small talk. Occasionally the small talk ran out, and there was an uncomfortable silence, which underlined that we didn't really know each other well. I was still angry at him for the way he'd treated me, but I didn't bring that up. I didn't want a huge confrontation, because it would have ruined the day, and because I was still scared of him: my life had changed so much over the years, but our relationship was still frozen in 1958. We watched the match from the director's box. Watford got hammered 3–1 – we hadn't been long in the First Division, and the team just seemed overawed by playing in a huge stadium like Anfield – but I still think he enjoyed it, although it was hard to tell. I suppose, deep down, I'd hoped that he might be impressed by the fact that I was now chairman of the club he'd taken me to see as a kid, that Watford fans now chanted 'Elton John's Taylor-made army' when we scored or pushed

Britain's least likely pop star accepts his gold discs. Stephen James, Bernie, me and Dick James at the DJM offices.

(*left*) With my lovely nan, Ivy Sewell; (*right*) Doing my best to upstage Rod Stewart, as usual.

(*above*) Her Royal Highness Tony King, with loyal subject John Lennon emerging from her skirts.

(*right*) Luggage tags from the SS *France* trip, where I wrote *Captain Fantastic and the Brown Dirt Cowboy* by day, and took on all-comers at bingo by night.

Rehearsing with John at the Record Plant, NYC, the day before the Thanksgiving show at Madison Square Garden.

With Bernie at Tower Grove Drive, LA, in the 1970s. The ongoing effects of a disastrous hair-dye experiment on the John cranium are clearly visible.

Onstage with Stevie Wonder, Wembley, 1977. Unbeknown to everybody present, I'm about to announce my retirement from live performance, yet again.

(*above*) At Studio 54, for Roberta Flack's party. With me are Andy Warhol, Jerry Hall and Ahmet Ertegun. It's clearly early in the evening because both my eyeballs are pointing in the same direction.

(*left*) In Leningrad with Ray Cooper in 1979.

On the runway with the Starship, freshly repainted to my specifications.

'I won't be able to sing in it? You let me worry about that': the master of shy understatement takes the stage, mid-70s.

Driving a gold-painted golf cart with illuminated glasses and a bow tie on
the front to the unveiling of my star on the Hollywood Walk of Fame.
You can see how overjoyed I was by this turn of events.

With the wonderful Billie Jean King and Bernie, respectively
the inspiration for, and the writer of, 'Philadelphia Freedom'.

(*left*) Wearing the Donald Duck costume, in which I couldn't walk or sit down properly, playing Central Park in September 1980.

(*below*) The other great partnership of my career: Watford manager Graham Taylor discusses tactics with the chairman, 1983.

Backstage at Live Aid with the magnificent Freddie Mercury, who had both just stolen the show and blithely informed me I looked like the Queen Mother onstage.

George Michael wanted to leave the frivolity of pop music behind – so naturally I turned up at Wham!'s farewell concert in June 1986 dressed as Ronald McDonald.

forward on the pitch. If I couldn't get a 'well done, son, I'm proud of you' out of him for my music, then maybe I could for what we'd achieved at Watford. But it never happened. I've turned it over in my mind since, and I can't work out whether he had a problem expressing things like that to me, or whether he felt embarrassed over being wrong about the choices I'd made against his wishes. Still, we parted on relatively good terms. I never saw him again. I couldn't see the point. There was no real relationship to repair. Our lives had been completely separate for decades. There weren't beautiful childhood reminiscences to be picked over and savoured.

In December 1983 we went back to Montserrat. *Too Low for Zero* had been a huge hit, the biggest album I'd made for nearly a decade – platinum in Britain and America, five times platinum in Australia – so for the follow-up, we decided to repeat the formula: Bernie writing all the lyrics, the old Elton John Band providing the music, Chris Thomas producing. In fact the only real change to the team was that Renate Blauel was promoted from tape operator to engineer. She was conscientious and everyone liked her – the other musicians, the crew, Chris. She was quiet but tough and self-possessed. Recording studios in those days were a real boys' club, you really didn't find many women working in them, but she was making a career for herself just by being incredibly good at what she did; she'd stepped up and worked as an engineer for The Human League and The Jam.

I flew out on Boxing Day and arrived in a foul mood. My mum and Derf had come to Woodside for Christmas, and Mum had immediately slipped into her old role of managing the house and being foul to the staff. She'd had a huge row with one of the cleaners, which had turned into a huge row with me, and she and Derf had stormed out on Christmas Eve.

But I perked up on arrival. Tony King had flown in the day before me – he'd come out to stay over New Year. He was living in New York now, working for RCA with Diana Ross and Kenny Rogers. He'd given up drinking, joined AA and looked great, although he had some terrifying stories about what was happening in the gay community in Greenwich Village and on Fire Island as a result of a new disease called AIDS. We messed around in the studio, me inventing characters – an elderly aristocrat called Lady Choc Ice, a lugubrious, Nico-like singer called Gloria Doom – and Tony pretending to interview them. We both thoroughly approved of the boy who took Renate's old tape operator job, Steve Jackson: he was blond and gorgeous.

After a few days, Tony left to go back to New York. I called him there a couple of weeks later, and told him I had some news.

'I'm getting married,' I said.

Tony laughed. 'Oh yes? And who are you getting married to? That glamorous tape operator? Are you going to be Mrs Jackson?'

'No,' I said. 'I'm getting married to Renate.'

Tony kept laughing.

'Tony,' I said, 'I'm serious. I've asked Renate to marry me and she's said yes. The wedding's in four days' time. Can you get a plane to Sydney?'

The laughter at the other end of the phone stopped very abruptly.

I had arrived in Montserrat with my latest boyfriend in tow, an Australian called Gary, who I'd met in Melbourne a couple of years before. It was another in an endless line of young, blond, pretty hostage situations. I'd fallen for him, then set about my usual foolproof course of making both our lives a misery. I had convinced him to leave Australia and come and live with me at Woodside, showered him with gifts, then become bored and got Bob Halley to send him home. We would get in touch again, I'd have a change of heart and ask him to come back to Woodside, then get bored and tell Bob to book him a ticket back to Brisbane. It was going nowhere, other than round and round in circles. Why was it always like this? I knew I was at fault, but I was too stupid to work out what I was doing wrong. Cocaine's like that. It makes you egotistical and narcissistic; everything has to be about what you want. And it also makes you completely erratic, so you actually have no idea *what* you want. That's a pretty dismal cocktail for life in general, but for any kind of personal relationship, it's lethal. If you fancy living in a despondent world of unending, delusional bullshit, I really can't recommend cocaine highly enough.

But back in Montserrat, the songs came thick and fast, and there was one other bright side to the recording sessions. I started spending more and more time with Renate. I really enjoyed her company. She was smart and kind and very, very funny – she had a very British sense of humour. She was very beautiful, but didn't seem aware of it, always dressed down in jeans and a T-shirt. She seemed a little isolated and lonely, a woman in a man's world, and isolated and lonely was exactly how I felt inside. We got on incredibly well; so well, I became more interested in talking to her than I was in spending time with Gary. I would invent reasons for us to hang out together, ask her back to the studio after dinner on the pretext of listening to the day's work, just so we could talk. On more than one occasion, I found myself idly reflecting that she was everything that I would have wanted a woman to be, if I was straight.

Obviously, that was a big if. In fact, it was an if so immense that it would have taken an astonishing amount of convoluted, irrational thinking to see it as anything other than completely insurmountable. Luckily, convoluted, irrational thinking was very much my forte in those days, and I quickly set to. What if the problem with my relationships wasn't me? What if it was the fact that they were gay relationships? What if a relationship with a woman could make me happy in a way that relationships with men had thus far failed to do? What if the fact that I enjoyed Renate's company so much wasn't a kind of affectionate bond between two lonely people a long way from home, but a sudden and unexpected stirring of heterosexual desire? What if I'd only spent the last fourteen years sleeping with men because I hadn't found the right woman yet? And what if I now had?

The more I thought about it, the more I thought that it was true. It was a tricky line of argument that didn't really hold up to close scrutiny, or indeed any scrutiny whatsoever. But tricky as it was, it was easier than facing up to the real problem.

We were both drunk in a restaurant called the Chicken Shack when I first mooted the idea of getting married. Renate understandably laughed it off, assuming it was a joke. Up to that point, there hadn't been any hint of actual romance between us, not so much as a kiss. If I'd had any sense, I would have left it at that. But by now I'd absolutely convinced myself that this was the right thing. It was what I wanted; it was going to solve all my problems at a stroke. In my own way, I was infatuated: with the idea of getting married, with Renate's company. I missed her when she wasn't there. It felt remarkably like I was in love.

So when the whole entourage moved from Montserrat to Sydney – me and the band to prepare for an Australian tour, Renate and Chris Thomas to mix the album – I took her out for dinner to an Indian restaurant and asked her again. I loved her and I wanted to spend the rest of my life with her. We should get married. We should do it right away, here in Australia. It was 10 February 1984 – we could get married on Valentine's Day. I could make this happen. It was insanity, but it sounded romantic. Renate said yes.

★

W e rushed back to the hotel we were staying in, the Sebel Townhouse, assembled everyone in the bar and announced the news: 'Hey! Guess what?' It was greeted by a sea of aghast faces, not least Gary's, who'd travelled to Australia with us and now suddenly found himself my ex-boyfriend once more. I asked John Reid and Bernie to be my best men. The resulting party broke the record for the amount of money spent in the bar in one night. Everyone clearly needed a stiff drink in order to process what had just happened.

The next few days passed by in a blur. There was a reception to organize, a church to find, problems with getting a marriage licence at short notice to overcome. I spoke to Renate's father on the phone, asking for her hand in marriage. He was a businessman from Munich, and extremely gracious, given that he had just been informed, out of the blue, that his daughter was going to marry a famously homosexual rock star in four days' time. I rang my mum and Derf and told them. They seemed as bemused as everyone else, although, like everyone else, they didn't attempt to stop me. There was no point. At that stage in my life, what I said went and if anyone tried to challenge me, people got screamed at and inanimate objects got thrown and smashed. It's nothing to be proud of, but that's how it was. Instead, some friends tried to make sense of what I was doing, usually coming to the conclusion that I was getting married because I'd decided I wanted children. I let them think that – in all honesty, it was a more plausible explanation than the truth – but nothing could have been further from my mind. Nearly forty, and more than capable of behaving like a child myself, the last thing I needed was an actual child thrown into the equation. Perhaps if she'd had more time to mull it over, Renate might have changed her mind. But I don't think she would have done.

The wedding itself was as straightforward as any wedding can be at which one of the groom's best men is his former lover, to whom he lost his virginity. Renate wore a white lace dress with a gold and diamond pendant I'd bought her as a wedding gift. She had flowers in her hair. She looked beautiful. Neither my parents nor Renate's were there, but plenty of friends flew in: Tony King, Janet Street-Porter. Bernie's new wife Toni was one of the brides-maids. Rod Stewart couldn't make it, but his manager Billy Gaff sent a telegram: 'You may still be standing, dear,' it read, 'but the rest of us are on the fucking floor.'

On the steps of the church, we were surrounded by fans and paparazzi. People were cheering and applauding. Out of a nearby window, someone cranked their stereo up and played 'Kiss The Bride' from *Too Low for Zero*, which, despite its title, is about the least appropriate song to play at a wedding this side of Tammy Wynette's 'D.I.V.O.R.C.E.'. Over the strains of me singing 'Don't say "I do" – say "bye-bye"', a voice rang out, offering congratula-tions in a very Australian way. 'You finally did it!' the voice bellowed. 'Good on you, you old poof!'

The reception was back at the Sebel and was every bit as inconspicuous and understated as you might expect. White roses had been flown in from New Zealand, where we were to honey-moon. There was lobster and quail and loin of venison, vintage Château Margaux and Puligny-Montrachet, a five-tier wedding cake, a string quartet. As was traditional, there were speeches and the reading of telegrams. As was also traditional, John Reid later punched someone, a guy from the *Sun* newspaper, to whose reporting of the wedding he'd taken exception.

Later, the party moved up to my hotel suite, where there was more booze and cocaine. At this point, I should say that Renate and I agreed when we divorced that we would never publicly discuss the intimate details of our marriage. And I am respecting that. The truth is I don't have anything bad to say about Renate at all. Nor does anyone else who met her. The only person who was cold towards her was my mother, and that was nothing to do with Renate, or her personality. I just think my mother hated the idea of the apron strings finally being cut, of someone else occupying the lead role in my life.

The problem was me. I was still capable of locking myself away, alone, with a load of cocaine whenever I felt like it. Everyone at Woodside was now well accustomed to my drug use, and just treated it as a fact of life. I can remember Gladys, one of the cleaners, discreetly taking me aside one day and saying, 'I found your special white medicine on the floor while I was cleaning your room, so I put it in your bedside drawer,' and there it was, still on the mirror where I'd been chopping out lines. I suppose I'd thought that being in a settled relationship might somehow bring an end to that kind of behaviour. But it didn't work like that. It didn't work like that at all.

ten

It's worth pointing out that Renate didn't just marry a gay drug addict. That would have been bad enough. But she married a gay drug addict whose life was about to go haywire in ways he hadn't previously thought possible. I had a couple of years that were normal enough, at least by my standards. I watched Watford lose the FA Cup Final. I made another album, called *Ice on Fire*. Gus Dudgeon produced it, the first time we'd worked together since the mid-seventies. In Britain, the big hit was 'Nikita', a love song to a Russian, who Bernie, whether by accident or out of mischief, had given a man's name. At Live Aid I set up an area backstage with fake grass and a barbecue, so other artists could drop by. Freddie Mercury arrived, still on a high from Queen's show-stealing performance, and offered a very Freddie-esque appraisal of the hat I'd chosen to perform in: 'Darling! What the fuck were you wearing on your head? You looked like the Queen Mother!' I went to Wham!'s farewell concert at Wembley in the summer of 1986, where I marked George Michael's momentous decision to leave the frivolity of pop music behind and announce himself a mature singer-songwriter by turning up in a Reliant Robin, dressed as Ronald McDonald. George wanted to sing 'Candle In The Wind' as a mark of his new seriousness, but onstage

I struck up with a pub piano version of 'When I'm Sixty-Four' instead.

But later that year, things started to go seriously off-piste for me. It began when I noticed there was something wrong with my voice while on tour in America. It was very odd. I was playing Madison Square Garden and I could sing fine, but found I couldn't speak in anything louder than a whisper offstage. I decided the best course of action would be to rest my voice between shows and make a joke out of it. I got hold of a Harpo Marx wig and a raincoat and took to wearing it backstage, honking a horn instead of speaking.

But my voice got worse when we got to Australia. Just as we arrived, my new album came out. It was called *Leather Jackets*, and it was about as close to an unmitigated disaster as anything I've ever released. I had always tried to be strict about not using drugs in the studio, but this time, that rule went completely out of the window. The coke had precisely the impact on my creative judgement you might expect. I stuck any old crap on *Leather Jackets*. The big single was meant to be 'Heartache All Over The World', a song so lightweight you could have lifted it up with your little finger. There were old out-takes, songs that weren't good enough for earlier albums but that, after a couple of lines, I suddenly recognized as lost masterpieces the public needed to hear as a matter of urgency. There was a terrible song I co-wrote with Cher called 'Don't Trust That Woman', the lyrics of which were beyond belief: 'you can rear-end her, oooh, it'll send her'. You could tell what I thought of that by the fact that I declined to put my own name to it, crediting the song to Cher and my old made-up studio character Lady Choc Ice. Of course, if you hate a song so much that you won't actually admit you wrote it, it's generally speaking a good idea not to record and release it, but I was so wasted that any kind of logic was completely beyond me.

It wasn't all bad: 'Hoop Of Fire' was pretty classy, especially compared to the company it was keeping, while a ballad called 'I Fall Apart' was another example of Bernie's uncanny ability to put words in my mouth that so perfectly expressed my personal situation I might have written them myself. But there was no getting around the fact that, overall, *Leather Jackets* had four legs and a tail and barked if a postman came to the door.

So I wanted the subsequent tour to be something special, an event so ambitious and spectacular it would obliterate the memory of the album that preceded it. I told Bob Mackie to go as crazy as he liked on the costume front, which is how I ended up onstage in Australia variously wearing a giant pink Mohican wig with leopardskin sides, another wig based on the explosive hairstyle made famous by Tina Turner in the eighties, and an outfit that made me look like Mozart had joined a glam rock band – a white sequinned suit teamed with an eighteenth-century powdered wig, white make-up and a fake beauty spot. The Mozart outfit was intended as a wry comment on the second half of the show, during which I was performing with the Melbourne Symphony Orchestra. If anyone thought I was being pretentious, a rock star carrying on like a great classical composer, well, I had made the connection first.

Going on tour with an orchestra and playing rock and roll was something that no one had ever tried before. It meant that, for the first time, I could perform the songs from my early albums live exactly as they had been recorded, complete with Paul Buckmaster's beautiful arrangements. Gus Dudgeon flew out to oversee the sound. We miked up every instrument in the orchestra individually, which no one had ever done before either, and the effect was astonishing: when the strings came in on 'Madman Across The Water', it took the top of your head off. They made a hell of a sound – with the bass cellos and the double basses in full flight, I could feel the stage vibrating underneath me – which was just as well, as the star attraction was struggling to make any sound whatsoever.

For a singer, it was the most bizarre, disconcerting sensation: whenever I opened my mouth onstage, I had absolutely no idea what was going to happen. Sometimes I would sound fine. Other times I would rasp and croak and wheezily fail to hit the notes. For some reason, it particularly seemed to affect me when I spoke rather than sang. I'd try to introduce a song and literally nothing would come out at all. It was as if someone had answered certain critics' long-held prayers by discovering a way of switching me off.

Something was clearly very wrong. For a while, I kept faith in the old sore throat remedy that Leon Russell had given me back-stage at the Troubadour in 1970, gargling with honey, cider vinegar and water as hot as I could stand. It made no difference whatsoever. Eventually, after a show in Sydney during which the loudest sounds I emitted came not during the songs but between them – when I was racked by coughing fits and spat up gunk in a variety of colours so lurid that Bob Mackie's costumes looked sober by comparison – sanity prevailed and I agreed to see an ear, nose and throat specialist called Dr John Tonkin.

He examined my larynx and told me I had cysts on my vocal cords. He didn't know at this stage whether they were cancerous or benign. If they were cancerous, that was it – my larynx would have to be removed and I would never speak again, let alone sing. He wouldn't know for sure until he performed a biopsy. Then he looked at me and frowned. 'You smoke dope, don't you?' he said.

I completely froze. I'd only started smoking spliffs to take the edge off all the cocaine I was doing, but had quickly discovered I enjoyed them in their own right. It was a different kind of drug to coke and booze, which I thought made me more sociable, despite an ever-increasing mountain of evidence to suggest they were making my behaviour about as antisocial as it was possible to get.

But marijuana didn't make me want to go out and party, or stay up for days on end. It just made me laugh and made music sound fantastic. I had a particular love for getting stoned and listening to Kraftwerk: their music was so simple and repetitious and hypnotic. Of course, being me, I couldn't just occasionally smoke a spliff and enjoy listening to *Trans-Europe Express* or *The Man Machine*. I immediately became as gung-ho for weed as I was for everything else. By the time of the Australian tour, one member of the road crew was more or less specifically employed just to roll joints. He went everywhere we did, carrying a shoebox full of the things.

When Dr Tonkin questioned whether I smoked dope, I decided to skip over the finer details of the spliff-roller on staff. 'A bit,' I croaked. Dr Tonkin rolled his eyes, firmly said, 'I think you mean "a lot",' and told me to stop. It might well have directly caused the cysts, and even if it hadn't, it certainly wasn't helping. I never smoked another joint. I wasn't exactly the master of personal resolve when it came to drink and drugs at that point. I lost count of the times I told myself 'never again' while in the grip of a terrible hangover, only to forget I'd ever said it when the hangover wore off. Sometimes I would stick to my decision for months but, sooner or later, I always ended up going back. It turns out there's nothing like being absolutely terrified to help you quit something, and nothing like the word 'cancer' to make you absolutely terrified. Dr Tonkin also told me I should cancel the rest of the Australian tour, but I refused: there was still a week of shows in Sydney to go. For one thing, the cost of cancelling would have been astronomical – there were over a hundred musicians involved, we were supposed to be making a film of the shows and recording them for a live album. But more importantly, if there was a chance I was never going to sing again, I at least wanted to put off the day I stopped as long as I could.

I decided I would take the same stoic, show-must-go-on attitude when I told the band and crew what had happened. Instead, I walked into the bar of the Sebel Townhouse – yes, there again – croakily announced, 'They think I've got throat cancer,' and then burst into tears. I couldn't help it. I was so scared. Even if the operation was successful, even if the biopsy came back clear, I might still be done for, at least as a singer – Julie Andrews had come out of an operation to remove a cyst on her vocal cords with her voice completely destroyed.

We finished the tour. Sick and terrified, I stormed out of the final gig at the Sydney Entertainment Centre, which was being broadcast live on TV, minutes before the show was about to start. I could hear the orchestra playing the overture as I hurried out of the venue. I passed Phil Collins, who was coming in: he was taking his seat at the last moment so as not to be bothered by fans. He looked quite startled to see the star attraction heading in the opposite direction.

'Oh, hello, Elton . . . hang on, where are you *going*?'

'Home!' I shouted, not stopping.

I had a bit of a history of storming out of venues when I was meant to be onstage. A few years previously I had walked out of a Christmas show at the Hammersmith Odeon in a fury in between the end of the set and the encore. My car got as far as the Hogarth Roundabout before I calmed down and decided to return: it's about ten minutes away from the venue, but when we turned the car around, we realized the route back was going to take even longer, because it involved going round a one-way system. Amazingly, the audience were still there when I got back.

This time, I didn't even make it to the car before I had a change of heart. It turned out to be the best show of all. The thought that I might never sing again carried me through it. The highlight was 'Don't Let The Sun Go Down On Me'. My voice was rough and raspy, but I don't think I've ever performed that song better: it was always pretty show-stopping with the orchestra thundering away, but that night, every line seemed to have a new meaning, a different emphasis.

After the tour, I went into hospital in Australia and had the operation. It couldn't have gone better. There was no cancer. The cysts were removed. After I recovered, I realized that it had changed my voice for good, but I liked how it sounded. It was deeper and I couldn't sing falsetto anymore, but there was something about the sound I liked. It felt more powerful, more mature; it had a different kind of strength. I couldn't believe my luck. I thought 1987 had got off to a bad start, but now, the only way was up. I couldn't have been more wrong.

The first headline appeared in the *Sun* in February 1987 – ELTON IN VICE BOYS SCANDAL. But, in retrospect, it was always only a matter of time until the *Sun* came after me: I was gay, I was successful, I was opinionated, which in the *Sun's* eyes made me fair game for a vendetta. Its editor at the time was called Kelvin MacKenzie, a man so toxic the Environment Agency should have cordoned him off. Under his control the *Sun* wasn't really a newspaper so much as a spirited daily attempt to see how much racism, misogyny, xenophobia and, especially, homophobia could be crammed into sixty-four tabloid pages. It's hard to get across to anyone who doesn't remember the *Sun* in the eighties just how nasty it was. It treated people like shit, whether they were famous or not. It found a loophole in the law that enabled it to identify rape victims if no one had been arrested for the crime. It offered homosexuals money to leave Britain: FLY AWAY GAYS AND WE WILL PAY. When a TV actor called Jeremy Brett was dying of heart disease, the *Sun* sent journalists along to confront him in hospital and ask him if he had AIDS, a disease it also told its readers they couldn't contract through straight sex.

I read the story about me with my mouth hanging open. The irony was that there were dozens of men, all around the world, who could theoretically have sold a sex and drugs exposé on me: ex-boyfriends, disgruntled one-night stands. On the evidence of their first exposé, however, the *Sun* had managed to unearth someone I'd never actually met, who'd sold them a story about an orgy somewhere I hadn't been – the home of Rod Stewart's manager Billy Gaff.

In fairness, though, had they found someone who had actually slept with me, they couldn't have got a story like this. It wasn't so much that it was completely fabricated, although it was. It was that it seemed to have been completely fabricated by a raving lunatic. I had allegedly readied myself for the orgy by donning a pair of 'skimpy leather shorts'. *Leather shorts?* I've worn some ridiculous old tat in my time, but I've never, ever prepared for a night of passion by squeezing into a pair of leather shorts – you know, I'm trying to get someone to sleep with me, not take one look and run in the opposite direction, screaming. Furthermore, I was apparently 'twirling a sex aid' between my fingers and 'looking like Cleopatra'. Ah, of course, Cleopatra: last ruler of the Ptolemaic dynasty, lover of Julius Caesar and Mark Antony, and history's most celebrated dildo-twirler and wearer of leather shorts.

On one level, it was laughable, but on another, it wasn't funny at all. It was implying that the rent boys involved had been underage. If you repeat a lie often enough, people think it's true, especially if it's in print. What if people actually believed this? What the hell was I supposed to do? My mum and Derf were going to read this; maybe my grandmother. Oh God, Auntie Win: she had a job in a newsagent. I could imagine her taking delivery of that morning's *Sun*, horrified; selling copies of it to people who knew who her nephew was and were laughing at her.

My initial reaction was to just lock myself away in Woodside and hit the vodka martinis. Then I got a phone call, from Mick Jagger. He'd seen the story and wanted to offer some advice. He told me I shouldn't, under any circumstances, try and sue them. When he'd issued a writ against the *News of the World* after they'd falsely claimed he'd bragged to an undercover reporter about his drug use in the sixties, they had reacted by spying on him and then setting up the famous drug bust at Redlands: he and Keith Richards had ended up in prison, before a public outcry caused their sentences to be overturned. Weirdly, the conversation had the opposite effect to the one Mick intended. As I pointed out to Mick, I didn't really care what the press said about me. I'd occasionally get upset about a bad review or a hurtful remark, but that's the way it goes if you put yourself in the public eye. You just have to suck it up and get over it. But why should I let them get away with telling lies about me?

I could prove that what they were saying wasn't true. On the date I was supposed to have been at Billy Gaff's house, dressed up like an extra in a Village People video and waving a dildo around like a majorette, I had been in New York, having lunch with Tony King and discussing the finer points of my Tina Turner wig with Bob Mackie. There were hotel bills, restaurant receipts and plane tickets to prove it. I had the money to take them to court. Fuck them. I was going to sue.

After I issued the first writ, the *Sun* published more and more stories, filled with more and more lies: every time one appeared, I issued another libel writ against them. Some of the lies were really unpleasant – they claimed I'd paid rent boys to let me urinate on them – and others were just bizarre. There was a claim I kept Rottweiler dogs with their voice boxes cut: ELTON'S SILENT ASSASSINS. The only problem with this story was that

I didn't own any Rottweiler dogs, only two German shepherds, both of whom nearly deafened the RSPCA when they came down to check on their welfare. The *Sun* kept going even when it became apparent that the public didn't want to know. What they were doing clearly wasn't affecting my popularity at all – the stories were reported all around the world, but the live album we'd recorded on the Australian tour was a huge hit, platinum in America, and the version of 'Candle In The Wind' released from it as a single unexpectedly went Top Ten on both sides of the Atlantic. What they were affecting was the *Sun* itself. Every time they put a story about me on the front of the paper, the news-paper's sales dipped. I don't know whether people realized it was all untrue, or whether they saw it as a vendetta against me and thought it was unfair, or whether they were just bored stiff of hearing about it.

Knowing they were in trouble, the *Sun* became increasingly frantic in their attempts to get something on me, anything that would actually stick. I was followed everywhere I went. When I stayed at the Century Plaza in Los Angeles, the penthouse suite was bugged. We had been warned by our solicitors that it might be – it was the suite where President Reagan always stayed – so we had the room swept by the FBI. Someone was trying to frighten me, trying to make me call the lawyers off. They offered to pay any rent boy £500 to say he'd slept with me. Not surprisingly, they were inundated with candidates, but they were all so obviously making it up that even the *Sun* baulked at using them.

The best they could manage was to get hold of some Polaroids that had been stolen from my house. They were about ten years old. One of them featured me giving a guy a blow job. They printed them in the paper, which was mortifying. I tried to console myself with the thought that at least I could claim it as another first in my career – first artist in history to debut at the top of the

US charts with two consecutive albums; first artist in history to have seven American Number Ones in a row; first artist in history to appear in a national newspaper giving someone a blow job. Besides, it seemed like a sign of desperation on the part of the *Sun*. Gay man sucks penis: it's not exactly a Pulitzer-winning scoop. In addition, it was written up in a way that I couldn't help but think told you more about the journalist than about me. It was all 'disgusting' this and 'private perversion' that. How boring does your sex life have to be for a blow job to count as the height of unimaginable depravity?

It went on and on, for months and months, until I'd issued seventeen libel writs against them. I'd love to tell you that I never wavered in my conviction that I would defeat them, but it wasn't like that. Some days I would be fine, righteously angry, ready to take them on. Other days I would be in tears, totally despairing, even ashamed. I hadn't done any of the things they had said I'd done, but I knew I'd laid myself open to something like this happening. My drug use was an open secret. I certainly hadn't slept with anyone underage, but then nor had I always been hugely discriminating in my choice of partners. A few years before, someone I slept with had helped themselves to a sapphire and diamond ring, a watch and some cash before they left. I worried about the court case, about having my private life dissected in public, about what the *Sun* would do to try and smear me.

The thought of it made me do what I'd always done when things got too much. I would shut myself away in my room, just like I had as a kid when my parents were fighting, and try and ignore what was happening. The only difference was that now I would shut myself away with an abundant supply of booze and drugs. I wouldn't eat for three days, then I would wake up starving and stuff myself with food. I would panic about gaining weight and make myself sick by jumping up and down until I puked.

I had developed bulimia, although at the time I didn't know what bulimia was. What I did know was that certain foods were easier to throw up straight away than others. Anything stodgy like bread was difficult; you ended up bent over the toilet, retching and retching. I realized that you had to stick to things that were soft, so my diet became bizarre. When I was bingeing, my idea of a meal became two jars of Sainsbury's cockles and a pint of Häagen-Dazs peanut butter ice cream. I'd shovel it in then bring it up again, sneaking off to make myself sick, thinking that no one would notice. Obviously they did – you come back smelling of puke, looking as if you've been crying, because throwing up makes your eyes water – but of course no one would dare to confront me about it, for fear of the consequences. Everything about it, from what I ate, to how I behaved, seems completely disgusting now, but back then, it became second nature to me; it was just how I was.

Still, when things got really bad, I would eventually pull myself out of it, consoling myself with two thoughts. One was that, as far as the *Sun* went, I was absolutely in the right – if a single word of what they had said was true, then I would never have dared sue them. And the other was that, however bleak things seemed, I knew of people far, far worse off than me, people who'd found the strength to deal with problems that made mine look completely insignificant. I'd first read a *Newsweek* magazine feature about an American teenager called Ryan White in a doctor's waiting room a couple of years before. I was simultaneously horrified and inspired by his story. He was a haemophiliac from Indiana, who had contracted AIDS through a blood transfusion, and AIDS was a disease that had been playing on my mind a great deal. John Reid's PA Neil Carter was the first person I knew who died of it: he was diagnosed, then three weeks later he was dead. After that, the floodgates just seemed to open. Whenever I spoke to Tony King in America, where the epidemic was more advanced, he'd tell me of an old friend or a friend of a friend who was sick. John Reid's secretary, Julie Leggatt, was the first woman in Britain to be diagnosed with AIDS. My ex-boyfriend Tim Lowe had tested positive. So had another ex, Vance Buck, a sweet blond boy from Virginia, who loved Iggy Pop and whose photo was on the inside cover of my album *Jump Up!*, just below the lyrics to 'Blue Eyes', the song Gary Osborne and I had written with him in mind. It was horrible, but ask any gay man who lived through the seventies and eighties and they'll tell you a similar story: everyone lost someone, everyone can remember the climate of fear.

But it wasn't just the fact that Ryan White had AIDS. It was what had happened as a result of him contracting the disease. He had been ostracized in his hometown of Kokomo. The superintendent of his school district refused to let him attend classes, in case he infected his schoolmates. He and his mother Jeanne became involved in a protracted legal battle. When the Indiana department of education ruled in his favour, a group of parents filed an injunction to block his return: they were allowed to hold an auction in the school gymnasium to raise funds to keep him out. When that failed, they set up an alternative school, so that their children didn't have to go near him. He was abused in the street, his school locker was spray-painted with the word FAG and his possessions were vandalized. The tyres on his mother's car were slashed and a bullet was shot through the family's front window. When the local paper supported him, they received death threats. Even their Methodist church turned its back on them: when it came to the blessing at their Easter service, no one in the congregation would shake Ryan's hand and say 'peace be with you' to him.

Throughout it all, Ryan and his mother Jeanne behaved with unbelievable dignity, bravery and compassion. Christians who truly held to the teachings of Christ, they forgave the people who made their already difficult lives even more hellish. They never condemned, they just tried to educate. Ryan became an intelligent, sympathetic, articulate spokesman for people with AIDS at a time when AIDS was still being demonized as God's vengeance on gays and drug addicts. When I found out that he liked my music and wanted to meet me, I got in touch with his mother and invited them to a gig in Oakland, then took them to Disneyland the next day. I really adored them. Jeanne reminded me of the women in my family, especially my nan: she was working class, straight-talking, hard-working, kind but clearly built with an unbreakable core of steel. And Ryan seemed absolutely remarkable. He was so ill that I had to push him around Disneyland in a wheelchair, but he wasn't angry, he wasn't bitter, he never cracked. He didn't want pity or sympathy. Talking to him, I got the feeling that because he knew he didn't have much time left to live, he didn't want to waste it feeling sorry for himself or angry at others – life literally was too short. He was just a lovely kid, trying to lead as normal a life as possible. They were an incredible family.

We kept in touch afterwards. I would call, send flowers, ask if there was anything I could do to help. Whenever I could see Ryan, I saw him. When they couldn't stand it in Kokomo anymore, I loaned Jeanne the money to move her family to Cicero, a small town outside Indianapolis. I tried to just give her the money, but she insisted on it being a loan – she even wrote out a contract and made me sign it. Every time I felt hopeless about the situation I was in, I thought about them. That was real courage in the face of something truly appalling. So stop the self-pity. Just get on with it.

Nevertheless, I kept a low public profile until Michael Parkinson got involved. I'd been on his chat show in the seventies – I'd ended up playing a pub piano while Michael Caine sang 'Maybe It's Because I'm A Londoner' – and we'd subsequently become friends. He contacted me when the *Sun*'s stories first appeared and told me he had a new chat show on ITV called *One to One* – each episode was devoted to a single guest. Why didn't I come up to Leeds and appear on it? I said I wasn't sure, but he was persistent.

'I'm not doing this for me,' he said, 'I'm doing this for you. I know you, I know what the *Sun* are like. You're not saying anything publicly, and you need to. If you don't say anything, people will assume you've got something to hide.'

So I eventually did the show. If you look at the clips of it on YouTube, you can see the effect that events were having on me. I was unshaven, dressed down, I looked haggard and pale. But it went well. The audience were clearly on my side. Michael asked about the *Sun* and I told him that I'd just discovered they had tried to bribe the receptionist at my doctor's to hand over my medical records.

'I think they want to examine my sperm,' I said. 'Which is odd, because if you believe the stories they've been printing, they must have already seen bucketloads of it.'

Not long afterwards, the rent boy who had made the initial allegations in the *Sun* told another tabloid that he had made them all up, and that he'd never met me. 'I don't even like his music,' he added. The morning the first libel case was due to come to court, the *Sun* completely caved in. They offered to settle for £1 million. It was the biggest libel payout in British history, although it was a good deal for them – if it had gone to court, they would have ended up paying me millions. That night, rather than prepare to take my turn in the witness box, I went to see Barry Humphries at the Theatre Royal, Drury Lane, and laughed myself stupid at Dame Edna Everage. Afterwards, we waited around in the West End to see the first edition of the next morning's paper arrive at the news stands. When forced to apologize for making things up, the *Sun* was notorious for printing the correction as small as possible and burying it on page 28. But I said their apology had to be the same size as the initial allegations – a banner headline, front page: SORRY ELTON.

People subsequently said it was a landmark victory that changed British newspapers, but I'm not sure that it changed the *Sun* very much. Two years later, they printed the most notorious load of lies in their history, about the behaviour of Liverpool fans during the Hillsborough disaster, so it's not as if checking their facts suddenly became a huge priority. What did change was the way newspapers behaved around me, because they realized I would sue them if they made things up. I did it again a few years later, when the *Daily Mirror* claimed I'd been seen at a Hollywood party telling people I'd found a wonderful new diet, then chewing food and spitting it out instead of swallowing it: ELTON'S DIET OF DEATH. I hadn't even been in America at the time. I got £850,000 and gave it to charity. The money wasn't the point. The point was to make something very clear. You can say whatever you like about me. You can say I'm a talentless, bald old poof, if that's your opinion. I might think you're an arsehole for saying it, but if it was against the law to express colourful opinions about people, I'd have been locked up years ago. But you can't tell lies about me. Or I'll see you in court.

Renate and I divorced in early 1988. We had been married for four years. It was the right thing to do, but it was a horrible feeling. I'd broken the heart of someone I loved and who loved me unconditionally, someone I couldn't fault in any way. She could have taken me to the cleaners, and I wouldn't have blamed her: everything that had gone wrong was down to me and me alone. But Renate was too dignified and too decent for that. Despite all the pain, there was no acrimony involved at all. For years afterwards, whenever something happened to me, the press would turn up on her doorstep, looking for her to dish the dirt, and she never, ever has: she just told them to leave her alone.

I saw her once after we divorced. She had moved out of

Woodside to a beautiful cottage in a small village. For all that had happened, there was still a very real love there. When I had children, I invited her to Woodside, because I wanted her to meet them; I wanted to see her, I wanted her to be part of our lives, and us part of hers, in some way. But she didn't want to, and I didn't push the issue. I have to respect how she feels.

eleven

It was the state of the squash court that made me realize my passion for collecting had perhaps got the tiniest bit out of control. The squash court was one of the things that I'd liked about Woodside when I first moved in. I would challenge anyone who came over to a game. But no one had played squash at Woodside for some time, because no one could actually get into the court anymore. The place was full of packing cases, and the packing cases were full of things I'd bought: on tour, on holiday, from auctions, whatever. I hadn't been able to unpack any of it, because there was literally no room anywhere in the house to put any more stuff. Every inch of wall space was covered with paintings, posters, gold and platinum discs, framed awards. My record collection was piled up all over the place. I had a special room for it that was like a maze, with corridor after corridor of floor-to-ceiling shelving that housed everything I'd bought since I was a kid: I still had the 78s I'd spent my pocket money on in Siever's in Pinner, with 'Reg Dwight' written on the labels in ink and photos of the artists I'd cut out of magazines Sellotaped to the sleeves. But I'd managed to outgrow the room, by buying someone else's record collection as well. He was a BBC radio producer called Bernie Andrews who had worked on *Saturday Club* and with John Peel, and he owned every single released in Britain between 1958 and 1975, thousands and thousands of the things. Of course, loads of them were absolutely crap: even in pop's most miraculous years, the good releases were outweighed by the bad. But it appealed to my completist collector's mentality. Owning every single released in Britain! It was like some mad childhood fantasy come true.

If I'd just collected records, I might have been able to cope, but I didn't. I collected everything: art, antiques, clothes, chairs, jewellery, glassware. There were beautiful art deco vases and Gallé and Tiffany table lamps just sat on the floor, because there was no space left on any tables – a pretty incredible state of affairs given how much furniture I'd managed to cram into every room. Walking around the house was like taking part in the world's most expensive obstacle course. If you put a foot wrong, or turned round too quickly – which I can tell you for a fact is quite easy to do if you're spending a significant portion of your life drunk and on drugs – you could smash something worth thousands of pounds. It didn't really make for a terribly relaxing environment in which to live. I'd have people over and spend half my time bellowing at them to be careful or to watch what they were doing. I'd occasionally stick my head round the door of the squash court – there was just about enough room to do that, if you breathed in – and feel oddly despairing. Ever since I was a kid, owning things had always made me feel happy, but now it just made me feel overwhelmed. What was I going to do with all this stuff?

A few months after Renate and I separated, I came up with a radical solution. I was going to sell it. All of it. Every painting, every bit of memorabilia, every stick of furniture, every objet d'art. All the clothes, all the jewellery, all the glasses, all the gifts that fans had sent me. Everything in the house, except the records. I got in touch with Sotheby's, who had recently held a huge posthumous sale of Andy Warhol's possessions, and told them I wanted to auction the lot. They sent experts out to Woodside to have a nose around. The experts left looking a little faint. I couldn't work out whether they were floored by the quantity of stuff I was selling – one of them told me, in hushed tones, that I had the largest private collection of Carlo Bugatti furniture in the world – or whether they were just reeling from the sheer hideousness of some of it. I liked to think I had developed a good eye for art and furniture, but I also had a remarkably high threshold for gaudy kitsch. There were things in my home that made my old stage outfits look like the last word in understated good taste. There was a model of a bonobo gorilla in an Edwardian dress that a fan had sent me, with an accompanying note explaining that it was a sculpture representing the futility of war. There was a radio in the shape of a doll wearing a see-through negligee: the volume and tuning controls were mounted on her tits. There was a pair of brass bath taps with large Perspex testicles attached to them.

I decided that I should keep some original *Goon Show* scripts, complete with Spike Milligan's handwritten annotations, that I'd bought at an auction, and four paintings: two Magrittes, one Francis Bacon portrait of his lover George Dyer that people had told me I was crazy to spend £30,000 on back in 1973, and *The Guardian Readers*, the Patrick Procktor painting that had appeared on the cover of *Blue Moves*. Everything else could go.

Before you get the wrong idea, I should add that I had absolutely no intention whatsoever of leading a more simple and meaningful life, uncoupled from the yoke of consumerism and unencumbered by material possessions. If anyone thought that, they were swiftly disabused the first time I went to Sotheby's for a meeting about the upcoming auction: supposedly there to discuss disposing of my worldly goods, I instead ended up buying two paintings by Russian avant-garde artists Igor and Svetlana

Kopystiansky. It was more that I wanted a new start. I wanted to completely remodel and redecorate Woodside. I didn't want to live in a berserk pop star's house anymore, I wanted somewhere that felt like a home.

It took Sotheby's three days just to transport everything from Woodside to their London warehouse. There was so much to sell that there had to be four separate auctions. One was for stage costumes and memorabilia, one for jewellery, one for art deco and art nouveau and one called 'diverse collections', which had everything in it from Warhol silkscreens to suitcases to sporrans – at some point I appeared to have bought two of those.

I used a photo of some of the lots on the cover of my new album, which I'd called *Reg Strikes Back*: it seemed like the right title, after the events of 1987. Sotheby's held an exhibition before the auction. They only showed a quarter of what was up for sale, but it filled the Victoria and Albert Museum. Bizarrely, the former prime minister, Edward Heath, came to have a look at it: maybe he was in the market for a pair of bath taps with Perspex testicles attached. The auctions were a huge success. They had to put up crash barriers outside to cope with the crowds. Paintings sold for double the anticipated price. Things that I thought fans might pick up for a few quid went for thousands. Everything went: the bonobo gorilla representing the futility of war, the sporrans, the doll-in-a-negligee radio. They even sold the banners that hung outside Sotheby's advertising the auction.

I didn't go. I left Woodside the day the removal vans arrived. I didn't set foot in the house again for two years. I wasn't to know it then, but by the time I came back, my life would have changed even more than my home had.

★

I decided to move to London while the house was being emptied. At first I stayed in a hotel – the Inn On The Park, the location for the famous story about me ringing the Rocket office and demanding they do something about the wind outside that was keeping me awake. This is obviously the ideal moment to state once and for all that this story is a complete urban myth, that I was never crazy enough to ask my record company to do something about the weather; that I was simply disturbed by the wind and wanted to change rooms to somewhere quieter. Unfortunately, I can't tell you that, because the story is completely true. I absolutely was crazy and deluded enough to ring the international manager of Rocket, Robert Key, and ask him to do something about the wind outside my hotel room. I certainly didn't want to change rooms. It was 11 a.m., I'd been up all night and there were drugs everywhere: the last thing I needed was the hotel staff bustling in to help me move to a different floor. I angrily outlined the situation to Robert. To his lasting credit, he gave my request very short shrift. On the other end of the phone, I heard the muffled sound of Robert, with his hand over the receiver, telling the rest of the office, 'Oh God, she's finally lost it.' Then he spoke to me again. 'Elton, are you fucking insane? Now get off the phone and go back to bed.'

I started renting a house in west London, but I spent most of my time away on tour or in America. I'd fallen in love with a guy called Hugh Williams, who lived in Atlanta. But I also found myself in Indianapolis. Ryan White had been happier since moving to Cicero, but nothing could stop the progress of his disease. In the spring of 1990, his mother Jeanne called and told me that he had been rushed into the Riley Hospital for Children with a severe respiratory infection. He was on life support. I flew there straight away. For the next week, I tried to make myself useful around the hospital while Ryan slipped in and out of consciousness. I didn't know what else to do to help. I cleared up the room. I fetched sandwiches and ice cream. I put flowers in vases and bought stuffed animals for the other kids on the ward. I acted like Jeanne's secretary, fending off phone calls, doing the job that I paid Bob Halley to do for me. Ryan had been such a visible advocate for AIDS sufferers that he had become a celebrity. When the news that he was dying got out, Jeanne was deluged with people wanting to offer their support and it was too much for her to deal with. I held the phone up to Ryan's ear when Michael Jackson called. All Ryan could do was listen. He was too weak to answer.

When I went back to my hotel, I would think about Jeanne and her daughter Andrea. They were watching Ryan die, slowly and painfully. They had prayed for a miracle, but the miracle never came. They had every right to feel angry and resentful. But they didn't feel that way. They were stoic, they were forgiving, they were patient and kind. Even in the most awful circumstances I loved being around them, but they made me feel ashamed of myself, in a way I'd never felt before. I spent half my life feeling angry and resentful about things that didn't matter. I was the kind of person who got on the phone and shouted at people because the weather outside my Park Lane hotel didn't suit me. Whatever else had been wrong with my childhood, I hadn't been brought up to behave that way. How the fuck had I become like this? I'd always managed somehow to justify my behaviour to myself, or to make a joke of it, but now I couldn't: real life had barged into my celebrity bubble.

Because they knew I was in Indianapolis, I was asked to play a gig at the Hoosier Dome for Farm Aid, a charity set up by Neil Young, Willie Nelson and John Mellencamp. It was a huge event, with everyone from Lou Reed to Carl Perkins to Guns N' Roses performing. I had been happy to get involved, but now I didn't want to go, because I didn't want to leave Jeanne by Ryan's bedside; I knew he didn't have long left. I rushed over there and literally ran onstage in the same clothes I had been wearing at the hospital.

I played without a backing band, raced through 'Daniel' and 'I'm Still Standing', dedicated 'Candle In The Wind' to Ryan, then ran offstage again. I was back at the hospital within an hour, and I was there when Ryan died the next morning, 8 April, at 7.11 a.m. He was eighteen. It was a month before his high-school graduation.

Jeanne had asked me to be one of the pall-bearers at his funeral, and also to perform. I sang 'Skyline Pigeon' with a photo of Ryan on top of my piano. It was a song from my first album, *Empty Sky*, one of the first really good things Bernie and I had written, and it seemed to fit the occasion: 'dreaming of the open, waiting for the day that he can spread his wings and fly away again'. The funeral was a huge event. It was broadcast live on CNN. Michael Jackson and the First Lady, Barbara Bush, were there. There were press photographers everywhere and hundreds of people standing outside in the rain. Some of the mourners were people who had made the Whites' lives a misery back in Kokomo; they came and apologized and asked Jeanne to forgive them and she did.

Ryan was in an open casket. After the service, family and close friends filed towards his body to say goodbye. He was wearing his faded denim jacket and a pair of mirrored sunglasses – his choice of clothes to be buried in. I put my hands on his face and told him I loved him.

I went back to my hotel in a strange mood. It wasn't just grief, there was something else bubbling underneath: I was angry at myself. I kept turning over the fact that Ryan had done so much in such a short time to help people with AIDS. A kid with nothing, and he'd changed public perceptions. Ronald Reagan, who'd done his best to ignore AIDS while he was president, had written a piece that the *Washington Post* published that morning, praising Ryan and condemning the 'fear and ignorance' that surrounded the disease. I was the highest-profile gay rock star in the world. I'd spent the eighties watching friends and colleagues and ex-lovers die horribly; years later, I had all their names engraved on plaques and put them on the wall of the chapel at Woodside. But what had I done? Virtually nothing. I had made sure I got tested for HIV every year, and by a miracle I came up negative every time. I had played a couple of benefit gigs, and helped record a charity single, a version of Burt Bacharach's 'That's What Friends Are For', with Dionne Warwick, Stevie Wonder and Gladys Knight. It had been a huge success – it was the biggest-selling single of the year in America and it raised $3 million. I had attended some of Elizabeth Taylor's fundraising events, because I'd known Liz for years. She had a grand image, but she wasn't like that at all in real life. She was incredibly kind and welcoming and she was hilarious – she had a really filthy English sense of humour – although you had to watch your jewellery around her. She was obsessed. If you were wearing something she liked the look of, she'd somehow just charm you into giving it to her; you would walk into her dressing room wearing a Cartier watch and leave without it, never entirely sure how she'd managed to get it off you. I suppose she used exactly the same skill when it came to fundraising. She had the guts to stand up and do something, help- ing start the American Foundation for AIDS Research, forcing Hollywood to pay attention, despite everyone telling her getting involved with AIDS would damage her career.

I should have been doing the same. I should have been on the front line. I should have put my head on the chopping block the way Liz Taylor did. I should have been marching with Larry Kramer and ACT UP. Everything I'd done so far – charity singles, celebrity fundraisers – seemed superficial and showbizzy. I should have been using my fame as a platform to gain attention and make a difference. I felt sick.

I turned on the TV and watched the news coverage of the funeral, which only made things worse. It was a beautiful service, and my performance had been fitting. But every time the camera focused on me, I was horrified. I looked awful in a way that had nothing to do with the tragedy of Ryan's death and everything to do with the way I was living my life. I was bloated and grey. My hair was white. I looked worn out, exhausted, ill. I was forty-three years old, and I looked about seventy. God, the state of me. Something had to change.

But not yet. I left Indianapolis and life went back to my idea of normal. I had recorded a new album before Ryan got really sick, and now I had to promote it, something I had neglected to do while Ryan was dying. *Sleeping with the Past* had been recorded at a studio in rural Denmark called Puk. I think the idea was partly to try and avoid the press, who were crawling all over the place because of my divorce from Renate, and partly to try and avoid the kind of behaviour that had gone on during the making of *Leather Jackets*. In a sense it worked. Even I couldn't figure out how to source any drugs in the depths of the Danish countryside. It was the middle of winter, freezing cold, completely desolate: you would have had more luck finding a cocaine dealer on the moon. But every night we would head out to the nearest town, Randers, and hit the pubs, marvelling at the way that Danes drank. Lovely people, very friendly, always happy to appeal to my competitive nature by challenging us to a game of darts, but you see them around booze and the old Viking heritage becomes very apparent. I shouldn't have tried to keep up with them, but my competitive nature got the better of me there, too. The schnapps the locals drank was lethal – they called it North Sea Oil. I became quite used to waking up on the floor of someone else's room, with my tongue stuck to the roof of my mouth, gripped by the conviction that this particular case of alcohol poisoning was going to prove fatal. Other members of the crew fared even worse than me: on producer Chris Thomas's birthday, I hired a brass band to knock on his door first thing in the morning and launch into 'Happy Birthday

To You'. You can imagine how marvellous that sounded to a man with a raging hangover.

The schnapps, the pubs, the hangovers: it's worth pointing out that I'm describing the working week here. At weekends, I let my hair down a bit. I would fly to Paris and party. There was a gay club I loved on the rue de Caumartin, called Boy. In truth, I thought I was getting a bit too old for clubbing, but the music at Boy kept me coming back. Laurent Garnier and David Guetta DJ'd there – it was the start of house and techno taking over in Paris's clubs and it felt as fresh and exciting and bold as disco had back in the seventies. Whenever I hear 'Good Life' by Inner City, I think about the dance floor in Boy going crazy.

Despite my visits to Paris and the amount of North Sea Oil consumed during its making, *Sleeping with the Past* turned out really well. The idea was to make an album influenced by old soul music, the kind of thing I'd played in nightclubs in the sixties, hence the title. You can really hear it in songs like 'Amazes Me' and 'I Never Knew Her Name'. In fact, the only track I wasn't sure about was a ballad called 'Sacrifice'. Demonstrating again the infallible commercial instincts that led me to announce I was going to strangle Gus Dudgeon if 'Don't Let The Sun Go Down On Me' was ever released, I said I didn't want it on the album. I was talked round, but then the record company wanted to release it as a single, which just seemed stupid – it was a five-minute-long ballad, no one was going to play it. At first, they put it out on the B-side of a song called 'Healing Hands', which I thought was much more commercial. The single didn't do much until nearly a year later, in June 1990, when the DJ Steve Wright started ignoring what it said on the label and playing the other side on his Radio One show. Then it suddenly took off: within three weeks I had my first British solo Number One.

Remembering how I felt about my response to the AIDS crisis after Ryan's funeral, I decided to donate all the royalties to four

British AIDS charities, and announced I'd do the same thing with every single I released in future. I gave money to Stonewall, a new charity that was lobbying for LGBT rights in the wake of Section 28, a recent law that banned local governments and schools in Britain from 'promoting' homosexuality. When I appeared at the International Rock Awards, a televised ceremony, I called out the host, a homophobic comedian called Sam Kinison, who specialized in jokes about AIDS. A week after Ryan's funeral, he'd been on Howard Stern's radio show, sniggering about it. I said I was only there under protest, that Kinison was a pig and that the awards ceremony should never have employed him. His response was incredible. He started whining that I owed him an apology and that what I'd said was 'way out of line'. A man who went around laughing at 'faggots' dying, whose whole schtick was supposed to be about causing offence and saying the unsayable, was now apparently terribly offended himself about being called a name. He could dish it out, but he couldn't take it. He could whistle for his fucking apology.

And I played some benefit shows for Ryan's charity, at the opening of Donald Trump's new casino in Atlantic City. Jeanne White was my guest, but they weren't great gigs. I was propping myself up with booze and drugs, making mistakes onstage. It was nothing too drastic – the occasional forgotten lyric and the odd fluffed piano line. I doubt anyone in the audience even noticed, and no one in the band mentioned it. I've never been big on post-gig inquests, where you all sit around and talk about where things went wrong: tell people when they've played great, don't sit there nitpicking over little errors for hours, just let it go. But deep down I knew I'd broken one of my unwritten rules. I'd certainly raced offstage at the end of gigs before, pathetically eager to have a line, but I had made a point of never doing drugs before going on: that felt like letting an audience down.

★

Back in Atlanta, Hugh had some news for me. He was sick of drinking and taking drugs. He knew he couldn't stop without help. So he was going into rehab. He had booked into a residential treatment programme at Sierra Tucson, the same rehab centre that had treated Ringo Starr for alcoholism a couple of years before. He was leaving that day.

You might think after what had happened in Indianapolis – the shame I'd felt in the company of Ryan's mum and sister, the horror of seeing myself at the funeral – that this would have been news I welcomed. I should have asked to go with him. Instead, I went ballistic. I was furious. Hugh was my latest partner-in-crime: if he was admitting he had a problem, that meant I had a problem. By implication, he was accusing me of being a drug addict.

He wasn't the first person to suggest I needed help. After he'd stopped working for me, my valet, Mike Hewitson, had written me a very sane, level-headed letter – 'you've really got to stop this nonsense, stop putting that bloody stuff up your nose' – and I'd responded by refusing to speak to him for a year and a half. Tony King had tried to talk to me. He had visited me with Freddie Mercury, and afterwards Freddie had told him that I looked like I was in trouble and that Tony should get involved: 'You need to look after your friend.' Coming from Freddie, no saint when it came to booze and drugs himself, that judgement should have carried a lot of weight. Instead, I dismissed what Tony had to say as sanctimonious preaching from an alcoholic in recovery. And a couple of years before, George Harrison had tried to talk to me at an insane party I'd held at a house I was renting in LA. I'd had the garden strung with lights, got Bob Halley to fire up the barbecue and invited everyone I knew that was in town. By the middle of the evening, I was flying, absolutely out of my mind, when a scruffy-looking guy I didn't recognize wandered into the party. Who the hell was he? It must be one of the staff, a gardener. I loudly demanded to know what the gardener was doing helping himself to a drink. There was a moment's shocked silence, broken by the sound of Bob Halley's voice: 'Elton, that's not the fucking gardener. It's *Bob Dylan*.'

Coked out of my brain and keen to make amends, I rushed over and grabbed him, and started steering him towards the house.

'Bob! Bob! We can't have you in those terrible clothes, darling. Come upstairs and I'll fit you out with some of mine at once. Come on, dear!'

Bob stared at me, horrified. His expression suggested he was trying hard to think of something he wanted to do less than get dressed up like Elton John, and drawing a blank. This was the late eighties, and one of my recent looks had involved teaming a pink suit and a straw boater with a scale model of the Eiffel Tower on top of it, so you couldn't really blame him. But full of cokey confidence, I wasn't deterred. As I continued propelling him out of the garden, I heard the unmistakable sound of George's mordant, Scouse-accented voice calling out to me.

'Elton,' he said. 'I really think you need to go steady on the old marching powder.'

Bob somehow managed to talk his way out of being dressed in my clothes, but it didn't change the fact that one of The Beatles was publicly telling me to do something about my cocaine habit. I just laughed it off.

This time, however, I didn't laugh it off. The full force of the Dwight Family Temper was unleashed. Maybe it hit home harder than before because, after Indianapolis, I knew for a fact that Hugh was right. The ensuing row was terrible. I screamed and shouted. I said the most hurtful, wounding things I could think of to Hugh, the kind of stuff so horrible it literally comes back to haunt you – you suddenly remember having said it years later, completely out of the blue, and still clench your teeth and wince. None of it made any difference. Hugh's mind was made up. He left for Arizona that afternoon.

Incredibly, given the way we had parted, Hugh later asked me to visit him at the treatment centre. Big mistake. I arrived and was gone within twenty minutes, which was long enough for me to cause a huge scene. I exploded again – this place was a total shithole, the therapists were a bunch of creeps, he was being brainwashed, he had to leave at once. When he wouldn't, I stormed out and got on a plane back to London.

On arrival, I went straight to my rented house and locked myself in. I holed up in the bedroom for two weeks, alone, snorting cocaine and drinking whisky. On the rare occasions when I ate, I made myself sick immediately afterwards. I was up for days on end, watching porn, taking drugs. I wouldn't answer the phone. I wouldn't answer the door. If anyone knocked, I'd sit for hours afterwards in complete silence, rigid with paranoia and fear, terrified to move in case they were still outside, spying on me.

Sometimes I listened to music. I played 'Don't Give Up' by Peter Gabriel and Kate Bush over and over and over again, crying at the lyrics: 'no fight left or so it seems, I am a man whose dreams have all deserted'. Sometimes I spent whole days writing out pointless lists of records I owned, songs I'd written, people I would like to work with, football teams I'd seen: anything to fill the time, to give me a reason to take more drugs, to stop myself going to sleep. I was supposed to have a Watford board meeting, but I rang them and told them I was unwell. I didn't wash, I didn't get dressed. I sat around, wanking, in a dressing gown covered in my own puke. It was sordid. Awful.

Sometimes I never wanted to see Hugh again. Sometimes I was desperate to speak to him, but I couldn't get hold of him. He had moved into a halfway house, and after the scene I'd created at the rehab centre, no one would tell me where he was. Eventually, I made myself so ill that I realized this was it. I couldn't take it anymore. If I carried on for a couple more days I genuinely would be dead: I'd either overdose or have a heart attack. Was that really what I wanted? I knew it wasn't. Despite my self-destructive behaviour, I didn't actually want to self-destruct. I had no idea how to live, but I didn't want to die. I'd managed to track down Hugh's ex-boyfriend, Barron Segar, who told me that he was in a halfway house in Prescott, a city four hours north of Tucson. I called Hugh. He sounded nervous. He said we could meet, but that there were conditions. I had to speak to his counsellor first. He wanted to see me, because there were things he wanted to say to me, but he wouldn't say them unless I had a counsellor present too. He didn't spell it out, but I suspected some kind of intervention was on the cards. I hesitated for a moment, but I was past convincing myself that, although things were bad, I was intelligent enough, successful enough and wealthy enough to sort them out on my own. I was too miserable and too ashamed of myself to even try. So I agreed: whatever it took.

Robert Key came with me and Connie Pappas met us at the airport in LA. I phoned Hugh's counsellor. He told me that the meeting had to form part of Hugh's therapy. We would both make a list of things we didn't like about each other and read it out. I was terrified, but I did it.

The next day, I was in a tiny hotel room in Prescott, facing Hugh. We sat so close that our knees were touching, holding our lists. I went first. I said that I didn't like the fact that Hugh was untidy. He left his clothes everywhere. He didn't put CDs back in their cases after he had played them. He forgot to turn the lights off after he left a room at night. Stupid, niggly little irritations, the kind of things that get on your nerves about your partner every day.

Then it was Hugh's turn. I noticed that he was shaking. He was more terrified than me. 'You're a drug addict,' he said. 'You're an alcoholic. You're a food addict and a bulimic. You're a sex addict. You're co-dependent.'

That was it. There was a long pause. Hugh was still shaking.

He couldn't look at me. He thought I was going to explode again and storm out.

'Yes,' I said. 'Yes, I am.'

Both Hugh and his counsellor looked at me. 'Well, do you want to get help?' his counsellor asked. 'Do you want to get better?'

I started to cry. 'Yes,' I said. 'I need help. I want to get better.'

twelve

Lutheran Hospital,
Park Ridge,
Illinois
10 August 1990

We've lived together, you and I, for sixteen years, and boy, have we had some great times. But now it's time for me to sit down and tell you how I really feel about you. I loved you so much. At first, we were inseparable – we seemed to meet so often, either at my house, or at other people's. In the end, we were so fond of each other that I decided I couldn't be without you. I wanted us to be a great couple and to hell with what other people thought.

When I first met you, you seemed to bring out everything that had been suppressed before. I could talk about anything I wanted for the first time in my life. There was something in your make-up that brought all my walls and barriers crashing down. You made me feel free. I was never jealous if other people shared you. In fact, I liked turning other people on to your charms. I realize how stupid I must have been, because you never really cared for me. It was all one-sided. You only care about how many people you can trap in your web.

My body and brain have suffered greatly because of my love for you – you have left me with permanent physical and mental scars. Remember that romantic saying, 'I would die for you'? Well, I nearly did. Still, you're a hard lady to get rid of. We've split so many times before but I always went back to you. Even though I knew it was a mistake, I still did. When there was no one else to comfort me, you were only a phone call away at any hour of the day or night. You never cease to amaze me – I've sent cars to pick you up and I even sent planes so that you and I could spend some hours or days together. And when you finally arrived, I was ecstatic to embrace you once more.

We had great parties with people. We had great, intense talks about how we were going to change the world. Of course, we never did, but boy, could we talk! We had sex with people we barely knew and who we really didn't give a damn about. I didn't care who they were as long as they slept with me. But, in the morning, they were gone, and I was alone again. You had gone too. Sometimes I wanted you so insatiably, but you had vanished. With you by my side, I was all-conquering, but with you gone I was just a sad little child again.

My family never liked you at all. In fact, they hated the spell you had me under. You managed to push me away from them and lots of my friends. I wanted them to understand how I felt about you, but they never listened, and I would feel anger, and hurt. I felt ashamed because I cared more about you than I did about my own flesh and blood. All I cared about was myself and you. So I kept you to myself. In the end, I didn't want to share you anymore.

I just wanted us to be alone. I became more miserable, because you ruled my life – you were my Svengali.

I guess I'll try and come to the point of this letter. It's taken me sixteen years to realize that you've taken me nowhere. Whenever I tried to have a relationship with someone else, I always brought you along at some point. So I have no doubts that it was me who was the user. But I found no compassion and love – what love I had for anyone was always superficial.

I had grown tired and hateful towards myself, but recently, I met someone again – someone I loved and trusted, and that person was adamant that this was going to be a two-way love affair, not a three-way one. He made me realize how self-centred I had become, and he made me think about my life and my sense of values. My life has ground to a halt. I now have the opportunity to change my way of living and thinking. I am prepared to accept humility, and therefore have to say goodbye to you for the final time.

You have been my whore. You have kept me from any sort of spirituality and you have kept me from finding out who I really am. I don't want you and I to share the same grave. I want to die a natural death when I go, at peace with myself. I want to live the rest of my life being honest and facing the consequences rather than hiding behind my celebrity status. I feel as though, after sixteen years with you, I was dead anyway.

Once more, white lady – goodbye. If I run into you somewhere – and, let's face it, you're such a woman about town – I'll ignore you and leave immediately. You've seen me enough over the years and I'm sick of you. You've won the fight – I surrender.

Thanks but no thanks,

Elton

The moment the words 'I need help' came out of my mouth, I felt different. It was like something had been switched back on inside me, like a pilot light that had gone out. I somehow knew that I was going to get well. But it wasn't as straightforward as that. First of all, they couldn't find a clinic anywhere in America that would take me. Almost all of them specialized in treating one addiction at a time, and I had three: cocaine, alcohol and food. I didn't want them treated consecutively, which would have meant spending something like four months going from one facility to another. I wanted them all treated at once.

Eventually they found somewhere. When I saw it, I nearly refused to go in. Hugh's treatment centre – which, you may remember, I loudly declared to be a total shithole – was really luxurious. It was set in the countryside outside Tucson, with incredible views of the Santa Catalina mountains. It had a vast swimming pool, around which there were yoga classes. Mine was just an ordinary general hospital: the Lutheran, in a suburb of Chicago called Park Ridge. It was a big, grey, monolithic building, with mirrored glass windows. It didn't seem much like a place that offered yoga classes by the pool. The only thing it had a view of was a shopping centre car park. But Robert Key was still with me, and I felt too embarrassed to turn tail. Besides, there was nowhere else to go. He dropped me in reception, gave me a hug, then went back to England. I checked in, under the name George King, on 29 July 1990. They told me I had to share a room, which didn't go down very well, until I saw my room-mate. His name was Greg, he was gay and very attractive. At least there was *something* nice to look at around here.

I checked out again six days later. It wasn't just that it was tough in there, although it was. I couldn't sleep: I would lie awake all night, waiting for the daily alarm call at 6.30 a.m. I had panic attacks. I suffered from mood swings – not from high to low, but low to even lower, a fog of depression and anxiety that thickened and thinned but never cleared. I felt ill all the time. I felt weak. I was lonely. You weren't allowed to make phone calls or speak to anyone outside. They allowed me to bend that rule once, when the news broke on TV that the guitarist Stevie Ray Vaughan had been killed in a helicopter crash. He was on tour with Eric Clapton at the time and his helicopter was part of a convoy that had taken off, carrying the artists and their crews. Ray Cooper was in Eric Clapton's band. The news that was coming through was confusing – at one point, they incorrectly reported that Eric had died too – and I had no idea whether Ray was in the helicopter that had crashed. After a lot of tearful pleading, they let me find out: Ray was OK.

And, most of all, I was embarrassed. Not because of my addictions, but because we were expected to do things for ourselves – clean our rooms, make our beds – and that was something I was completely unused to. I'd allowed myself to get to the stage where I shaved and I wiped my arse, and paid other people to do everything else for me. I had no idea how to work a washing machine. I had to ask another patient, a woman called Peggy, to show me. After she realized that I wasn't joking, she was kind and helpful, but that didn't change the fact that I was a forty-three-year-old man who didn't know how to clean his own clothes. When it came time to spend my $10 a week allowance on stationery or chewing gum, I realized I had no idea how much things cost. It was years since I'd done any shopping myself that didn't involve an auction house or a high-end designer boutique. It was shameful: the completely unnecessary bubble that fame and wealth lets you build up around yourself, if you're stupid enough to allow it. I see it all the time now, especially with rappers: they turn up everywhere with huge, pointless entourages, far bigger than the one I saw around Elvis that so shocked me at the time. They're often doing it out of a spirit of charity – they're giving a job to their friends from back home, when back home is somewhere no one would want to be

– but it's a dangerous thing to do. You think you're surrounding yourself with people and making your life easier. But in reality you're just isolating yourself from the real world, and, in my experience at least, the more isolated you are from reality – the more removed you become from the person you're naturally supposed to be – the harder you're making your life and the less happy you become. You end up with something like a medieval court, with you as the monarch and everyone around you jockeying for position, scared of losing their place in the pecking order and fighting each other to see who can be closest to you, who can exert the most influence on you. It's a grotesque, soul-destroying environment to live in. And you've created it yourself.

But the real problem was that the treatment was based around the Alcoholics Anonymous 12-step programme, and as soon as my counsellor started talking to me about God, I flipped out. I didn't want to know about religion: religion was dogma, it was bigotry, it was the Moral Majority and people like Jerry Falwell saying that AIDS was God's judgement on homosexuals. It's a stumbling block for a lot of people. Years later, when I tried to convince George Michael to go into rehab, he dismissed it out of hand for the same reason: 'I don't want to know about God, I don't want to join some cult.' I tried to explain that I had thought exactly the same thing too, but that just made things worse: he thought I was being patronizing and smug. But I really had been there too. That afternoon in Chicago, I stormed out of the meeting, went back to my room, packed my bag and left.

I got as far as the pavement outside. I sat down on a bench with my suitcase and burst into tears. I could easily make some phone calls and get out of here, but where was I going to go? Back to London? To do what? Sit around in a dressing gown covered in puke, doing coke and watching porn all day? It wasn't a very appealing prospect. I lugged my suitcase sheepishly back into the hospital. A couple of days later, I nearly walked out again.

My counsellor suggested that I wasn't taking rehab seriously: 'You're not working hard enough, you're just here for the ride.' I really lost my temper. I told him that if I hadn't been taking rehab seriously, I would have left long ago. I said he was picking on me because I was famous. He dismissed my arguments – it was like he wasn't listening. So I called him a cunt. That seemed to get his attention. I was hauled up before a disciplinary board and warned about my language and behaviour.

But it was also agreed I would get a different counsellor, a woman called Debbie, who seemed less concerned about making an example of me because of who I was, and I started to make progress. I liked the routine. I liked doing things for myself. I got to grips, if not with the idea of God, then of a higher power. It made sense. I only had to look at my life, all the moments where instinct, or fate, had driven me along: everything from Ray Williams putting me in touch with Bernie almost as an after-thought, to the fact that I'd picked up that magazine with Ryan White's story in it in the doctor's waiting room, to the decision to clear out the contents of Woodside, which was starting to look less and less like a rash impulse and more and more like a pre-monition that my life was about to change. I started to embrace the AA meetings. After a while I was allowed visitors: Billie Jean King and her partner Ilana Kloss came to see me, so did Bernie and my friends Johnny and Eddi Barbis. I had to write all the time, including a farewell letter to cocaine – which Bernie read when he visited and broke down in tears – and a list of conse-quences of my drug and alcohol abuse. It was hard at first, but once I got started, I couldn't stop. When I'd arrived at the hospital, a consultant had asked me how I was feeling, and I told him the truth: I didn't know, I wasn't sure if I'd had any real feelings for years, or whether everything was the result of the constant see-sawing of emotions brought on by taking drugs and booze. Now, though, it all came gushing out. The list of consequences went on and on for three pages. Self-hatred. Severe depression. Going onstage under the influence of drugs.

It was cathartic, but the group meetings would throw my problems into sharp relief. There were people there who had undergone the most horrifying things. At one, we were told to talk about our worst, dirtiest secret. I talked a little about my past relationships, about my unerring ability to take over other people's lives for my own selfish, deluded reasons. Then it was the turn of a girl from somewhere in the Deep South of America, who was there for help with food addiction. It took her forty-five minutes to tell her story – at first because she was sobbing so hard she couldn't get the words out and eventually because she was struggling to make herself heard over the sound of everyone else crying. She had grown up being abused by her father. When she was a teenager, she had become pregnant. She was too scared to tell anyone, so she ate more and more in order to put weight on to disguise her pregnancy. In the end she had delivered the baby herself, frightened and alone.

So the meetings were no place for the faint-hearted, but I grew to love them. They forced me to be honest, after years of deceiving other people and myself. If someone else has the guts to stand there and tell you about being abused by their own father, it compels you to step up and tell the truth about yourself – it's just insulting their bravery to do anything else. When you're an addict, it's all about lying, covering your tracks, telling yourself you don't have a problem, telling other people you can't do something because you're ill, when in reality you're just wasted or hungover. Being honest was hard, but it was freeing. You got rid of all the baggage that came with lying: the embarrassment, the shame.

Whenever someone had tried to help before, my standard way of dismissing their concern was to say that they didn't understand; they weren't Elton John, how could they possibly know what it was like being me? But it quickly became apparent that the other addicts in the meetings did understand. They understood only too well. At one meeting, everyone was asked to write down what they liked and didn't like about me. They made two lists on a board – my good points and my bad points. I started talking about what had been said, turning it over and over, calmly accepting the criticisms. I thought I was doing well, but after a while, someone stopped me, and pointed out that I had gone on and on about the negative comments, but never mentioned any of the positive ones. They said that was a sign of low self-esteem. I realized they were right. Perhaps that's why I loved performing so much. You find it hard to accept personal compliments, so your life becomes about finding a more impersonal alternative: chart placings, crowds of nameless faces applauding. No wonder I always claimed my problems melted away onstage. No wonder my life offstage had become such a mess. I went back to my room and wrote I AM WORTHY, I AM A GOOD PERSON on the blue folder I kept my writing in. It was a start.

After six weeks, I was ready to leave. I flew back to London where I called in at the Rocket office and told everyone I was taking some time off. No gigs, no new songs, no recording sessions for at least a year, maybe eighteen months. That was unheard of – I hadn't taken more than a few weeks off a year since 1965 – but everyone accepted it. The only thing I would do was honour an unbreakable commitment to a short private charity show with Ray Cooper at the Grosvenor House hotel, which was terrifying, but we got through it. While I was there, I saw the artwork for a career-spanning box set I had planned before going into rehab and asked for it to be changed. I liked the title, *To Be Continued . . .* – it seemed positive and hopeful, even prescient, given that I'd chosen it before I cleaned up. But I wanted it to feature a current photo, rather than a collection of old shots from the seventies and eighties; that way, the title seemed like a comment on my life now, rather than on my past. And that was the only work I did for the next year, unless you count unexpectedly turning up onstage in full drag at one of Rod Stewart's Wembley Arena gigs and sitting on his lap while he tried to sing 'You're In My Heart'. And I don't: spoiling things for Rod has never felt like work, more a thoroughly enjoyable hobby.

I spent some time in Atlanta with Hugh, but our relationship began to peter out. Both our counsellors had warned against us staying together: they kept telling us that it wouldn't work, that the dynamic of the relationship would change irrevocably now that we were sober. We both dismissed that as nonsense: half the writing I'd done in rehab had been about how much I loved Hugh, how much I missed him. So we rented an apartment, moved in together and discovered to our immense surprise that the dynamic of our relationship appeared to have changed irrevocably now that we were sober, and it wasn't working out. It wasn't a horrible split, we weren't screaming and shouting at each other, but it was sad. We had been through a lot together, but it was time for us both to move on.

So for most of the next eighteen months I was in London, where I settled into a quiet routine. I bought the house I'd been renting, where I had holed up on my final binge. I lived alone. I didn't bother with employing staff; I liked doing things myself. I bought myself a Mini and I got a dog from Battersea Dogs Home, a little mutt called Thomas. Every day, I would get up at 6.30 a.m. and take Thomas for a walk. I adored it. It's a real recovering addict's cliché to say that you notice things about your surroundings that you never saw while you were using – oh, the beauty of the flowers, the wonders of nature, all that crap – but it's only a cliché because it's true. I'm sure that's one of the reasons why I started collecting photography when I got sober. I'd been around incredible photographers for most of my career – Terry O'Neill, Annie Leibovitz, Richard Avedon, Norman Parkinson – but I just thought of it as a form of publicity, never an art, until I stopped drinking and using drugs. I went to the south of France for a holiday and visited a friend of mine, Alain Perrin, who lived outside Cahors. He was looking through black and white fashion photographs with a view to buying some. Idly peering over his shoulder, I was suddenly transfixed. They were by Irving Penn, Horst and Herb Ritts. I knew Herb Ritts – he'd taken the photo for the cover of *Sleeping with the Past* – but it felt like I was seeing his work in a completely new way. I loved everything about the photos Alain was looking at – the lighting, the shapes it had created and contorted; it all seemed extraordinary. I ended up buying twelve of them, and that was the start of an obsession that's never stopped: photography is the love of my life in terms of visual art.

But I first felt that change in how I saw things walking around London. A hot summer had turned into a mild autumn. It was lovely being up and out early in the cool sunshine, walking Thomas around Holland Park or the grounds of St James's church, watching the leaves gradually turn. Previously I had only ever been up at that time of the morning if I was still awake from the night before.

After the dog was walked, I would get in my Mini and drive to see a psychiatrist. I'd never visited one before, and it turned out to involve a steep learning curve. Some of the psychiatrists I've seen over the years have been great; they really helped me get an understanding of myself. And some of them turned into a bit of a nightmare: more interested in my celebrity and what associating with me could do for them. One of them was even struck off for molesting his patients – the female ones, I should add, lest anyone think I was among his victims.

I spent most of my time at meetings. I had left Chicago with strict instructions from my sponsor to go to an AA meeting the moment I cleared customs in London. Starved of football after weeks in America, I went to see a Watford game instead. That night, my sponsor rang. When I told him what I'd done, he yelled at me. A man who worked as a driver for the city of Chicago's sanitation department and spent most of his life communicating with his colleagues over the noise of his garbage truck, he could really yell. That night, he sounded like he was trying to make himself heard on the other side of the Atlantic without the aid of a telephone. More used to shouting at people than being shouted at, I was taken aback, but I was also abashed. He was a good man – I eventually ended up being his son's godfather – but he was genuinely angry, and his anger was born out of concern for me.

So I followed his advice. I became very strict about attending meetings: Alcoholics Anonymous, Cocaine Anonymous, Anorexics and Bulimics Anonymous. I went to meetings in Pimlico, on Shaftesbury Avenue, in Marylebone, on Portobello Road. Sometimes I went to three or four meetings a day. I went to a hundred in a month. Some of my friends began expressing the opinion that I was now addicted to going to meetings about addiction. They were probably right, but it was a substantial improvement on the things I'd been addicted to previously. Perhaps there was a meeting I could attend to deal with it.

At the very first meeting I went to, a photographer leapt out and got a shot of me leaving. Someone must have recognized me there and tipped them off, which was obviously against the rules. It was on the front page of the *Sun* the next day: ELTON IN ALCOHOLICS ANONYMOUS. As, this time, they neglected to suggest that I attended in leather shorts or twirling a dildo, I let it pass. I didn't mind who knew. I was taking a positive step. I kept going to the meetings because I enjoyed them. I liked the people I met. I always volunteered to make the tea, and I made lasting friends, people I'm still in touch with today: ordinary people, who saw me as a recovering addict first and Elton John second. In a weird way, the meetings reminded me of being at Watford FC – there was no special treatment laid on for me, and there was that same sense of people pulling together towards the same goal. You heard the most extraordinary things. Women in the Anorexics and

Bulimics meetings would talk about taking a single pea, cutting it into four and eating a quarter for lunch and a quarter for dinner. I would think, 'that's *insane*', but then I would remember how I'd been a few months before – unwashed and pissed out of my mind at 10 a.m., literally doing a line of coke every five minutes – and realized they must have thought exactly the same about me.

Not everything that happened in the months after I got sober was wonderful. My father died at the end of 1991: he had never really recovered from the heart bypass operation eight years before. I didn't go to his funeral. It would have seemed hypocritical, plus the press would have turned up en masse and the whole thing would have become a circus. My father didn't share in my fame, so why inflict the effects of it on him at the end? Besides, I'd already done enough mourning for my relationship with my dad, and I'd reached a peace, of sorts: I wished that things had been different, but it was what it was. Sometimes you have to look at the hand you've been dealt and throw in the cards.

And then there was Freddie Mercury. He hadn't told me he was ill – I'd just found out, through mutual friends. I visited him a lot when he was dying, although I could never stay for much longer than an hour. It was too upsetting – I didn't think he wanted me to see him like that. Someone so vibrant and so *necessary*, someone that would have just got better with age and gone from strength to strength, dying in such a horrible, arbitrary way. A year later, they could have kept him alive with antiretroviral drugs. Instead, there was nothing they could do for him. He was too frail to get out of bed, he was losing his sight, his body was covered in Kaposi's sarcoma lesions, and yet he was still definitely Freddie, gossiping away, completely outrageous: 'Have you heard Mrs Bowie's new record, dear? What does she think she's doing?' He lay there, surrounded by catalogues of Japanese furniture and art, interrupting the conversation to telephone auction houses in order to bid for items he liked the look of: 'Darling, I've just bought this, isn't it wonderful?' I couldn't work out whether he didn't realize how close to death he was, or if he knew perfectly well but was determined not to let what was happening to him stop him being himself. Either way, I thought it was incredible.

Eventually he made the decision to stop taking any medication other than painkillers, and died at the end of November 1991. On Christmas Day, Tony arrived at my front door, carrying something in a pillowcase. I opened it up and it was a watercolour by an artist whose work I collected called Henry Scott Tuke, an Impressionist who painted male nudes. There was a note with it: 'Darling Sharon – thought you'd love this. Love, Melina.' While he was lying there, he'd spotted it in one of his auction catalogues and bought it for me. He was thinking about Christmas presents for a Christmas he must have known in his heart he wouldn't see; thinking about other people when he was really too ill to think of anyone but himself. Like I said before: Freddie was magnificent.

Some people really struggle when they come out of addiction into sobriety, but I was the opposite. I was elated. I never really wanted to use again; I was just happy waking up every morning without feeling like shit. Bizarrely, I would dream about cocaine all the time. I still do, almost every week, and it's been twenty-eight years since I last did a line. It's always the same dream: I'm snorting coke when I hear someone coming into the room, usually my mother. Then I try to hide what I'm doing, but I spill it and it goes everywhere – all over the floor, all over me. But it never made me hanker after cocaine. Quite the opposite. When I wake up, I can almost feel the numbing sensation of the coke sliding down the back of my throat – always the part of doing it that I hated – and I just think 'thank God that's over'. I sometimes wish I could have a glass of wine with my dinner, or a beer with friends, but I know I can't. I don't mind people drinking around me at all: it's my problem, not theirs. But I never feel like having a line, and I can't bear being anywhere near people who are doing it. The second I walk into a room, I know. I can just sense people are on it. The way they're talking – their voices pitched slightly louder than they need to be, not really listening – and how they're behaving. I just leave. I don't want to do cocaine, and I don't want to be around people who are doing it, because, quite frankly, it's a drug that makes people act like arseholes. I wish I'd realized that forty-five years ago.

Every time I went to a foreign country to play live, I found out where the AA or NA meeting was and went there as soon as I landed. I went to meetings in Argentina, France, Spain. I went to meetings in Los Angeles and New York. And I went to meetings in Atlanta. Even though I'd broken up with Hugh, I was still in love with the city. I'd met a great circle of friends through Hugh, people from outside the music business, whose company I enjoyed. It was a great music town – there was a big soul and hip-hop scene – but it was strangely relaxed; I could go to the cinema or the shopping mall on Peachtree Road and no one would bother me.

I was spending so much time there that I eventually decided to buy an apartment, a thirty-sixth-floor duplex. The views were beautiful, and so, I couldn't help noticing, was the real-estate agent who sold it to me. He was called John Scott. I asked him out, and we became a couple.

Eventually, I stopped going to meetings. I had gone virtually every day for three years – something crazy like 1,400 meetings – but I'd finally decided that they had done all they could for me. I got to a point where I didn't want to talk about alcohol or cocaine or bulimia every day. I suppose because I was a high-profile addict who turned his life around very publicly, I became someone that my peers looked to if they had a problem. It's become a bit of a running joke – Elton always springing into action whenever a pop star has an issue with drink or drugs – but I don't mind at all. If someone is in a state and needs help, I call them, or leave my number with their manager, just saying, 'Listen, I've been there,

I know what it's like.' If they need to contact me, they can. Some of those people everyone knows about. I got Rufus Wainwright into rehab – he was taking so much crystal meth that, at one stage, he'd gone temporarily blind – and I'm Eminem's AA sponsor. Whenever I ring to check in on him, he always greets me the same way: 'Hello, you cunt', which I guess is very Eminem. And some of them no one knows about, and I'm not going to spill the beans now: they wanted to keep their problems private, and that's fine. Either way, it's incredibly rewarding. Helping people to get sober is a wonderful thing.

But some people you can't help. It's a horrible feeling. You end up just looking on from the sidelines, knowing what's going to happen, knowing that there's only one way their story's going to end. It was like that with Whitney Houston – her aunt, Dionne Warwick, asked me to call her, but either the messages I left didn't get through, or she didn't want to know. And George Michael *really* didn't want to know. I nagged at him because I was worried and because mutual friends kept contacting me, asking if I could do something. He wrote an open letter to *Heat* magazine, most of which was concerned with telling me, at considerable length, to fuck off and mind my own business. I wish we hadn't fallen out. But more than that, I wish he was still alive. I loved George. He was ludicrously talented, and he went through a lot, but he was the sweetest, kindest, most generous man. I miss him so much.

George was one of the first people I performed with after I got sober. As much as I enjoyed my time off, I knew it couldn't last forever and I didn't want it to last forever – I wanted to get back to work, even if getting back to work felt daunting. I'd started thinking about playing live again, and to test the water a little, I agreed to appear onstage at one of George's gigs. He was doing a run of shows at Wembley Arena. This time, I didn't turn up in a Ronald McDonald costume or drive a Reliant Robin. I dressed down in a baseball cap and we sang 'Don't Let The Sun Go Down

On Me' together, as we had at Live Aid six years before, in 1985. It felt great. The audience went insane when my name was announced, and when the duet was released as a single, it went to Number One on both sides of the Atlantic. I booked a studio in Paris and tentatively suggested recording a new album, which ended up being called *The One*.

The first day there, I managed twenty minutes before leaving in a panic. I can't remember now what the problem was. I suppose I thought I couldn't make an album without drink or drugs, which made no sense whatsoever. You only had to listen to *Leather Jackets* to realize that the opposite was true: it was pretty compelling evidence that I couldn't make an album *while* taking drugs. I went back the next day, and I gradually settled into things. The only real problem came with a track called 'The Last Song'. Bernie's lyrics were about a man dying of AIDS being reconciled with his estranged father, who had excommunicated him when he found out he was gay. They were beautiful, but I just couldn't cope with singing them. It was just after Freddie's death. Somewhere in Virginia, I knew Vance Buck was dying, too. Every time I tried to get the vocal down, I started crying. Eventually I managed it and 'The Last Song' was subsequently used as the finale of *And the Band Played On*, a docudrama about the discovery of, and the fight against, HIV. They played it over a montage of images of prominent AIDS victims. Half of them were people I knew personally: Ryan; Freddie; Steve Rubell, the owner of Studio 54.

By then, I had started the Elton John AIDS Foundation. I had kept doing charity work, but the more I did, the more I realized I needed to do. The thing that shook me the most was volunteering for a charity called Operation Open Hand that delivered meals to AIDS patients all over Atlanta. I did it together with my new boyfriend John. At some houses we delivered to, the person inside would only open the door a crack when we knocked. They were covered in lesions and didn't want to be seen, because the stigma attached to AIDS was so great. Sometimes they wouldn't open the door at all. You would leave the meal on the step, and as you walked away you would hear the door open, the meal would be snatched in and the door would slam shut again. These people were dying horribly, but worse, it seemed as if they were dying in shame, alone, cut off from the world. It was horrendous, like something you read about happening in the Middle Ages – sick people being cast out of society because of fear and ignorance – but it was happening in the 1990s, in America.

I couldn't get it out of my head. Eventually, I asked John if he would help me start a charity of our own, concentrating on helping people protect themselves from HIV, and on the basic things that people with HIV needed to live a better, more digni-fied life: simple stuff like food, lodging, transportation, access to doctors and counsellors. For two years, John ran it from his kitchen table in Atlanta. Virginia Banks, who worked on my team in LA, became the secretary. There was a staff of four, including me. We didn't have any experience, we didn't know anything about infrastructure, but I did know that we had to keep overheads down. I'd seen too many charity foundations, especially celebrity ones, wasting money. You'd turn up to a fundraiser and everyone would have been flown in and chauffeured around at the charity's expense. Even now, nearly thirty years later, our overheads are minimal. We put on some pretty glitzy events, but they're all sponsored. The charity doesn't pay a thing towards them.

I really threw myself into the AIDS Foundation. In rehab, my counsellor had asked me what I was going to do with the spare time and energy I would have now I was sober, time and energy that had previously been consumed by taking drugs or recover-ing from taking them. They called it the hole in the doughnut and they wanted to know how I planned to fill it. I talked wildly about my grand plans – I would learn to speak Italian *and* to cook. Of course, neither of those things happened. I suppose the AIDS Foundation was the thing that filled the hole in the dough-nut – it gave me a new sense of purpose outside of music. I was determined that it was going to work: so determined, I auctioned off my record collection to raise funds to get it started. There were 46,000 singles, 20,000 albums, even the old 78s with 'Reg Dwight' proudly written on the sleeves in biro. It went in one lot, for $270,000 to an anonymous bidder. I talked anyone I thought could help into getting involved: businessmen who could show us how to run things as efficiently as possible; people who worked at my record label; Robert Key from Rocket; Howard Rose, the agent who'd steered my live career from the moment I first turned up in America.

I tapped friends for ideas. Billie Jean King and Ilana Kloss came up with Smash Hits, an annual fundraising tennis tourna-ment that's been running since 1993: tennis stars were really keen to get involved because of Arthur Ashe's death. Competitive as ever, I often took part myself, although the most famous thing I've done on a tennis court remains falling flat on my arse while trying to sit in a director's chair courtside at the Royal Albert Hall. Another breakthrough was the Academy Awards Viewing Party. It was effectively given to us by a guy called Patrick Lippert, a political activist who founded Rock the Vote. He always held a fundraising Oscars party for one of his causes, but after being diagnosed with HIV, he decided to turn the event into an AIDS foundation fundraiser, and asked if we wanted to be involved. The first party was held in 1993 at Maple Drive, the restaurant owned by Dudley Moore. There were 140 people there – that's all the restaurant held – and we raised $350,000, which seemed like an enormous amount of money at the time. The next year we did it again, and more stars turned out: I ended up sitting in a booth with Tom Hanks, Bruce Springsteen and his wife Patti, Emma Thompson and Prince. But Patrick wasn't there. He died of AIDS three months after the first party, aged thirty-five. Like Freddie Mercury, he just missed out on the antiretroviral drugs that could have saved his life.

Since then, the Elton John AIDS Foundation has raised over $450 million, and we've hosted some incredible events. The last time Aretha Franklin performed live was at our twenty-fifth anniversary gala, at the Cathedral of St John the Divine in New York. She had been supposed to play the previous year, but had to pull out as she was too sick. She was dying of cancer, and had announced her retirement, but she made an exception for us. When she arrived, I was shocked: I wasn't prepared for how thin and frail and unwell she looked. Backstage, I found myself asking her if she wanted to sing. I suppose I was really asking whether she was well enough to sing. She just smiled and nodded and said, 'I would never let you down again.' I think she must have known that this was the last time she would perform, and she liked the fact that it was for the charity and that the gala was in a church, where her singing career had begun. She sang 'I Say A Little Prayer' and 'Bridge Over Troubled Water' and she tore the roof off. However sick she was, it hadn't affected her voice – she sounded astonishing. I stood at the front of the stage watching the greatest singer in the world sing for the final time, crying my eyes out.

The AIDS Foundation has given me experiences I would never otherwise have had and taken me to places I would never have visited. I've had to speak before Congress several times – asking for the US government to increase AIDS funding – which strangely wasn't quite as nerve-racking as I expected. Compared to trying to convince Watford Borough Council's planning committee to let us build a new football stadium, it was a walk in the park. I thought I would get a hostile audience from the more right-wing, religiously zealous Republicans, but no: once again, compared to some members of Watford Borough Council's planning committee, they were the absolute model of open-mindedness, flexibility and sweet reason.

And, unexpectedly, working with the AIDS Foundation would indirectly lead to the most profound and important change that's ever taken place in my life. But we'll come to that later.

thirteen

I don't want to sound mystical – or even worse, smug – but it was sometimes hard to escape the feeling that life was patting me on the back for getting sober. *The One* became my biggest-selling album worldwide since 1975. After two years, the renovations at Woodside were finished and I moved back in. I loved it. It finally looked like somewhere a normal human being might live, rather than a coked-up rock star's preposterous country pile. Ten years after we'd last written a song together, Tim Rice phoned up out of the blue, asking me if I was interested in working with him again. Apparently Disney were making their first animated film based on an original story rather than an existing work, and Tim wanted me involved. I was intrigued. I'd written a movie soundtrack before, for *Friends*, a 1971 film that got some pretty hair-raising reviews – I remember Roger Ebert calling it 'a sickening piece of corrupt slop', but not all the critics enjoyed it as much as that. I'd given soundtracks a wide berth ever since, but this was clearly something different. The songs had to tell a story. The plan was that we wouldn't write the usual Broadway-style Disney score, but try and come up with pop songs that kids would like.

It was a strange process. Tim wrote the same way as Bernie,

lyrics first, so that was fine. In fact, writing a musical was like writing the *Captain Fantastic* album, because there was a storyline: there was a specific sequence that you had to follow; you always knew in advance which order the songs had to go in. But I would be lying if I said I never had doubts about the project or, rather, my place within it. I have many flaws, but being an artist who takes himself too seriously is something you could never accuse me of. Even so, there were days when I'd find myself sat at the piano, thinking long and hard about the path my career seemed to be taking. You know, I wrote 'Someone Saved My Life Tonight'. I wrote 'Sorry Seems To Be The Hardest Word'. I wrote 'I Guess That's Why They Call It The Blues'. And there was no getting around the fact that I was now writing a song about a warthog that farted a lot. Admittedly, I thought it was a pretty good song about a warthog who farted a lot: at the risk of appearing big-headed, I'm pretty sure that in a list of the greatest songs ever written about warthogs who fart a lot, mine would come in somewhere near the top. Still, it felt a long way from The Band turning up backstage and demanding to hear my new album, or Bob Dylan stopping us on the stairs and complimenting Bernie on 'My Father's Gun'. But I decided that something about the sheer ridiculousness of the situation appealed to me, and carried on.

It was the right decision. I thought the finished film was completely extraordinary. I'm not the kind of artist who invites people over to play them my new album, but I loved *The Lion King* so much that I arranged a couple of private screenings so friends could see it. I was incredibly proud of the whole thing; I knew we were on to something very special. Even so, I couldn't have predicted that it would become one of the highest-grossing films of all time. It introduced my music to a completely new audience. 'Can You Feel The Love Tonight?' won an Oscar for Best Original Song: three of the five nominations in that category had come from *The Lion King*: one of them was 'Hakuna Matata', the song about the farting warthog. The soundtrack sold eighteen million copies – more than any album I've ever released except my first *Greatest Hits* collection. As an added bonus, it kept *Voodoo Lounge* by The Rolling Stones off the number one spot in America all through the summer of 1994. I tried not to be too delighted when I heard that Keith Richards was furious, grumbling about being 'beaten by some fuckin' cartoon'.

Then it was announced that they were turning it into a stage musical, for which Tim and I were asked to come up with more songs. Once more demonstrating my uncanny ability to predict exactly what isn't going to happen, I kept telling people that turning an animated film into a stage show was both impossible and doomed to failure – I couldn't see it at all.

But the director, Julie Taymor, did an amazing job. It opened to rave reviews, was nominated for eleven Tony Awards, won six, and became the most successful theatrical production in the history of Broadway. The whole thing looked astonishing – the sheer ingenuity they had used in staging it was breathtaking, but I still found the experience of actually sitting through it oddly awkward. It had nothing whatsoever to do with the show itself. It was just that I was used to making albums where I had the last word, or to being completely in charge of my live shows. Here was some- thing I'd helped create, and yet once it was onstage, it was unfolding completely out of my control. The arrangements were different from the way I had recorded the songs, and so were the vocals. In musical theatre, every word has to be clearly enunciated, it's a completely different way of singing to anything a rock or pop artist does. It was a totally new experience for me: simultaneously amazing and slightly unnerving. I was completely outside of my comfort zone, which, it slowly dawned on me, was an extremely good place for an artist to suddenly find himself, forty years into his career.

Disney were absolutely overjoyed with *The Lion King*'s success – so overjoyed, they came to me with a deal. It was for a ridiculous amount of money. They wanted me to develop more films, do TV shows and books; there was even some talk about a theme park, which boggled the mind a little. There was just one problem. I'd agreed to make another film with Jeffrey Katzenberg, who had been chairman of Disney when *The Lion King* was made but then left a few months after the film was released and set up DreamWorks with Steven Spielberg and David Geffen. But he didn't just exit: his leaving prompted one of the great Hollywood wars between studio executives, so epic that people have literally written books about it. The Disney deal was exclusive: it was particularly exclusive of anything involving Jeffrey, who was now suing them for breach of contract and $250 million, which he eventually got. There wasn't anything in writing with Jeffrey, but I'd given him my word – he was one of the people who had brought me in to *The Lion King* in the first place. So I regretfully turned Disney's deal down. At least the world was spared an Elton John theme park.

But while my world still seemed to be full of new ideas and opportunities, the one thing sobriety hadn't helped at all was my love life. My relationship with John Scott had petered out some time before, and since then: nothing. I tried not to think about how long it was since I'd last had sex, in case the sound of me howling in anguish frightened the staff at Woodside.

I realized that I didn't really know any available gay men. When I got sober, I stopped going to the kinds of places I might meet them. I didn't think I'd be tempted to have a vodka martini if I went to a club or a bar, but there didn't seem any point in testing this theory. And besides, even before I'd gone into rehab, I'd begun thinking I was getting a bit old for that sort of thing. I'm sure the music at Boy would have sounded as wonderful as ever, but there does come a point where, in that environment, you start to feel like the dowager duchess at the debutantes' ball, peering down your pince-nez at the latest arrivals.

It all came to a head one Saturday afternoon, when I was rattling around the house feeling thoroughly sorry for myself. I had one eye on the football, where Watford were doggedly trying to make my mood worse by getting hammered 4–1 away at West Brom. I was contemplating another thrilling evening in front of the TV when I came up with an idea. I rang a friend in London and explained my predicament. I asked if he could round some people up and invite them to come to dinner that evening. It was short notice, but I'd send a car to London for them. As I said it, I realized that it all sounded a bit pathetic, but I was desperate to meet some gay men who weren't in Alcoholics Anonymous. I wasn't even looking for sex, I was just lonely.

They turned up around seven: my friend and four guys he'd roped in. They said they had to leave early to get to a Halloween party back in London, but I didn't care. Everyone who had come along seemed really nice. They were funny and chatty. We ate spaghetti bolognese and had a great laugh – I'd almost forgotten what it was like to have a conversation that didn't revolve around either my career or sobriety. The only one who didn't seem terribly pleased to be there was a Canadian guy in a tartan Armani waistcoat called David. He was clearly shy and didn't say much, which I thought was a shame: he was very good-looking. I later discovered that he'd heard a lot of gossip on the London gay scene about the inadvisability of having anything whatsoever to do with Elton John, unless you had a burning desire to be showered with gifts, forced to put your life on hold in order to be whisked away on tour, then summarily dumped – usually by his personal assistant – when he met someone else, or lost his temper with you during a post-cocaine comedown, or announced he was getting married to a woman. I should have been outraged, but, taking into account my past behaviour, the gossips of the London gay scene had a point.

Eventually, he volunteered the information that he was interested in film and photography, which got the conversation going. I offered to give him a tour of the house and show him my collection of photographs. The more I talked to him, the more I liked him. He was quiet but self-assured. He was obviously very smart. He said he was from Toronto but had moved to London a few years before. He lived in Clapham and worked for the advertising company Ogilvy and Mather in Canary Wharf – at thirty-one, he was one of their youngest board directors. I thought I could sense something resonating between us, a flicker of chemistry. But I tried to put it out of my mind. The new, improved, sober Elton John wasn't going to decide he'd fallen madly in love with someone within minutes of meeting them.

Still, when it came time for them to leave, I asked for his number in what I thought was a casual way, suggestive merely of further stimulating conversations about our shared interest in photography somewhere down the line. He wrote his full name down – David Furnish – handed it over and off they went.

The next morning found me pacing around the house, trying to work out what was the earliest you could call someone who'd been out the previous night at a Halloween party, without looking like the kind of person they'd eventually have to get a restraining order out against. I decided eleven thirty was reasonable. David picked up. He sounded tired, but not entirely surprised to hear from me. It transpired that my casual request for his number hadn't looked quite as casual as I thought. Judging by the reaction of his friends, who'd spent the entire journey back to London mercilessly teasing him and singing the chorus of 'Daniel' at him, I might as well have dropped to my knees, tearfully grabbed his ankles and refused to let go until he handed it over. I asked if he wanted to meet up again, and he did. I asked what he was doing that evening, when I just happened to be in London. I behaved as if this was a remarkable coincidence, but frankly, if David had been in Botswana, I suspect I would have happened to be there that evening too: 'The Kalahari Desert? What a stroke of luck! I've got a meeting there tomorrow morning!' I suggested he come over to the house in Holland Park, and I would order a Chinese takeaway.

I put down the phone, told my driver that my plans for the day had changed and we were going to London immediately. I rang the most famous Chinese restaurant I could think of, Mr Chow in Knightsbridge, and asked if they did deliveries. Then I realized I didn't know what kind of food he liked, so I played it safe and ordered an immense selection from the menu.

David looked a bit startled when the Chinese takeaway arrived, or rather didn't stop arriving – by the time they'd finished delivering all the boxes, the place looked like the squash court at Woodside before I had the auction – but other than that, our first date went incredibly well. No, I definitely wasn't imagining it, there really was something resonating between us. It wasn't just a physical attraction; our personalities clicked. Once we started talking, we didn't stop.

But David had some reservations about us getting involved. For one thing, he wasn't keen on the idea of being seen as Elton John's Latest Boyfriend, with all the attention that would bring. He had his own life, a career, and didn't like his independence being turned upside down because of who he was seeing. And for another, he was only half out of the closet. His friends in London knew he was gay, but his family didn't, and nor did his workmates, and he didn't want them to find out via a paparazzi photo in a tabloid.

So for the first few months our relationship was very quiet and discreet: we were, to use an old-fashioned phrase, courting. We mostly based ourselves at the house in Holland Park. Every weekday morning, David would get up and go to work in Canary Wharf, and I would head off to the studio or to do promotion for the album of duets I'd just released. I made a video for the version of 'Don't Go Breaking My Heart' I'd recorded with RuPaul: for once, I actually looked happy while I was making a video. I *was* happy. There was something about the relationship that I couldn't quite put my finger on. Then I realized what it was. For the first time in my life, I was in a completely normal relationship, that felt equal, that had nothing to do with my career or the fact that I was Elton John.

Each Saturday, we would send each other a card, to commemorate the fact that we had met on a Saturday, and – if you've eaten recently, you may want to skip to the next sentence in case you become nauseous – listen to Tony! Toni! Toné!'s 'It's Our Anniversary'. There were a lot of cosy dinners and clandestine weekends away. If I called him at work, I had to use a false name – George King, the pseudonym I'd used when I booked into rehab. I thought it was terribly romantic. A secret love! The only kind of secret love I'd had before was the kind you have to keep secret because the other person clearly isn't interested in you.

But much as I adored the idea of a secret romance, I was pretty hopeless at the practicalities of it. It quickly became apparent that after twenty-five years of earning a living by being as extravagant and OTT as possible, my notion of keeping things low-key was wildly at odds with everyone else's. If you're trying not to draw attention to a relationship, it's perhaps not the best idea to regularly send your partner two dozen long-stemmed yellow roses at work, particularly if he works in an open-plan office. With the benefit of hindsight, the Cartier watch was probably a mistake as well. It was so expensive that David had to wear it all the time. He couldn't leave it at home, in case his flat got burgled, because he didn't have any insurance. Questioned by his colleagues as to where it came from – and if it might in some way be linked to the fact that his desk suddenly looked like a stand at the Chelsea Flower Show – he invented a beloved grandmother back in Canada, who had recently died and left him some money in her will, then spent an awkward afternoon fending off a succession of sad smiles, supportive hugs and expressions of condolence. When we arranged a weekend in Paris and I went to meet him off his plane at Charles de Gaulle Airport, I was fully briefed about the need to go unnoticed by any photographers or fans who happened to be there. Waiting in the arrivals lounge, I became aware of a degree of nudging and pointing going on around me. By the time David appeared, I was in a state of considerable agitation.

'Get in the car quickly,' I hissed. 'I think I've been recognized.'

David smiled. 'Really? I wonder why?' he said, directing his gaze to my outfit. The clothes I had decided would enable me to pass unnoticed through the airport consisted of a pair of harlequin-check leggings and an oversized shirt decorated in brightly coloured rococo patterns, accessorized with an enormous jewelled crucifix around my neck. I could possibly have drawn more attention to myself, but only if I'd turned up with a piano and started playing 'Crocodile Rock'.

The leggings and the oversized shirt were by Gianni Versace, my favourite designer. I wore his clothes all the time. I'd discovered his little shop in Milan at the end of the eighties and immediately become obsessed. I thought I had stumbled across a genius, the greatest menswear designer since Yves Saint Laurent. He used the very best materials, but there was nothing starchy or po-faced about his designs: he made men's clothes that were fun to wear. My already high opinion skyrocketed when I was introduced to the man behind them. Meeting Gianni was almost weird, like finding out I had a long-lost twin brother in northern Italy. We were virtually identical: same sense of humour, same love of gossip, same interest in collecting, same unquiet mind. He couldn't switch off; he was always thinking, always coming up with some new way of doing what he did, which was everything. He could design children's clothes, glassware, dinner services, album covers – I got him to design the sleeve for *The One*, which he did beautifully. He had exquisite taste. He would always know of a little Italian church down a side street that had the most beautiful mosaic work in the nave, or a tiny workshop that made the most incredible porcelain. And he was the only person I've ever met who could shop like me. He would go out to buy a watch and come back with twenty.

Actually, he was worse than me. Gianni was so extravagant, that by comparison I looked like the embodiment of frugal living and self-sacrifice. He thought Miuccia Prada was a communist, because she had designed a handbag made from nylon, rather than crocodile or snakeskin or whatever preposterously opulent material he was working with that season. He would try and encourage me to buy the most outrageously expensive things.

'I 'ave found you the most incredible tablecloth, you must buy it, for dinner on Christmas Day. Made by nuns, it takes them thirty years to make, look at it, it's wonderful. It costs a million dollars.'

Even I baulked at that. I said I thought a million dollars was perhaps a little excessive for something that would be completely destroyed the second anyone spilt a bit of gravy on it. Gianni looked horrified, as if he was considering the possibility that I might be a communist too.

'But Elton,' he spluttered, 'it's beautiful . . . the craftsmanship.'

I didn't buy the tablecloth, but it didn't affect our friendship. Gianni became my closest friend. I used to love picking up the phone and hearing his voice, delivering its usual greeting: ''Allo, bitch.' I introduced him to David and they got on like a house on fire. Of course they did; there was nothing not to like about Gianni, unless you designed handbags out of nylon. He had the biggest heart and he was hilarious. 'When I die,' he would cry dramatically, 'I want to be reincarnated even more gay. I want to be super-gay!' David and I would exchange puzzled glances, wondering how that could conceivably be possible. There were leather bars on Fire Island less obviously homosexual than Gianni.

Sometimes, being in a normal relationship made me realize how abnormal my own life frequently was. I arranged a small lunch party, so David could meet my mother and Derf. By then our relationship wasn't secret anymore. Someone from David's office had spotted us getting out of a car outside the Planet Hollywood restaurant in Piccadilly. He'd been called in to see his boss, told him everything, then made plans to go back to Toronto for Christmas and come out to his family. I was incredibly nervous: David had said his father was very conservative, and I knew how horrific coming out could be if your family weren't supportive. In Atlanta, I'd had an affair with a guy called Rob, whose parents were very religious and anti-gay. He was a sweetheart, but you could tell the conflict between his sexuality, religion and his parents' views was constantly eating away at him. We stayed friends, and after we broke up he came to see me on my birthday and brought me some flowers. The next day, he walked onto the freeway and threw himself in front of a truck.

It turned out that David's family couldn't have taken the news better – I think, more than anything, they were pleased he wasn't keeping secrets from them anymore – but I had still held off as long as I could from introducing him to my mother. Ever since I broke up with John Reid, she had developed a habit of . . . not seeing off my partners exactly, but being cold towards them, making their lives and mine more difficult, as if she resented the presence of anyone who detracted attention from her.

But the problem with the lunch party wasn't really my mum. It was one of the other guests, a psychiatrist, who at the last minute informed me that his client Michael Jackson was in England, and asked if he could bring him along. This didn't sound like the greatest idea I'd ever heard, but I could hardly refuse. I'd known Michael since he was thirteen or fourteen: after a gig I played in Philadelphia, Elizabeth Taylor had turned up on the Starship with him in tow. He was just the most adorable kid you could imagine. But at some point in the intervening years, he started sequestering himself away from the world, and away from reality, the way Elvis Presley did. God knows what was going on in his head, and God knows what prescription drugs he was being pumped full of, but every time I saw him in his later years I came away thinking the poor guy had totally lost his marbles. I don't mean that in a light-hearted way. He was genuinely mentally ill, a disturbing person to be around. It was incredibly sad, but he was someone you couldn't help: he was just gone, off in a world of his own, surrounded by people who only told him what he wanted to hear.

And now he was coming to the lunch at which my boyfriend was scheduled to meet my mother for the first time. Fantastic. I decided the best plan was to ring David and drop this information into the conversation as nonchalantly as possible. Perhaps if I behaved as if there was no problem here, he might take it in his stride. Or perhaps not – I hadn't even finished nonchalantly mentioning the change in lunch plans before I was interrupted by an anguished yell of 'are you fucking KIDDING me?' I tried to reassure him by lying through my teeth, promising that the reports he had heard of Michael's eccentricities had been greatly exaggerated. This probably wasn't very convincing, given that some of the reports of Michael's eccentricities had come directly from me. But no, I insisted, it wouldn't be as strange as he might expect.

In that respect at least, I was absolutely right. The meal wasn't as strange as I might have expected. It was stranger than I could have imagined. It was a sunny day and we had to sit indoors with the curtains drawn because of Michael's vitiligo. The poor guy looked awful, really frail and ill. He was wearing make-up that looked like it had been applied by a maniac: it was all over the place. His nose was covered with a sticking plaster which kept what was left of it attached to his face. He sat there, not really saying anything, just giving off waves of discomfort the way some people give off an air of confidence. I somehow got the impression he hadn't eaten a meal around other people for a very long time. Certainly, he wouldn't eat anything we served up. He brought his own chef with him, but didn't eat anything he made, either. After a while, he got up from the table without a word and disappeared. We finally found him, two hours later, in a cottage in the grounds of Woodside where my housekeeper lived: she was sitting there, watching Michael Jackson quietly playing video games with her eleven-year-old son. For whatever reason, he couldn't seem to cope with adult company at all. While all this was going on, I could see David though the gloom, sitting at the other end of the table, valiantly trying to make bright conversation with my mother, who was doing her bit to add to the strained atmosphere by spending most of the meal telling him that she thought psychiatry was a waste of time and money in a voice loud enough for Michael Jackson's psychiatrist to hear. Whenever she paused for breath, I noticed David glancing around, as if looking for someone who might explain what the hell he'd got himself into.

It didn't take an unexpected visit from Michael Jackson to make the world David was entering seem completely bizarre. I could make it seem that way myself, without any help from the self-styled King of Pop. Rehab had curbed most of my worst excesses but not all of them: the Dwight Family Temper seemed particularly resistant to any kind of treatment or medical intervention. I was still perfectly capable of throwing appalling tantrums when I felt like it. I think the first time David really saw one up close was the night in January 1994 when I was due to be inducted into the Rock and Roll Hall of Fame in New York. I didn't want to go, because I don't really see the point of the Rock and Roll Hall of Fame. I loved the original idea of it – honouring the true pioneers of rock and roll, the artists who laid the path in the fifties that the rest of us followed, especially the ones who got ripped off financially – but it quickly became something else entirely, a big televised ceremony with tickets that cost tens of thousands of dollars. It's just about getting enough big names involved each year to put bums on seats.

The smart thing would have been to politely decline the invitation, but I felt obliged. I was being inducted by Axl Rose, who I really liked. I had got in touch with him when he was being ripped apart in the press: I know how lonely it can feel when the papers are giving you a kicking, and I just wanted to offer some support. We got on great and ended up performing 'Bohemian Rhapsody' together at the Freddie Mercury Tribute gig. I got a lot of flak for that, because a Guns N' Roses song called 'One In A Million' had homophobic lyrics. If I'd thought it reflected his personal views, I wouldn't have touched him. But I didn't – I thought it was pretty obvious the song was written from the point of view of a character who wasn't Axl Rose. It was the same with Eminem: when I performed with him at the Grammys, the Gay and Lesbian Alliance Against Defamation gave me a really hard time, but it was obvious that his lyrics were about adopting a persona – a deliberately repugnant persona at that. I didn't think either of them were actually homophobes any more than I thought Sting was actually going out with a prostitute called Roxanne, or Johnny Cash actually shot a man in Reno just to watch him die.

So I went along to the Rock and Roll Hall of Fame. As soon as I got there, I decided I'd made a mistake, turned round and left, ranting all the way about how the place was a fucking mausoleum. I dragged David back to the hotel, where I immediately felt guilty for blowing them out. So we went back. The Grateful

Dead were performing with a cardboard cut-out of Jerry Garcia, because Jerry Garcia wasn't there: he thought the Rock and Roll Hall of Fame was a load of bullshit, and had refused to attend. I decided Jerry had a point, turned round and left again, with David dutifully in tow. I had got out of my suit and into the hotel dressing gown when I was once more struck by a pang of guilt. So I got back into my suit and we returned to the awards ceremony. Then I got angry at myself for feeling guilty and stormed out again, once more enlivening the journey back to the hotel with a lengthy oration, delivered at enormous volume, about what a waste of time the whole evening was. By now, David's sympathetic nods and murmurs of agreement were starting to take on a slightly strained tone, but I convinced myself he was probably rolling his eyes like that at the manifest failings of the Rock and Roll Hall of Fame rather than at me. This made it easier to decide – ten minutes later – that all things considered, we had better go back to the ceremony yet again. The other guests looked quite surprised to see us, but you could hardly blame them: we'd been backwards and forwards to our table more often than the waiting staff.

I'd like to tell you it ended there, but I fear there may have been another change of heart and furious return to the hotel before I actually got onstage and accepted the award. Axl Rose gave a beautiful speech, I called Bernie up onstage and gave the award to him, then we left. We drove back to the hotel in silence, which was eventually broken by David.

'Well,' he said quietly, 'that was quite a dramatic evening.' Then he paused. 'Elton,' he asked plaintively, 'is your life *always* like this?'

I suspect nights like that got David interested in making *Tantrums and Tiaras*, although it was my idea to begin with. A film company wanted to make a documentary about me, but I thought it would be more interesting if it was made by someone close to me, who had access I would never give anyone else. I didn't want a load of whitewashed bullshit, I wanted people to really see what it was like being me: the funny parts, the ridiculous aspects. And I got the feeling David wanted the world to know what he had to put up with. It was like a way of making sense of this insane life that he'd become part of, that had become his life, too. So he set up a little office in the tram I'd bought in Australia – you see, I knew it would come in useful one day – and started filming.

I wasn't afraid about people seeing the monstrous, unreasonable side of me. I'm perfectly aware how ridiculous my life is, and perfectly aware of what an arsehole I look like when I lose my temper over nothing – I go from nought to nuclear in seconds and then calm down just as quickly. My temper was obviously inherited from my mum and dad, but I honestly think that, somewhere within them, every creative artist, whether they're a painter, a theatre director, an actor or a musician, has the ability to behave in a completely unreasonable way. It's like the dark side of being creative. Certainly, virtually every other artist I had become friends with seemed to have that aspect to their character too. John Lennon did, Marc Bolan, Dusty Springfield. They were wonderful people, and I loved them to bits, but everyone knows they all had their moments. In fact, Dusty had so many that she told me she'd worked out the secret of throwing a tantrum successfully: if you got to the stage where you started hurling inanimate objects around the room, you had to make sure you didn't hurl anything that was expensive or difficult to replace. I'm just more honest about it than a lot of people, especially these days. Today, record labels give pop stars media training; they literally school them to try and cover up any flaws in their character, to never say anything out of line.

You don't have to be an expert on the subject of my career to know that I come from a different era, before anyone thought pop stars needed to be told what they should and shouldn't say to the media. I'm really glad, even though I've said things that have caused a lot of controversy and kept newspapers in articles head-lined THE BITCH IS BACK for decades. It probably was a bit cruel to say that Keith Richards looked like a monkey with arthritis, but, in fairness, he'd been pretty foul about me: he got as good as he gave. The only time I caused real trouble was when I told an American Sunday newspaper magazine called *Parade* that I thought Jesus might well have been a very intelligent, super-compassionate gay man. I just meant that no one really knows anything about Jesus's personal life, and that you can extrapolate all sorts of ideas from his teachings about forgiveness and empathy. But the religious nuts didn't take it that way: the big idea they seemed to have extrapolated from Jesus's teachings was that you should go around inciting people to kill anyone who says something you don't like. I ended up with officers from the Atlanta police force sleeping in my guest room for a week. There were protesters outside the apartment building, waving banners, one of which said ELTON JOHN MUST DIE – not really what you want to see on your doorstep when you come home of an evening. The guy holding it posted a video on YouTube threatening to kill me. He ended up being arrested, and the protests died down.

Even so, I still think a world in which artists are coached not to say anything that might upset anyone and are presented as perfect figures is boring. Furthermore, it's a lie. Artists aren't perfect. *No one* is perfect. That's why I hate whitewashed docu-mentaries about rock stars where everyone's telling you what a wonderful person they were. Most rock stars can be horrible sometimes. They can be fabulous and charming and they can be outrageous and stupid, and that's what I wanted to show in *Tantrums and Tiaras*.

Not everyone thought it was a good idea. George Michael watched some of the footage and he was horrified: not because of what he saw – he already knew what I was like – but because I was actually going to put it out. He thought it was a terrible mistake. John Reid said he was on board with the idea, but then quietly went around trying to sabotage the whole project. After my mother agreed to be interviewed for it, he went behind my back and told her not to get involved because it was just going to be about sex and drugs.

I was furious about that, but I didn't care what other people thought. I usually can't stand to watch myself in anything, but I loved *Tantrums and Tiaras*, because it was real. David and the producer Polly Steele just followed me around on my 1995 world tour with little Hi-8 camcorders, and most of the time I forgot I was being filmed. It's hilarious: me making these completely ridiculous threats, screaming that I'm never coming to France again because a fan waved at me while I was trying to play tennis, or that I'm never making another video because someone's inadvertently left my clothes in the back of a car. Watching it was cathartic, and I think the shock of seeing myself changed the way I behave – well, that and a lot of therapy. I've still got a temper – you can't change your genes – but I'm a lot more aware of what a waste of energy it is, how completely stupid I feel once I've calmed down, so I try to keep it in check: admittedly with varying degrees of success, but at least I'm making an effort.

In fact, the only thing I regret about *Tantrums and Tiaras* is how influential it became. It really spawned that whole genre of reality TV where you see into a celebrity's life, or worse, someone who's become a celebrity for being on reality TV. You know, it's not exactly the most edifying thing having *Being Bobby Brown* and *The Anna Nicole Show* on your conscience. There's a sense in which *Keeping Up with the Kardashians* might ultimately be my fault, for which I can only prostrate myself before the human race and beg their forgiveness.

★

antrums and Tiaras was finally released in 1997: David was coming back from a press conference in Pasadena for its American launch when I found out Gianni Versace had been murdered. I had bought a house in Nice and Gianni was meant to be flying out to France to have a holiday with David and me the following week – the tickets were booked – when a serial killer shot him outside his mansion in Miami: he'd already murdered men in Minnesota, Chicago and New Jersey and was supposed to have become obsessed with Gianni after meeting him briefly at a nightclub years before, although I don't think anyone knows whether he actually met him or not.

When John Reid rang and told me what had happened, I completely went to pieces. I turned on the TV in the bedroom and sat there, watching the coverage, bawling. Gianni had been out doing his morning routine. Each day, he got every international paper, every magazine. There were always piles of them lying around his house, with Post-it notes all over them: ideas that had caught his attention, things he thought he could work with, stuff he found inspiring. And now he was dead. It was like John Lennon's death – there was no explanation, nothing whatsoever about it that made it any easier to comprehend, no way of rationalizing it in your head, even slightly. Another random murder.

His family asked me to perform at his memorial service, at the Duomo in Milan. They wanted me to duet with Sting: the 23rd Psalm again, the same piece I'd sung in the cathedral in Sydney after John died. The service was mayhem. There were paparazzi everywhere, film crews and photographers even in the church. It was claustrophobic but, in a weird way, it's what Gianni would have wanted. He loved publicity, to the point where it was the one thing about him that drove me up the wall. You would go on holiday with him to Sardinia, and every single place you went, Gianni's PR people would have rung up the press beforehand and tipped them off. I'd tell him I hated it, but he didn't get that at all: 'Oh, Elton, but they love you, they want to take your picture, is beautiful, no? They love you.' At the cathedral, two officials – monsignors or cardinals or whatever they were – called me and Sting out in front of the congregation and started quizzing us about our performance: I think they didn't really want us to sing because we weren't Catholics. It was horrible, like being dragged out before the school by the headmaster at assembly but in the middle of a memorial service in a church filled with TV cameras and flashes going off.

We were eventually allowed to sing and got through the performance, which was a miracle. I couldn't stop crying. I don't think I've ever seen a human being look so beside themselves with grief as Allegra, Gianni's little niece. She was eleven when he died, and he doted on her: he left his share of the business to her in his will. She somehow blamed herself for his death, because she used to go and get the papers with him every morning, but the morning he died, she'd been in Rome with her mum. She thought that if she had been with her uncle, he wouldn't have been killed. After his death, she developed a terrible eating disorder. She would go missing and they would find her hiding in wardrobes in the house, clutching his old clothes, things that still smelt of him. It was awful. Just awful.

In fact, the whole Versace family went to pieces after Gianni's death. Donatella had always had a cocaine problem. Everyone knew, except Gianni. He was incredibly naive about drugs. He didn't even drink: he would have a glass of red wine and put Sprite and ice cubes in it, which I imagine tastes revolting enough to put you off investigating alcohol any further. At Versace events, he would go to bed early, and then the party would really start, with Donatella leading the charge. He realized that something was wrong with her, but he couldn't work out what it was. I remember walking around the garden at Woodside with him, listening to him going, 'I don't understand my sister – one day she's good, one day she's bad, she has moods, I don't understand it.' I told him that she was a cocaine addict, that I'd done coke with her many times before I got clean. He couldn't believe it – he had no inkling whatsoever of what her life was like when he wasn't around.

But after his murder, Donatella's coke use got completely out of control. I didn't see much of her – she was avoiding me because she knew I disapproved – but then, one night, she turned up backstage at a gig I was playing in Reggio Calabria out of her mind, really high. While I was playing, she sat at the side of the stage in floods of tears. She never stopped crying throughout the entire show. Either she *really* hated my performance or she was asking for help.

So we decided to stage an intervention. David and her publicist Jason Weisenfeld arranged it, at Allegra's eighteenth birthday party in Gianni's old apartment on Via Gesù. I was there, with David and Jason and our friends Ingrid Sischy and her partner Sandy, all waiting in this little sitting room. Donatella and Allegra came in, wearing these unbelievably extravagant, gorgeous Atelier Versace gowns, and sat on a divan as everyone spoke in turn. There was an awful silence. You never know how an intervention is going to go: if the person it's aimed at isn't ready to admit they've got a problem, it just turns into a disaster. Suddenly, Donatella spoke up. 'My life is like your candle in the wind!' she cried dramatically. 'I want to die!'

We got her on the phone to a rehab facility called The Meadows in Scottsdale, Arizona. We could only hear her side of the conversation, which was extraordinary. 'Yes, yes . . . cocaine . . . also pills . . . oh, a handful of this pill, a handful of that pill, and if that doesn't work I take all the pills and mix them together . . . yes . . . OK, I come now, but one condition: NO OILY FOOD.'

Having presumably been assured that oily food wasn't on the menu, off she went, still in her gown. The next day, we got a phone call from Jason Weisenfeld, who told us she had been admitted. Apparently the facility's rule that residential patients weren't allowed to wear make-up had gone down pretty badly, and there had been a bit of fuss when Donatella realized she'd forgotten to pack a deodorant but, other than that, she was fine: she went on to complete the programme and get clean. We congratulated Jason on pulling the whole thing off.

'Yeah,' he said glumly. 'All I have to do now is walk around Scottsdale trying to find a fucking Chanel deodorant.'

After the funeral, we invited Gianni's partner Antonio to come and stay with us in Nice. He was distraught, and he never really got on with the rest of Gianni's family. It was a very strange, sombre summer, sitting in the house we'd just bought, that we'd decorated in a style influenced by Gianni's taste, that we'd been waiting to show off to him and get his opinion on. One night, David said very firmly that it was time I thought about hiring professional security. I'd never bothered before, not even after John was murdered. I had employed a guy called Jim Morris as a bodyguard in the seventies, but that was more a camp affectation than anything. He was a bodybuilder who'd been crowned Mr America, and openly gay – no small thing for a black tough guy to be in those days – and he spent more time carrying me onstage on his shoulders than anything else. Now it seemed we genuinely needed security. Things had changed.

And our summer was about to get stranger still. One Sunday morning, at the end of August, we were woken by the sound of the fax machine going off. David went to look at it and came back with a sheet of paper, with a handwritten message from a friend in London: 'so sorry to hear about this awful news'. Neither of us knew what it meant. It couldn't possibly be referring to Gianni – he had been dead for six weeks now. With a mounting sense of dread, I switched the television on. And that was how I found out Princess Diana had died.

fourteen

I first met Diana in 1981, just before she and Prince Charles
were married. It was at Prince Andrew's twenty-first birthday
party at Windsor Castle; Ray Cooper and I were supposed to be
providing the entertainment. It was a completely surreal evening.
The outside of the castle was illuminated with psychedelic lighting,
and before we performed, the entertainment in the ballroom came
courtesy of a mobile disco. Because the Queen was there, and no
one wanted to cause any offence to the royal sensibilities, the
disco was turned down about as low as you could get without
switching it off altogether. You could literally hear your feet
moving around on the floor over the music. Princess Anne asked
me to dance with her to 'Hound Dog' by Elvis Presley. Well, I
say dance: I ended up just awkwardly shuffling from foot to foot,
trying to make as little noise as I could so that I didn't drown
out the music. If you strained your ears and concentrated hard,
you could just about make out that the DJ had segued from
Elvis into 'Rock Around The Clock'. Then the Queen appeared,
carrying her handbag. She walked over to us and asked if she
could join us. So now I was trying to dance as inaudibly as possible
with Princess Anne and the Queen – still holding her handbag
– while what appeared to be the world's quietest disco played Bill

Haley. Weirdly, it made me think of The Band barging into my dressing room or Brian Wilson endlessly singing the chorus of 'Your Song' at me when I first went to America. It was eleven years later, my life had changed beyond recognition, and yet here I was, still desperately trying to act normal, while the world around me appeared to have gone completely mad.

And that was the thing about my interactions with the Royal Family. I always found them incredibly charming and funny people. I know the Queen's public image isn't exactly one of wild frivolity, but I think that's more to do with the nature of her job. I noticed it when I got the CBE, and then the knighthood. She has to spend two and a half hours handing the things out, making small talk with two hundred people, one after the other. Anyone would be hard pressed to come up with a string of brilliant witticisms in that position. She just asks you if you're busy at the moment, you say 'yes, Ma'am', she says 'how lovely' and moves on. But in private she could be hilarious. At another party, I saw her approach Viscount Linley and ask him to look in on his sister, who'd been taken ill and retired to her room. When he repeatedly tried to fob her off, the Queen lightly slapped him across the face, saying 'Don't' – SLAP – 'argue' – SLAP – 'with' – SLAP – 'me' – SLAP – 'I' – SLAP – 'am' – SLAP – 'THE QUEEN!' That seemed to do the trick. As he left, she saw me staring at her, gave me a wink and walked off.

Yet no matter how funny or normal the Royal Family seemed, whether they were complaining about the paint job on my Aston Martin, or asking me if I'd done any coke before I went onstage, or winking at me after slapping their nephew across the face, there would inevitably come a moment where I'd find myself feeling slightly out of place, thinking: 'This is just bizarre. I'm a musician from a council house on Pinner Road – what am I doing here?' But with Diana it wasn't like that. Despite her status and background, she was blessed with an incredible social ease, an ability to talk to anybody, to make herself seem ordinary, to make people feel totally comfortable in her company. Her kids have inherited it, Prince Harry in particular; he's exactly the same as his mum, completely without any interest in formality or grandeur. That famous photo of her holding an AIDS patient's hand at the London Middlesex Hospital – that was Diana. I don't think she was necessarily trying to make a big point, although obviously she did: in that moment, she changed public attitudes to AIDS forever. She just met someone suffering, dying in agony: why wouldn't you reach out and touch them? It's the natural human impulse, to try and comfort someone.

That night in 1981, she arrived in the ballroom and we immediately clicked. We ended up pretending to dance the Charleston while hooting at the disco's feebleness. She was fabulous company, the best dinner party guest, incredibly indiscreet, a real gossip: you could ask her anything and she'd tell you. The only peculiar thing about her was the way she talked about Prince Charles. She never mentioned him by name; it was always 'my husband', never Charles, certainly never an affectionate nickname. It seemed very distant, cold and formal, which was very strange, because the one thing Diana wasn't was formal: she was always incredulous at how starchy and proper some other members of the Royal Family could be.

But if I was bowled over by Diana, it was nothing compared to the impact she could have on straight men. They seemed to completely lose their minds in her presence: they were just utterly bewitched. When I was making *The Lion King*, Jeffrey Katzenberg, the head of Disney, came over to England, and we threw a dinner party for him and his wife Marilyn at Woodside. I asked them if there was anyone in Britain they really wanted to meet and, straight away, they said 'Princess Diana'. So we invited her, and George Michael, Richard Curtis and his wife Emma Freud, Richard Gere and Sylvester Stallone, all of whom were in the country at the time. The most peculiar scene developed. Straight away, Richard Gere and Diana seemed very taken with each other. She was separated from Prince Charles by this point, and Richard had just broken up with Cindy Crawford, and they ended up sitting on the floor in front of the fireplace together, locked in rapt conversation. As the rest of us chatted, I couldn't help notice a slightly strange atmosphere in the room. Judging by the kind of looks he kept shooting them, the sight of Diana and Richard Gere's newly blossoming friendship was not going down very well with Sylvester Stallone at all. I think he might have turned up to the party with the express intention of picking Diana up, only to find his plans for the evening unexpectedly ruined.

Eventually, dinner was served. We moved into the dining room and seated ourselves at the table. Or at least, most of us did. There was no sign of Richard Gere, or indeed Sylvester Stallone. We waited. Still no sign. Finally, I asked David to go and find them. He came back with both of them, but he was wearing a fairly ashen expression.

'Elton,' he mumbled. 'We have . . . a *situation.*'

It transpired that when David had gone out to find them, he'd discovered Sylvester Stallone and Richard Gere in the corridor, squaring up to each other, apparently about to settle their differences over Diana by having a fistfight. He'd managed to calm things down by pretending he hadn't noticed what was going on – 'Hey, guys! Time for dinner!' – but Sylvester clearly still wasn't happy. After dinner, Diana and Richard Gere resumed their position together in front of the fire, and Sylvester eventually stormed off home.

'I never would have come,' he snapped, as David and I showed him to the door, 'if I'd known Prince fuckin' Charming was gonna be here.' Then he added: 'If I'd wanted her, I would've taken her!'

We managed to wait until his car was out of sight before we started laughing. Back in the living room, Diana and Richard Gere were still gazing raptly at each other. She seemed completely unruffled. Maybe she hadn't realized what was happening. Or maybe stuff like that happened all the time and she was used to it. After she died, people started talking about something called the Diana Effect, meaning the way she managed to change the public's attitudes to the Royal Family, or to AIDS or bulimia or mental health. But every time I heard the phrase, I thought about that night. There was definitely another kind of Diana Effect: one that could bring Hollywood superstars to the verge of a punch-up over her attentions at a dinner party, like a couple of love-struck teenage idiots.

She was a very dear friend for years, and then, completely unexpectedly, we fell out. The cause was a book Gianni Versace put together called *Rock and Royalty*. It was a collection of portraits by great photographers: Richard Avedon, Cecil Beaton, Herb Ritts, Irving Penn, Robert Mapplethorpe. The proceeds were going to the AIDS Foundation, and she agreed to write the foreword. Then she got cold feet. I think Buckingham Palace didn't like the idea of a member of the Royal Family having anything to do with a book that featured shots of naked guys with towels draped around them. So, at the last moment, Diana withdrew her foreword. She said she had no idea of the book's contents, which just wasn't true: Gianni had shown her the whole thing and she had said she loved it. I wrote back to her, calling her out, telling her how much money she had cost the AIDS Foundation, reminding her that she had seen the book. The letter I got back was very formal and severe: 'Dear Mr John . . .' And that seemed to be the end of that. I was angry with her, but I was also worried. She seemed to be losing touch with all sorts of really close friends, who would be honest with her and tell her the truth. She was surrounding herself instead with people who told her what she wanted to hear, or who would listen and nod when she came out with some of the more paranoid theories she'd developed about the Royal Family since her divorce.

I knew from personal experience that wasn't a healthy situation.

I didn't speak to her again until the day Gianni was murdered. She was the first person to call me after John Reid rang and told me he was dead. I don't even know how she got hold of the number; we hadn't had the house in Nice for long. She was just down the coast, in St-Tropez, on Dodi Fayed's yacht. She asked how I was, if I'd spoken to Donatella. Then she said, 'I'm so sorry. It was a silly falling-out. Let's be friends.'

She came with us to the funeral, looking incredible: tanned from her holiday, wearing a pearl necklace. She was the same warm, caring, tactile person she had always been. When she walked in, the paparazzi in the church went crazy: it was like the biggest star in the world had arrived, which I suppose she had. They didn't let up throughout the service, although I feel I should point out that the famous shot they got of her supposedly consoling me – where she's leaning forward towards me, speaking, while I'm red-eyed and glazed with grief – is one moment in the service where she wasn't doing anything of the sort. They snapped her just as she was leaning past me, reaching for a mint that David offered her. The warm words of comfort coming from her lips at that exact moment were actually, 'God, I'd love a Polo.'

I wrote to her afterwards, thanking her, and she wrote back offering to be a patron of the AIDS Foundation and asking if I would get involved in her landmine charity. We were going to meet up next time we were both in London to have lunch and discuss it. But there wasn't a next time.

A couple of days after her death, I got a phone call from Richard Branson. He told me that when people signed the book of condolence at St James's Palace, a lot of them were writing down quotations from the lyrics of 'Candle In The Wind'. Apparently, they were playing it a lot on the radio in the UK as well – stations had changed from their usual musical format and were broadcasting sombre-sounding music to reflect the public mood. Then he asked if I would be prepared to rewrite the lyrics and sing it at the funeral. I hadn't been expecting that at all. I think Richard had been contacted by the Spencer family, because they felt the funeral should be something that people would really connect to: they didn't want a severe, remote royal event full of pageantry and protocol, because that wouldn't have fitted Diana's character at all.

So I called Bernie. I thought it was an incredibly tough gig for him. Not only was whatever he wrote going to be broadcast live to literally billions of people – it was obvious that the funeral would be a huge, global, televised event – it had to be vetted by the Royal Family and the Church of England. But he was fantastic: he acted as if writing a song that the Queen and the Archbishop of Canterbury had to check through first was all in a day's work. He faxed the lyrics over the next morning, I faxed them to Richard Branson and they were waved through.

Even so, when I went to rehearse at Westminster Abbey the day before the funeral, I had no idea what to expect. The memory of Gianni's memorial service, the fact that the church officials clearly hadn't thought it appropriate for me to perform, played on my mind. And that was just singing a hymn at a private service, not performing a rock song at a state event. What if people didn't really want me here either?

But it couldn't have been more different. The Archbishop of Canterbury was incredibly nice and hugely supportive. There was a real sense of camaraderie, that everyone had to pull together to make this thing work. I insisted on having a teleprompter by the piano, with Bernie's new lyrics on it. Up until then, I had been against their use. Partly because it seemed antithetical to the spontaneous spirit of rock and roll – you know, I'm pretty sure Little Richard wasn't reading the words off an autocue when he recorded 'Long Tall Sally' – and partly because I just thought: come on, do your job properly. You've really only got three things to do onstage – sing in tune, play the right notes and remember the words. If you can only be bothered to do two of them you may as well go and find another job instead – it's why I have such a problem with artists miming onstage. But this time, I thought I could relax the rules slightly. It was a completely unique experience, a one-off. There was a sense in which it was the biggest gig of my life – for four minutes, I was literally going to be the centre of the world's attention – but equally, it wasn't an Elton John moment, it wasn't about me at all. It was very strange.

Just how strange was underlined when we arrived at Westminster Abbey the next day. David and I went with George Michael; this was long before we fell out over his drug problems. He had rung up and asked if we could go to the funeral together. On the car journey there, we just sat in silence: George was too upset to speak, there was no conversation, nothing. The place was full of people I knew: Donatella Versace was there, David Frost, Tom Cruise and Nicole Kidman, Tom Hanks and Rita Wilson. It all felt slightly surreal, like a dream you were having rather than something that was actually happening in real life. We were seated in the inner sanctum of the church, right where the Royal Family came in. William and Harry looked completely shell-shocked. They were fifteen and twelve, and I thought the way they were treated that day was absolutely inhuman. They were forced to walk through the streets of London behind their mother's coffin, told to show no emotion and look straight ahead. It was a horrendous way to treat two kids who'd just lost their mum.

But I barely took any of it in. I wasn't suffering from nerves, exactly. I'd be lying if I said the thought that two billion people were watching never crossed my mind, but at least I was performing in front of the part of the church where they had put all the representatives from the charities Diana supported, so there were friends from the Elton John AIDS Foundation there – Robert Key, Anne Aslett and James Locke. But it was less stage fright than a very specific fear: what if I went into autopilot and *sang the wrong version*? I'd performed 'Candle In The Wind' hundreds of times. It really wasn't beyond the realms of possibility that I might lose myself in the performance, forget about the teleprompter al-together and start singing the original lyrics. How bad could it be if I did that? Appalling. People might have been quoting lines from them in the book of condolence at St James's Palace, but huge chunks of the lyrics were obviously completely inappropriate for the occasion. You'd have a hard time bluffing your way out of singing about Marilyn Monroe being found dead in the nude, or how your feelings were something more than sexual, at a state funeral, in front of a global audience of two billion people or whatever it was supposed to be.

And then an odd thing happened. I found myself zoning out of the funeral and thinking about an incident from years before, on my first tour of America. I had been booked to appear on *The Andy Williams Show* with Mama Cass Elliot from The Mamas and The Papas and Ray Charles. When I arrived, the producers blithely informed me that we weren't just going to be performing on the same show, we were going to be performing *together*. They seemed to think this was a wonderful surprise for me, that I was going to be delighted about it. They thought wrong: Mama Cass, fine, Andy Williams, fine, but *Ray Charles*? Are you joking? Ray Charles! Brother Ray! The Genius! An artist I'd spent hours fantasizing about being when I was a kid, hiding in my bedroom with my record collection, miming away to his *Ray Charles at Newport* live album. And now some idiot had decided that it was a marvellous idea for him to go on national TV and sing with me, as if a completely unknown English singer-songwriter was some kind of perfect musical counterpart for the man who'd basically single-handedly invented soul music. If it wasn't the worst idea I'd ever heard, it sounded so much like it as to make no difference. And there was absolutely nothing I could do about it. My career was just beginning, it was my first appearance on US TV. I was in no position to start upsetting American television executives by being difficult. So I did it. I got up and sang 'Heaven Help Us All' with Ray Charles – him playing a white piano, me playing a black piano. It went perfectly. Ray Charles was gracious and kind and encouraging – 'Hey, sweetheart, how you doin'?' – as artists who don't have anything to prove tend to be.

And it really taught me something important. Sometimes, you just have to step up to the plate, even if the plate is miles outside your comfort zone. It's like going deep inside yourself, forgetting about whatever emotions you may have and thinking: no, I'm a performer. This is what I do. Get on with it.

So I got on with it. I don't remember much about the performance itself, but I remember the applause afterwards. It seemed to start outside Westminster Abbey and sweep into the church itself, which I guess meant that Diana's family had achieved their aim in getting me to sing: it connected with the people outside. After the funeral, I went straight to Townhouse Studios in Shepherd's Bush, where George Martin was waiting: they were going to release the new version of 'Candle In The Wind' as a single to raise money for a charity memorial fund set up in Diana's name. I sang it twice, live at the piano, and went home, leaving George Martin to overdub a string quartet on it. When I got back to Woodside, David was standing in the kitchen, watching the coverage on TV. The funeral cortège had got to the M1: people were throwing flowers at Diana's hearse from the bridges over the motorway. That was when I finally broke down. I hadn't felt able to show emotion all day. I had a job to do, and how I felt about Diana's death might have interfered with my ability to do it; the funeral wasn't about me, it was about her. So up until that point, I couldn't afford to be upset.

The response to the single was crazy. People were queuing up outside record stores, then rushing in and grabbing armfuls of CD singles and buying them. There were all these preposterous statistics about it. At one point, it was supposed to be selling six copies a second; it was the fastest-selling single ever released; it was the biggest-selling single of all time in *Finland*. I got sales awards for it from the most bizarre places: Indonesia, the Middle East. And it just went on and on and on. It was Number One in America for fourteen weeks. It was in the Top Twenty in Canada for three years. There was part of me that couldn't understand it: why would anyone want to listen to it? Under what circumstances would you play it? I never did. I sang it three times – once at the funeral and twice in the studio – then I listened back to it once to OK the mix and that was it: never again. I suppose people were just buying it to give money to the charity, which was great, although a huge chunk of the £38 million it raised was ultimately wasted. The charity got involved in defending her image rights against people who were making Diana merchandise – plates and dolls and T-shirts – and the money started getting swallowed up by lawyers' fees. It lost a case against an American company called Franklin Mint and ended up paying them millions, settling a case of malicious prosecution out of court. Whatever the rights and wrongs of the situation, I felt it made them look bad, as if they were more interested in using the money raised to fight over trademarks than in clearing landmines or helping disadvantaged women, or all the other work they were doing.

In the end, it reached a point where I started feeling really uncomfortable with the charity single's longevity. Its success meant there was footage of Diana's funeral week after week on *Top of the Pops* – it felt as if people were somehow wallowing in her death, like the mourning for her had got out of hand and they were refusing to move on. It seemed unhealthy to me – morbid and unnatural. I really didn't think it was what Diana would have wanted.

I thought the media had gone from reflecting the public mood to deliberately stoking it, because it sold papers.

It was getting ridiculous, and I didn't want to do anything to prolong it any further. So when Oprah Winfrey asked me onto her talk show in the US to discuss the funeral, I said no. I wouldn't let them put the funeral version of 'Candle In The Wind' on a charity CD released to commemorate her life. It's never appeared on any *Greatest Hits* album I've put out and it's never been re-released. I even stopped singing the original version of 'Candle In The Wind' live for a few years: I just assumed people needed a rest from hearing it. When I went back on tour that autumn, I kept well away from it, and remembered Gianni and Diana by singing a song called 'Sand And Water', from an album by the singer-songwriter Beth Nielsen Chapman that was released the day Gianni was murdered. I'd played it over and over in Nice: 'I will see you in the light of a thousand suns, I will hear you in the sound of the waves, I will know you when I come, as we all will come, through the doors beyond the grave'. I always tried to avoid the topic with journalists: the chart nerd in me loved the fact that I'd made the biggest-selling single since the charts began, but the circumstances around it were such that I didn't want to dwell on it. When it was the twentieth anniversary of Diana's death, I did one interview, about her AIDS work, because Prince Harry specifically asked me to.

Perhaps there was also something personal bound up in my feelings about the single. It had been such a strange, horrible summer. From the moment Gianni died, it had felt like the world had spun off its axis and gone mad: his murder, the memorial service, the reconciliation with Diana, the weeks in the house in France looking after his partner Antonio, Diana's death, her funeral, the bedlam around 'Candle In The Wind'. It wasn't that I wanted to forget any of it – I just wanted life to return to some semblance of normality. So I got back to work. I went on tour. I sold off a

(*above*) Bernie and me with Ryan White in 1988. I didn't know it then, but meeting Ryan was going to save my life.

(*right*) Clean and sober, but still intent on ruining things for Rod Stewart whenever possible. I'm about to wander onstage unannounced and sit on his lap.

Taken by Herb Ritts in 1992. I'd known Liz Taylor for years –
she was hilarious, and had the guts to force Hollywood to
pay attention to AIDS long before I did.

(*left*) Backstage at Earls Court with Princess Diana in May 1993; (*right*) Working with
Tim Rice on *The Lion King*. I thought the finished film was extraordinary.

(*left*) With David Furnish, madly in love and fully Versace'd;
(*right*) David, Gianni Versace, me and Gianni's partner
Antonio D'Amico at Gianni's home on Lake Como.

The Oscar party fundraisers for my AIDS Foundation started in 1993 and
have become a yearly event. This is from the tenth party, with Denzel Washington
and Halle Berry, who won best actor and best actress that night.

David and me, shot by Mario Testino at the Ritz Paris, 1996.

Mum and Derf with me and David the day I received my knighthood in 1998.

Ingrid Sischy, who felt like my missing sister when I met her, demonstrating the transformative power of one of my wigs.

(*left*) 21 December 2005: the day David and I became civil partners. I was as happy as I had ever been; (*right*) I was genuinely worried we'd be facing crowds of protesters outside the Guildhall in Windsor but people turned up with cakes and presents.

With Auntie Win at the party after our civil partnership.
Mum, being an appalling pain in the arse, is not pictured.

(*left*) Our son Zachary taking his first steps in 2011 in Los Angeles.

(*below*) Having breakfast with Zachary in Nice. Fatherhood was the most unexpected event of my life – and the best.

(*above*) Passing on my expertise in shopping to the boys.

(*right*) Lady Gaga, underdressed as usual, performing godmother duties.

Bring your kids to work day. Zachary and Elijah onstage with me at Caesars Palace in Vegas.

Backstage with Aretha Franklin before her final live performance at the Elton John AIDS Foundation twenty-fifth anniversary gala in New York, November 2017.

Backstage at the farewell tour with Bernie, 2018. Still a study in opposites fifty years on. Still best friends.

load of my old clothes for the AIDS Foundation, in an event I called 'Out of the Closet'. I recorded a song for the cartoon series *South Park*, which seemed about as far away from singing 'Candle In The Wind' at a state funeral as I could possibly get. I started discussing setting up a joint tour with Tina Turner, a nice idea that quickly turned into a disaster. While it was still at the planning stage, she rang me up at home, apparently with the express intention of telling me how awful I was and how I had to change before we could work together. She didn't like my hair, she didn't like the colour of my piano – which for some reason had to be white – and she didn't like my clothes.

'You wear too much Versace, and it makes you look fat – you have to wear Armani,' she announced.

I could hear poor old Gianni turning in his grave at the very idea: the houses of Versace and Armani cordially hated each other. Armani said Versace made really vulgar clothes, and Gianni thought Armani was unbelievably beige and boring. I got off the phone and burst into tears: 'She sounded like my fucking *mother*,' I wailed at David. I like to think I've developed a thick skin over the years, but listening to one of the greatest performers of all time – an artist you're meant to be collaborating with – explain in detail how much they hate everything about you is a very depressing experience.

It wasn't the greatest start to our working relationship, but, incredibly, our working relationship got worse. I agreed to perform with her at a big event called VH1 Divas Live: we were going to do 'Proud Mary' and 'The Bitch Is Back'. My band went to rehearsals a couple of days before me, to get a feel for working with a different singer. When I arrived, I was greeted not by the joyful sight of musicians bonding over the common language of music, but the news that if I went on tour with Tina Turner, none of my band was planning on coming with me, on the grounds that Tina Turner was 'a fucking nightmare'. I asked what the problem was.

'You'll see,' sighed Davey Johnstone ominously.

He was right. Tina wouldn't address any of the musicians by name – she just pointed at them and bellowed 'Hey, you!' when she wanted to get their attention. We started playing 'Proud Mary'. It sounded great. Tina stopped the song, unhappy.

'It's you,' she shouted, pointing at my bass player, Bob Birch. 'You're doing it wrong.'

He assured her he wasn't and we started the song again. Once more, Tina yelled for us to stop. This time it was supposed to be my drummer Curt's fault. It went on like this for a while, stopping and starting every thirty seconds, every member of the band being accused of messing up in turn, until Tina finally discovered the real source of the problem. This time, her finger was pointed in my direction.

'It's you! You're not playing it right!'

I begged her pardon.

'You're not playing it right,' she snapped. 'You don't know how to play this song.'

The subsequent debate about whether or not I knew how to play 'Proud Mary' became quite heated quite quickly, before I brought it to a conclusion by telling Tina Turner to stick her fucking song up her arse and storming off. I sat in the dressing room alternately fuming and wondering what her problem was. I've thrown plenty of tantrums in my time, but there are limits: there's an unspoken rule that musicians don't treat their fellow musicians like shit. Maybe it was insecurity on her part. She'd been treated appallingly earlier in her career, suffered years and years of being ripped off, beaten up and pushed around. Maybe that had an effect on how she behaved towards people. I went to her dressing room and apologized.

She told me that the problem was that I was improvising too much – adding in little fills and runs on the piano. That's how I've always performed, ever since the early days of the Elton John

Band, when we would shift and change songs around onstage as the mood took us. It's part of what I love about playing live – the music is always a little fluid, not carved in stone; there's always room for manoeuvre, the musicians rub off each other and it keeps things fresh. There's nothing better onstage than hearing someone in your band do something you're not expecting that sounds fantastic in that moment. You catch their eye and nod and laugh – *that's what it's all about*. But Tina didn't think that way. Everything had to be exactly the same every time; it was all rehearsed down to the slightest movement. That made it obvious the tour wasn't going to work, although we made up later: she came for dinner in Nice, and left a big Tina Turner lipstick kiss in the visitors' book.

Instead, I arranged another series of live dates with Billy Joel. We'd been touring together since the early nineties: both of us onstage at the same time, playing each other's songs. I thought it was a fantastic idea. We were both pianists, there was a similarity in our approach to music, although Billy is a very American, East Coast kind of writer, like Lou Reed or Paul Simon. They're all very different, but you could tell they were from New York even if you knew nothing about them. We played together for years, although it ended badly, because Billy had a lot of personal problems at the time, and the biggest one was alcohol. He would wash medication for a chest infection down with booze in his dressing room, then fall asleep onstage in the middle of singing 'Piano Man'. Then he would rouse himself, take a bow and immediately head back to the hotel bar and stay there until 5 a.m. Eventually, I suggested that he needed the kind of help that I had got, which didn't make me very popular. He said I was being judgemental, but I genuinely wasn't. I just couldn't stand to watch a nice guy do that to himself any longer. But that was in the future. At first the tours with Billy were great: they were different, fun to play, audiences loved them, they were really successful.

So I had a lot going on, enough to make me feel like the madness of the summer was in the past. But the rest of the world apparently had no desire to stop going mad. The next time we went to Milan, I noticed that everywhere I went, people on the street would step away from me. When they saw me, women would cross themselves and men would grab their crotches. Because of my association with Gianni and Diana, they thought I was cursed, as if I had the evil eye or something. I couldn't have got a worse reception if I'd turned up wearing a shroud and carrying a scythe.

And then, as if a load of Italians carrying on like I was the angel of death wasn't crazy enough, something really insane happened. I was in Australia, where I'd just started touring with Billy in March 1998, when I got a phone call from David. He was at home at Woodside. He said that the girls who did the flower arrangements at the house each week had called round to tell him that they couldn't work for us anymore because they hadn't been paid for over a year and a half. He had rung up John Reid's office to find out what was going on and was told that the florists hadn't been paid because there wasn't any money to pay them. Apparently, I was going broke.

It didn't make any sense to me. The official position of John Reid and his office was that I'd spent it all, and more besides. Don't get me wrong, I know exactly what I'm like, and clearly no one would call me the living embodiment of frugality and thrifty housekeeping – well, with the possible exception of Gianni. I spent a lot of money – I had four houses, staff, cars, I bought art and porcelain and designer clothes – and occasionally, I'd get a stern accountants' letter telling me to cut back, which I would of course ignore. But I still didn't understand how I could be spending more than I earned. I never stopped working. I played live all the time, long tours, a hundred or a hundred and fifty shows in the biggest venues you could play, and the shows always sold out. My recent albums had all gone platinum around the world, and there was a constant stream of compilations coming out, that sold so well I wondered who could possibly be buying them. It seemed inconceivable that anyone who liked 'Your Song' or 'Bennie And The Jets' didn't already own it. *The Lion King* soundtrack had sold sixteen million copies, the film had grossed nearly a billion dollars, the musical was breaking box office records on Broadway.

I felt something wasn't right, but I had no idea what it might be. I honestly wasn't that interested in money. I've been extremely lucky and I've earned a lot, but earning a lot was never my motivation. Obviously, I would be lying if I said I didn't enjoy the fruits of my success, but the mechanics of how money was made didn't interest me at all: if they had, I'd have applied to accountancy school instead of joining Bluesology. I just wanted to play and make records. I was competitive; I would always ask how many albums or gig tickets I'd sold, and I'd watch my chart placings like a hawk, but I never asked how much money I'd earned, never really wanted to examine the contracts and the royalty cheques. I've never been a tax exile: I'm British and I want to live primarily in Britain. I'm not judging anyone who does it, but I don't see the point. You might save money, but I don't think that's going to be a great deal of comfort when you look back on your life and realize you've spent half of it sitting around feeling sorry for yourself in Switzerland, surrounded by other tax exiles who don't really want to be there either. And creatively, I want to be where things are happening in music, and that's not Monaco. I'm sure the principality has many things to recommend it, but when did you last hear of an amazing new band from Monte Carlo?

Besides, I didn't need to keep a close eye on my finances. As far as I was concerned, that was what John Reid did for me. It was the basis of a new management deal we'd done in St-Tropez in the eighties. I paid him 20 per cent of my gross earnings – an enormous amount by most artists' standards – on the understanding he would look after absolutely everything. I think the phrase used for this arrangement was 'Rolls-Royce service'. I could live a blissful life of creativity and pleasure, unencumbered by trifling irritations like examining tax returns, or looking at bank statements, or reading through the small print on contracts. It made sense to me because I trusted John implicitly. We'd been together for what seemed like forever, in one way or another. It was a relationship founded on something more than a business arrangement: however close other artists claimed to be to their managers, I doubted any of them had lost their virginity to them. I trusted him, even though there were occasionally moments when I wondered if his Rolls-Royce service might not be in need of an MOT. There was the time a tabloid newspaper managed to get hold of a load of my financial details, including one of the letters from the accountants warning me to curb my spending. I was convinced they had been leaked, but it turned out a guy called Benjamin Pell had found them by going through the rubbish bins outside John Reid's office. They'd just dumped confidential information on the street without shredding it, which didn't say a great deal for the firm's security or how they were looking after my interests: it certainly seemed their pro-cedures for dealing with personal data could use a revamp.

And then there was the plan John came up with to sell my master recordings. It meant that I would get a huge lump sum, and whoever bought them would get a royalty every time one of my records sold or a song of mine was played on the radio. It was an enormous deal, because it encompassed not just everything I'd recorded in the past but all the songs I would record in the future. John brought in lawyers and music industry figures who told me what a great idea it was, and I agreed. But the lump sum turned out to be far less than I'd anticipated and what I thought my master recordings would be worth. It seemed like everyone had been focusing on the gross figure rather than the net. After John had taken his commission and the lawyers and tax had been paid, the money left over really didn't look like enough to justify signing away every song I'd ever recorded and ever would record. But I put it out of my mind. It had still been enough to buy the house in Nice, fill it with art and furniture and make sure everyone around me benefited. John got his commission, I decided to pay off the mortgages of a lot of people who worked for me: my PA Bob Halley, Robert Key, my driver Derek, Bob Stacey, who'd been my roadie and looked after my wardrobe for decades. And besides, I didn't want a big confrontation with John about it.

But now, I felt something clearly wasn't right. David and I decided to get some professional advice, from a lawyer called Frank Presland who had worked for me before. He agreed that something seemed amiss and said I should have John Reid Enterprises independently audited. I told John, and to be fair he said he thought it was a good idea and would help in any way he could.

I was in Australia when the auditors went in, and I started dreading David's phone calls, with his daily report from his meetings with Frank Presland and the accountants. One night he rang, sounding audibly rattled: Benjamin Pell, the same guy who'd been snooping through the rubbish outside John Reid's office, had contacted him, saying that David was being watched and our phone lines were tapped, and that he should be careful what he said. That sort of activity was rife in the UK press at the time. How much worse could this get?

In the end the auditors raised a number of issues with the way various financial matters had been handled. I was avoiding John's calls and left it to Frank Presland to set out what we were disputing. To cut a long and extremely painful story short, John agreed to settle the potential dispute and, taking into account his financial situation at the time, he agreed to pay me $5 million.

I couldn't tell you how I really felt, because how I really felt changed every minute. I was heartbroken. I felt betrayed – whatever the legal rights and wrongs, I believed John would put my interests first and warn me if there was anything I should be concerned about. I was furious, with myself as much as John. I felt like a fucking idiot, because I'd been so eager to wriggle out of getting involved with my own business affairs. I felt embarrassed. But most of all, I felt like a coward. It was crazy: I was still terrified of confronting him about the situation and of rocking the boat. We'd been together so long that I couldn't imagine my world without John in it. From the moment he'd turned up in the lobby of the Miyako Hotel, our lives had been completely entwined. We'd been lovers, friends, partners, a team that had survived everything: fame, drugs, punch-ups, all the stupidity, all the extremes that came with me becoming Elton John. You name it, it had happened, and we'd stuck together: Sharon and Beryl. Whenever someone told me he was aggressive, or complained about his temper, I thought of the line Don Henley used about The Eagles' manager, Irving Azoff: 'he may be Satan, but he's *our* Satan'. And now it was over.

John severed his management contract and gave up his claim on my future earnings. He closed John Reid Enterprises and retired from management the following year. And I went back on tour. I had debts to pay off.

fifteen

One of the many things I love about Bernie is that he's someone who feels no compunction about telling you the last album you made together – an album which sold millions, went Top Ten around the world and spawned a string of hit singles – was a disaster of unimaginable proportions that required an immediate crisis meeting to ensure nothing like it ever happened again. Bernie and I had been on a commercial roll. We'd made two new albums, *Made in England* in 1995 and *The Big Picture* in autumn 1997, and they'd both done great: gone platinum everywhere from Australia to Switzerland. But *The Big Picture* was the problem, as far as Bernie was concerned. He hated everything about it: the songs, his lyrics, the production, the fact that we'd recorded it in England and he had to travel from the US for the sessions. The end result, he opined, as he sat on the terrace of our house in Nice three years later, was a load of clinical, boring, middle-of-the-road shit. In fact, he continued, clearly gathering steam, it was the worst album we'd ever made.

I wasn't a huge fan of *The Big Picture* myself, but I thought that was laying it on a bit thick. I certainly didn't think it was as bad as *Leather Jackets*, which in fairness wasn't saying much. *Leather Jackets*, you may remember, wasn't an album so much as an exercise in trying to make music while taking so much cocaine you've essentially rendered yourself clinically insane. But even that feeble defence cut no mustard. No, Bernie insisted, *The Big Picture* was even worse than that.

I didn't agree, but Bernie was clearly pissed off: pissed off enough to fly all the way from his home in America to the south of France to talk about it. And there definitely was something in what he said. I'd been listening to Ryan Adams' album *Heartbreaker* a lot. He was a classic country rock singer-songwriter, really – I could imagine him onstage at the Troubadour in the seventies. But there was a toughness and a freshness about it that did make *The Big Picture* sound weirdly dated and staid. Perhaps I had taken my eye off the ball when it came to my solo albums. Ever since the success of *The Lion King*, I'd become more and more interested in film and stage music. I'd written the soundtrack for a comedy called *The Muse*, and an instrumental piece for *Women Talking Dirty*, a British comedy-drama that David had produced. I wasn't writing songs, I was writing proper instrumental scores, where I had to sit watching the film and come up with thirty or sixty seconds of music to fit each given scene. I thought it would be boring, but I really loved it. When you get it right, it's incredibly inspiring, because you literally see the effect music can have: a little snatch of it can totally change how a scene feels, or how it works emotionally.

And Tim Rice and I had done the songs for the DreamWorks animation film *The Road to El Dorado* – the movie I'd promised Jeffrey Katzenberg I would make – then written another stage musical, *Aida*. That had been much harder work than *The Lion King*. There were problems with the set, the directors and designers were changed, and I stormed out of one of the Broadway previews midway through the first act, when I realized they hadn't changed the arrangements of a couple of the songs as I'd asked them to. If they weren't going to listen to me asking nicely, perhaps they would listen to me stomping up the aisle and out of the theatre. But the hard work – and indeed the stomping out – paid off. It ran on Broadway for four years, we won a Grammy, and a Tony Award for Best Score. And I already had another idea for a musical bubbling. We had been to see *Billy Elliot* at the Cannes Film Festival and I'm afraid I made rather a spectacle of myself. I had no idea what the film was about. I just assumed it was going to be a nice little British comedy with Julie Walters in it. I was completely unprepared for how much it was going to affect me emotionally. The scene where his father sees him dancing in the gym, and realizes that his son is really gifted at something, even though he doesn't understand it; the finale, where his dad goes to see him perform and feels proud and moved; it was just too close to home. It was as if someone had taken the story of me and my dad and written a happy ending for it, instead of what had actually happened in real life. I couldn't handle it at all. I was so upset that David literally had to help me out of the cinema. If he hadn't, there's every chance I would still be sat there now, heaving with sobs.

I pulled myself together enough to attend the reception afterwards. We were talking to the film's director Stephen Daldry and the writer Lee Hall, when David mentioned that he thought it would make a good stage musical. I thought he had a point. So did Lee, although he wanted to know who was going to write the lyrics. I told him he was: it was his story, he came from Easington, where the film was set. He complained that he'd never written a lyric in his life, but said he'd give it a go. I couldn't believe the stuff he came back with. Lee was a natural. I never had to change a single word that he'd written, and, better still, they were completely different from any words I'd worked with before. His lyrics were tough and political: 'You think you're smart, you Cockney shite, you want to be suspicious – while you were on the picket line, I went and fucked your missus.' There were songs about wishing Margaret Thatcher dead. There was a song that didn't make it into the final play called 'Only Poofs Do Ballet'. It was another completely new challenge. Perhaps the thought of recording a twenty-seventh Elton John album did seem a little routine by comparison.

Or maybe there was a way of changing that routine. In Nice, Bernie had started talking wistfully about the way we made albums in the seventies: how we used to record things on analogue tape, without too many overdubs, and with my piano at the front and centre of the sound. It was funny – I'd been thinking about the same thing. Perhaps it had to do with seeing Cameron Crowe's film *Almost Famous*, which was a kind of love letter to early seventies rock, personified by a fictional band called Stillwater. One scene uses 'Tiny Dancer': the band start singing along to it on their tour bus. In fact, that scene turned 'Tiny Dancer' into one of my biggest songs overnight. People forget that when it came out as a single in 1971, it flopped. It didn't make the Top Forty in America, and the record label in Britain wouldn't release it at all. When it turned up on the soundtrack of *Almost Famous*, I think a lot of people had no idea what it was, or who it was by. I think the film subconsciously put some ideas into my head, about the kind of artist I'd been back then, about how my music was made and how it was perceived, before I became absolutely huge.

It wasn't that I wanted to turn the clock back. I didn't have any interest in doing something retro. I think nostalgia can be a real trap for an artist. When you reminisce about the good old days, you naturally see it all through rose-tinted spectacles. In my case in particular, I think that's forgivable, because I probably was literally wearing rose-tinted spectacles at the time, with flashing lights and ostrich feathers attached to them. But if you end up convincing yourself that everything in the past was better than it is now, you might as well give up writing music and retire.

What I did like was the idea of recapturing that spirit, that directness, the same thing that I heard in Ryan Adams' music: stripping things down, just focusing on making music rather than worrying whether it was going to be a hit; going backwards to go forwards.

So that was how we made the next album, *Songs from the West Coast*. It came out in October 2001 and got the best reviews I'd had in years. Bernie wrote powerful, simple, direct lyrics: 'I Want Love', 'Look Ma', 'No Hands', 'American Triangle', which was a very harrowing, angry song about the homophobic murder of Matthew Shephard in Wyoming in 1998. We used a studio in LA, where we hadn't recorded for years, and a new producer, Pat Leonard, who was best known for working with Madonna, but was absolutely steeped in seventies rock. It was hilarious: he was the guy who co-wrote 'Like A Prayer' and 'La Isla Bonita', but he was completely obsessed with Jethro Tull. He'd probably have been happier if Madonna had played a flute while standing on one leg.

It ended up being a very Californian-sounding record. It's just different writing there, rather than making a record in London when it's pissing with rain every day. It's as if the warmth gets into your bones and relaxes you, and the sunlight somehow glows in the music you make. I loved the results, and I've used the same approach on a lot of albums I've made since then: thinking about what I'd done in the past, taking an idea and developing it differently. The follow-up, *Peachtree Road*, was the same: digging into the country and soul influences on *Tumbleweed Connection* and songs like 'Take Me To The Pilot'. *The Captain and the Kid* was a sequel to *Captain Fantastic and the Brown Dirt Cowboy*, with Bernie writing about what had happened to us after we went to America in 1970: everything from that stupid double-decker bus they picked us up from the airport in, to the way our partnership temporarily broke up. *The Diving Board* was me playing with just a bassist and drummer, the same as the original Elton John Band, but doing things I'd never done before, improvising instrumental passages between the songs. On *Wonderful Crazy Night*, I suppose I was thinking a little more of the pop side of *Don't Shoot Me I'm Only the Piano Player* and *Goodbye Yellow Brick Road*. I recorded it in 2015, and the news was just relentless misery: I wanted something light and fun, a sense of escape, lots of bright colours and 12-string guitar.

Those albums weren't flops, but they weren't huge commercial successes either. It's always frustrating at first when that happens to an album you think is brilliant, but you have to take it on the chin. They weren't commercial albums, they didn't have big hit singles built in; *The Diving Board* in particular was incredibly dark and depressing. But they were albums I wanted to make, albums I thought you would be able to play in twenty years' time and still feel proud of. Of course, I would have loved it if they'd gone to Number One, but that wasn't the most important thing anymore. I've had my moment selling zillions of records, and it was fabulous, but from the second it began, I realized it wouldn't last forever. If you believe it will, you can end up in terrible trouble. I honestly think that's one of the things that tipped Michael Jackson over the edge: he was convinced he could make an album bigger than *Thriller*, and was crushed every time it didn't happen.

Just before we started working on *The Captain and the Kid*, I got asked to do a residency at Caesar's Palace in Las Vegas. They had built a huge new theatre, the Colosseum. Celine Dion was playing there, and they wanted me to do a show as well. My immediate thought was that I didn't want to do it. In my head, Las Vegas was still linked to the cabaret circuit I'd escaped in 1967. It was The Rat Pack and Donny and Marie Osmond. It was the Elvis I'd met in 1976 – seven years on the Vegas strip visibly hadn't done *him* much good – and performers in tuxedos talking to the audience: 'You know, one of the wonderful things about showbiz . . .'

But then I started wondering if it was possible to do something completely different with a Vegas show. The photographer and director David LaChapelle had directed a great video for one of the singles from *Songs from the West Coast*, 'This Train Don't Stop There Anymore'. It featured Justin Timberlake lip-synching to the song, dressed as me backstage in the seventies, complete with a John Reid figure in the background, beating up a reporter and knocking a cop's hat off. I loved it and contacted him about getting involved with designing a whole show. I told him to do whatever he wanted, let his imagination run riot, be as outrageous as he wanted to be.

If you know anything at all about David's work, you'll realize this isn't a sentence you say to him lightly. He's brilliant, but at that stage in his career he couldn't take a holiday snap of someone without first getting them to dress up as Jesus and stand on top of a giant stuffed flamingo surrounded by neon signs and muscular boys in snakeskin jockstraps. This is a man who photographed Naomi Campbell as a topless wrestler stamping on a man's face in stiletto-heeled boots, while a crowd of masked men with dwarfism looked on. One of his fashion shoots featured an immaculately dressed model standing next to the corpse of a woman who'd been killed by an air-conditioning unit falling from a window, her head splattered into a bloody mess on the pavement. He somehow managed to convince Courtney Love to pose as Mary Magdalene, with what looked like Kurt Cobain's dead body draped over her knees. For my Vegas show, he designed a set full of neon signs and inflatable bananas and hot dogs and lipsticks: you didn't have to have a filthy imagination to notice that every last one of them looked remarkably like an erect penis. He directed a succession of videos for each song, arty and wild and unapologetically gay. There was a reconstruction of my suicide bid back in Furlong Road in the sixties – it was quite literally a dramatization in so far as it made my suicide bid look hugely dramatic rather than pathetic in the extreme. There were blue teddy bears ice-skating and feeding homoerotic angels honey. There were films of people sniffing cocaine off a boy's naked bum. There was a scene which featured the transsexual model Amanda Lepore naked, in an electric chair, with sparks flying out of her vagina. The show was called *The Red Piano*, an innocuous enough title given what it actually contained.

I thought it was all confirmation that David LaChapelle was a genius. I knew we'd got it right when I spotted a few people walking out in disgust, and when my mother told me she hated it. She came to the first night, expressed her aversion to what was happening onstage by theatrically putting on a pair of dark glasses after about five minutes, then came backstage afterwards with a face like thunder, telling everyone that it was so awful it was going to end my career overnight. Sam Taylor-Wood was there too – David and I knew her through the art world. I loved Sam's photography: I had bought her version of Leonardo da Vinci's *The Last Supper* and got her to direct a video for another single off *Songs from the West Coast*, 'I Want Love'. She couldn't believe my mum's reaction – 'I felt like taking my shoe off,' she said, 'and hitting her over the head with it' – but in fairness, she didn't know my mum that well. The drizzle of criticism that had started in the mid-seventies had continued pretty much unabated ever since: the woman didn't like *anything*. I'd got used to tuning it out, or laughing it off, but other people seemed to get a shock when they came into contact with it.

Some people hated *The Red Piano* because they hadn't got what they expected, which was the whole point. But what they expected proved they hadn't been paying much attention to the rest of my career. The whole thing had been founded on live performances that were outrageous and over-the-top. The Vegas residency worked because it fitted my character, and the way I'd presented myself in the past. It wasn't just a load of shocking visuals grafted on for effect, it was another form of going backwards to go forwards, an updated version of the seventies shows where I'd been introduced onstage by famous porn stars and brought Divine out in full drag. Despite the occasional angry letter to the management and Mum's dire imprecations, they were enormously successful shows, and I think they might have been groundbreaking, too. Maybe they changed the image of Las Vegas a little, made it seem less showbiz, a bit more edgy; it became a place where Lady Gaga or Britney Spears or Bruno Mars could perform without anyone raising an eyebrow.

I n Britain, the law around gay partnerships was changing. At the end of 2005 it became legal for same-sex couples to enter into civil partnerships: marriages in all but name, a couple of minor technical differences aside. David and I talked about it and decided we wanted to be first in line. We'd been together for over ten years, and it was an incredibly important piece of legislation for gay couples. As a result of AIDS, I'd seen so many people lose their partner, then discover they had no legal rights whatsoever as a couple. Their late boyfriend's family would come steaming in, cut them out of the equation entirely – out of greed, or because they never liked the fact that their son or brother was gay – and they would lose everything. Although we had discussed it very soberly and sensibly, I still managed to spring a surprise on David. I proposed to him in the middle of a dinner party we were hosting for the Scissor Sisters at Woodside. I did it properly and got down on one knee. Even though I knew he would say yes, it was still a really lovely moment. We had the rings we'd bought for each other in Paris – the weekend I thought I could remain incognito while wearing the entire Versace spring/summer menswear collection at once – re-blessed.

The new law came in at the start of December, and there was

a statutory fifteen-day waiting period. The first day we could legally become civil partners was 21 December. There was a lot to do. The ceremony itself was to be held at the Guildhall in Windsor, the same place Prince Charles got married to Camilla Parker Bowles. That was going to be a private, intimate event: just me and David, Mum and Derf, David's parents, our dog Arthur, Ingrid and Sandy and our friends Jay Jopling and Sam Taylor-Wood.

The original idea was to have a huge reception in the evening at Pinewood Studios, but the planner involved somehow managed to come back with a budget that even I thought was ridiculous, a not unimpressive feat in itself. I can remember looking at it and thinking, 'I could go mad in the Old Masters department of Sotheby's for that kind of money.' We couldn't find anywhere else to host our reception – it was just before Christmas, everywhere was already booked – so we decided to have the party at Woodside. We erected three interlinked marquees in the grounds: the first was a reception room, the second a dining room and the third housed a huge dance floor. There was going to be live entertainment: James Blunt was going to sing, and so was Joss Stone. There were six hundred guests, and David insisted on doing the seating plans himself. He was really meticulous. One of his pet hates is the kind of party where everyone is thrown together at random and you end up sitting next to a complete stranger. Besides, we needed to exercise a degree of caution, because the guest list was about as eclectic as it was possible to get: there were people invited from absolutely every area of our lives. I was quite proud of the fact that we were having a party where members of the Royal Family had been invited alongside a selection of star performers from the gay porn studio BelAmi, but it seemed perhaps best to ensure they weren't actually sitting together. So David very carefully arranged everything around what he called tribes: there was a table for the sports stars who were coming, a table for people from the fashion world, a table for the former Beatles and their associates. And then

I put my own personal mark on his painstaking efforts by ruining them.

There is a popular theory among psychologists that a person cursed with an addictive personality can get addicted to virtually anything. It was a theory I spent a lot of the early noughties attempting to prove with the aid of a paper shredder we'd bought for the office at Woodside. I'm not sure how my obsession with it began. Partly it was founded on a need for security: we had, after all, had our bank statements plastered all over the front pages of the press because some idiot in John Reid's office had thrown them out intact. But mostly it was because there's something incredibly, indefinably satisfying about using a paper shredder: the sound it makes, the sight of the paper slowly vanishing into it, the tendrils of shredded paper emerging from the other end. I loved it. I could sit in a room filled with priceless works of art and find none of them as compelling as the sight of an old tour itinerary being decimated.

But if I don't know where my obsession began, I can tell you exactly when it ended. It was about two minutes after I saw the state of the room in which David was working on the seating plan – there were sheets of paper all over the place – and decided that here was a great opportunity both to help him out by tidying up a bit and to feed my burgeoning passion for turning old documents into confetti. I can't remember how many pages of David's meticulously arranged seating plan I managed to feed through the shredder before he wandered back into the room and started shouting. I'd never heard him shout like that in my life: David was never a man for volcanic explosions of temper, but it appeared that over the course of our twelve years together, he'd been quietly taking notes from a master of the art and waiting for the right moment to put what he'd learned into action. He began wildly depicting scenes of unmanageable social disaster, in which the BelAmi stars ended up discussing their work on *Boys Like It Big 2* with his mum or my auntie Win. He was shouting so loudly you could hear him all over the house. You could certainly hear him very clearly upstairs in our bedroom. I know this for a fact because that's where I decided to hide, carefully locking the door behind me as a precaution. I didn't really think he was going to smash the paper shredder over my head, but all the same, the noise coming from downstairs suggested it wasn't entirely outside the realm of possibility.

But everything else in the run-up to the ceremony went remarkably smoothly. Our friend Patrick Cox threw us an incredible joint stag party at a Soho gay club called Too 2 Much. It was hilarious, a full cabaret performance. Paul O'Grady hosted the whole thing and sang a duet with Janet Street-Porter. Sir Ian McKellen came dressed as Widow Twankey. Bryan Adams sang and Sam Taylor-Wood did a version of 'Love To Love You Baby'. There were video messages from Elizabeth Taylor and Bill Clinton in between performances by the famous New York drag act Kiki and Herb and Eric McCormack, who played Will in *Will and Grace*, and was an old schoolfriend of David's back in Ontario. Jake Shears from the Scissor Sisters got so overexcited he ended up taking all his clothes off and demonstrating the pole-dancing skills he'd learned working in New York strip clubs before the band became successful. It was quite a night.

On the morning of the ceremony we woke up to a beautiful winter's day, sunny and crisp. There was a sort of magical Christmas Morning atmosphere in the house, amid all the bustle. We had guests staying with us: David's family had arrived from Canada; my old schoolfriend Keith Francis had flown all the way from Australia with his wife. Outside, there were people putting finishing touches to the marquees and checking the fairy lights in the trees. The night before, we had watched the TV news about the first civil partnerships to take place in Northern Ireland – there was a shorter registration period there – and how the couples had faced protests outside their ceremonies, evangelical Christians bellowing at them about 'sodomite propaganda', people throwing flour bombs and eggs. I was genuinely worried – if that was what was happening to everyday people, what kind of reception would a really famous gay couple get? David assured me everything would be OK: the police were fully aware of the threat and had set up an area for protesters, where they couldn't ruin the day. But now, the news from Windsor was that there were crowds lining the streets and a party atmosphere. No one wanted to attack us: instead, people had turned up with banners and cakes and presents for us. There were news trucks from CNN and the BBC parked outside, reporters doing pieces to camera.

I turned the TV off and told David not to watch anything either. I just wanted us to stay in the moment, together, without any distractions. I'd been married before, of course, but this was different. I was truly being myself, being allowed to express my love for another man in a way that would have seemed beyond comprehension when I realized I was gay, or when I first came out in *Rolling Stone* – partly because no one ever talked about gay marriage or civil partnerships in 1976, and partly because, back then, I seemed no more capable of ending up in a long-term relationship than I did of flying to Mars. And yet here we were. It felt intense: not just personal, but historic, too, like we were part of the world changing for the better. I was as happy as I could ever remember being.

And that was the moment my mother turned up, in character as a raving sociopath.

The first sign that there was something wrong was when she wouldn't get out of the car. She and Derf had arrived at Woodside as planned, but then point-blank refused to come into the house. Despite various entreaties to join us, they just sat there, stony-faced. David's family had to troop out to say hello through the car window. What the fuck was the matter with her? I didn't get a chance to ask. The security arrangements for the ceremony were that everyone was supposed to be travelling together to the Guildhall in a convoy of cars. But Mum announced that she wouldn't be joining the convoy, and nor would she be coming to the private lunch we were having at Woodside after the civil partnership, and suddenly drove off.

Oh, great. The most important day of my life and one of Mum's moods appeared to be upon us, the ones I'd lived in terror of when I was young. I'd inherited some of her capacity to sulk myself. The difference was that I snapped out of it quickly: I would realize what I was doing – shit, I'm not just behaving like an idiot, I'm *behaving like my mother* – and rush around issuing desperate apologies to everyone concerned. Mum never snapped out of it, never seemed contrite, never appeared to think she was in the wrong or behaving badly. The best you could hope for was a terrible argument – in which, as ever, she had to have the last word – followed by an awkward smoothing over, a shaky truce that lasted until she went off again. As the years passed, she had elevated sulking to an epic, awesome level. She was the Cecil B. DeMille of bad moods, the Tolstoy of taking a huff. I'm exaggerating only slightly. We're talking about a woman who didn't speak to her own sister for ten years as a result of an argument over whether Auntie Win had put skimmed milk in her tea or not. A woman whose dedication to sulking was such that, at its height, it literally caused her to pack her entire life up and leave the country. It happened in the eighties; she fell out with me and one of Derf's sons from his first marriage at the same time and, as a result, emigrated to Menorca. She would rather move to a foreign country than back down or apologize. There's not an enormous amount of point in trying to reason with someone like that.

I watched her car disappear down the drive and found myself

wishing she was in Menorca now. Or on the moon. Anywhere but heading to my civil partnership ceremony, which I had a terrible feeling she was going to try her best to stink up. I hadn't wanted her there in the first place. I had a nagging fear that she was going to do something like this, just as I had when I got married to Renate. That was one of the reasons I'd insisted on getting married so quickly, in Australia – I hadn't wanted Mum there. But I had changed my mind a few weeks beforehand, reasoning that not even Mum was crazy enough to pull a stunt like this. It appeared I was wrong.

She didn't – *couldn't* – spoil the day. It was too magical, with the crowds outside the Guildhall cheering, and later, the cars arriving at Woodside and what seemed like everyone I knew and loved climbing out to join the party, like your life flashing before your eyes in the loveliest of circumstances: Graham Taylor and Muff and Zena Winwood, Ringo Starr and George Martin, Tony King and Billie Jean King. But, in fairness to Mum, she absolutely gave it her best shot. When David and I exchanged our vows, she started talking, very loudly, over the top of us: rattling on about how she didn't like the venue and how she couldn't imagine getting married in a place like this. When the time came for the witnesses to sign the civil partnership licence, she signed her name, snapped, 'It's done, then,' slammed the pen down and stormed off. It was bizarre; my mood kept switching from complete euphoria to wild panic at what she was going to do next. Worse, I couldn't do anything about it. I knew from experience that trying to talk to her would just be lighting the blue touchpaper on a huge row that would ruin everything, and, better still, could quite easily take place in front of the world's media or six hundred guests. I wasn't keen on the coverage of Britain's most high-profile civil partnership featuring a section where Elton John and his mother entertained the nation by screaming at each other on the steps of the Windsor Guildhall.

At the party in the evening, she tutted and groaned and rolled her eyes during the speeches. She complained about the seating arrangements: apparently she wasn't close enough to me and David – 'you might as well have stuck me in Siberia' – although it was hard to see how she could have been any closer without actually sitting in our laps. I avoided her as the evening wore on, which was easy – there were so many friends to speak to, who wanted to wish us well. But out of the corner of my eye I could see a steady stream of people going to speak to her, then coming away very quickly, wearing extremely long faces. She was vile to everyone, no matter how innocuous their attempts at conversation. Jay Jopling made the fatal mistake of saying to her, 'Isn't this a lovely day?' which apparently counted as merciless provocation. 'I'm glad you fucking well think so,' snapped Mum in response. Tony King went to say hello – he'd known Mum and Derf for years – and, for his trouble, was informed that he was looking old. At one point, Sharon Osbourne sidled up to me as I was looking on.

'I know she's your mother,' she muttered, 'but I want to kill her.'

I didn't find out what had provoked all this until much later. She told the press she was upset because she'd been told she wasn't allowed in any of the photographs because she wasn't wearing a hat, which was just nonsense. David's mum had wanted a hat for the ceremony, he'd offered to take her and my mum shopping, but my mum had said she didn't want one. Fairly obviously this wasn't a problem at all, given that *she was in all the family photographs*. It turned out that David's parents knew what the problem was with her all along, but they didn't tell us before the ceremony, because they didn't want to upset us. They had rung her as soon as they arrived in the UK, having always got on well with Mum and Derf. They'd even gone on holidays together. My mother had told them they all had to work together to stop the civil partnership going ahead. She didn't approve of two men 'getting married', as she put it. She thought it was wrong that gay couples should be treated in the same way as straight couples. Everyone she had spoken to was horrified by the very idea. It was going to hurt my career. David's mum told her she was nuts, that their kids were doing something amazing and she should support them. My mother put the phone down on her.

She repeated the same line to me a couple of years later, in the middle of a blazing row. It didn't make sense. Mum had always been incredibly hard work, but she had never been homophobic. She was supportive when I told her I was gay and she had been unflappable when the press cornered her after I came out in *Rolling Stone*, telling them she thought I was brave and she didn't care if I was gay or straight. Why would she suddenly decide she had a problem with my sexuality thirty years later? Maybe she had all along, and had somehow managed to suppress it until now. As ever, I think the real problem was that she hated anyone being closer to me than she was. She'd been cold towards most of my boyfriends, and cold towards Renate, but this was on a different level. She knew the boyfriends were never going to turn into a long-term relationship: I was too erratic, because of all the coke I was taking. Even though I married Renate, Mum believed deep down it wasn't going to last, because she knew I was gay. But now I was sober and settled with a man I was deeply in love with. I'd found a life partner, and the civil partnership underlined that. She couldn't cope with the thought of the umbilical cord finally being cut: that idea had become so all-consuming that she couldn't see past it, didn't care about anything else, including the fact that I was finally happy.

Well, that was her tough luck. I *was* finally happy, and I wasn't going to change that for anybody, no matter how many moods they took. When she realized that, perhaps she would come round.

★

I had plenty to be happy about. Not just in my personal life: between the Vegas shows, *Billy Elliot* and the new albums, I was enjoying making music so much that my enthusiasm became infectious. David started getting interested in the stuff that had inspired me at the start of my career, artists and albums that he was a little too young to have experienced first-hand. He would make up iPod playlists of things I recommended to him. He took them with him to play in our hotel room when we went on holiday to South Africa, with our friends Ingrid and Sandy.

If you want an example of how a deep, lifelong friendship can be forged from the most unpromising start, Ingrid and I were it. I'd first met her when she was writing a profile about me for *Interview* magazine, which she edited. Or rather, I'd gone out of my way to avoid meeting her when she was writing a profile about me: I was in a foul mood and cancelled our interview. She rang back and told me she was coming anyway. I told her not to bother. She told me she was coming anyway. I told her to fuck off. She put the phone down and materialized at my hotel room door in what seemed like a matter of minutes. A matter of minutes later, I had fallen in love with her. Ingrid had balls. Ingrid had opinions. And Ingrid's opinions were worth listening to, because Ingrid was clearly as smart as hell. She'd been made the editor of *Artforum* magazine when she was twenty-seven and seemed to know everything there was to know about – and everyone there was to know in – the worlds of art and fashion. She took no shit from anybody, including, it had now become apparent, me. She was incredibly funny. By the end of the afternoon, she not only had her interview, she had a commitment from me to write a column for her magazine, and I had the same feeling I had when I met Gianni Versace for the first time: if he had seemed like my long-lost brother, Ingrid was my missing sister. We rang each other all the time; I loved talking to her, partly because she was a fabulous gossip, partly because whenever you spoke to her you learned something, but mostly because she always told you the truth, even if the truth wasn't what you wanted to hear.

Ingrid was originally from South Africa but had left when she was a kid. Her mother was in danger of being arrested for her involvement in the anti-apartheid movement, so the family moved first to Edinburgh then New York. But Ingrid loved South Africa, which is how she and Sandy ended up accompanying us on the holiday. One evening we were getting ready for dinner, with one of David's early seventies iPod playlists providing the soundtrack. While he was in the shower, 'Back To The Island' by Leon Russell came on. It caught me completely off guard. It's a beautiful song, but it's incredibly sad: about loss and regret and time passing. I sat on the bed and I started to cry. Leon coming into the dressing room at the Troubadour, the tours I did opening for him, and Eric Clapton, and Poco: it all suddenly seemed a very long time ago. I'd played this song over and over when I lived on Tower Grove Drive. I could still see it in my mind's eye. The dark wood of the interior; the suede on the master bedroom's walls; the way the sunlight fell on the swimming pool in the morning. A crowd of people stumbling through the front door after the Whiskey or the Rainbow or Le Restaurant finally threw us out; the clouds of heady Californian grass and the glasses filled with bourbon, and the blue eyes of a guy I lured up to the games room, who said he was straight but whose smile suggested he was persuadable. Dusty Springfield arriving back after a night touring the city's gay clubs and falling out of the car onto the drive. The afternoon Tony King and I tried mescaline and ended up with the screaming horrors, after someone in our party raided the kitchen and decided, in their altered state, that they'd invent a new kind of Bloody Mary, with a lump of raw liver on the side of the glass. Just the sight of it set us off.

But my memories of LA in the seventies were filled with ghosts. All the old Hollywood legends I'd gone out of my way to meet there had died of old age. So had Ray Charles. I'd been the last person to record a song with him, for an album of duets, thirty-four years after he'd invited me to appear on American television for the first time. We sang 'Sorry Seems To Be The Hardest Word', sitting down – he was too weak to stand. I asked the engineers for a copy of the tape, not so much for the music, but just to have a record of us chatting between takes. I suppose I wanted proof that it had really happened, that a kid who'd dreamed of being Ray Charles actually ended up talking to him like a friend. But there were other ghosts, too, people who didn't die of old age: people who AIDS took young, people who'd drunk or drugged themselves to death. People who'd died in accidents, people who'd been killed, people who'd died of the things that kill you in your fifties and sixties if you're unlucky. Dee Murray, my old bass player. Doug Weston, who ran the Troubadour. Bill Graham. Gus Dudgeon. John Lennon, George Harrison and Harry Nilsson. Keith Moon and Dusty Springfield. Endless boys I'd fallen in love with, or thought I'd fallen in love with, on the dance floor at the After Dark.

When he came back from the bathroom and saw me in tears, David's face fell.

'Oh God,' he sighed, 'what's the matter?'

By now bitterly experienced in dealing with my moods, his immediate thought was that I didn't like some minor aspect of the holiday and was going to start yelling about how we had to leave at once. I said it was nothing like that: I was just thinking about the past. On the iPod, Leon was still singing: 'Well all the fun has died, it's raining in my heart, I know down in my soul I'm really going to miss you'. God, that man could sing. What had happened to him? I hadn't heard anyone mention his name in years. I went to the phone and called my friend Johnny Barbis in LA and asked him if he could track Leon down. He came back with a Nashville number. I called it, and a voice answered. It sounded more gravelly than I remembered, but it was definitely him – that same Oklahoma drawl. I asked how he was. He said he was in bed, watching *Days of Our Lives* on TV: 'I'm all right. Just about making ends meet.' That was one way of putting it. Leon had made some bad business decisions, he had a lot of ex-wives, and times had changed. Now he was touring anywhere that would have him. One of the finest musicians and songwriters in the world, and he was playing sports bars and pubs, beer festivals and motorbike conventions, towns I'd never heard of in Missouri and Connecticut. I told him I was in the middle of nowhere in Africa, and I was listening to his music and thinking about the past. I thanked him for everything he'd done for me and told him how important his music was in my life. He sounded genuinely touched.

'Well, that's real nice of you,' he said. 'Thank you so much.'

After we'd finished talking, I put the phone down and looked at it. Something wasn't right. I couldn't explain it, but I just knew that wasn't why I had called him. I picked the phone up and dialled his number again. He laughed when he picked up.

'My God, forty-five years I don't hear from you and now twice in ten minutes?'

I asked him if he wanted to make an album, both of us, together. There was a long silence.

'Are you serious?' he said. 'Do you think I can do it?' He sighed. 'I'm really old.'

I told him I was pretty old, too, and if I could, he could, if he'd like to.

He laughed again. 'The hell I would – yeah.'

It wasn't an act of charity. It was more pure indulgence for me: if you'd told me in 1970 that I'd one day make a record with Leon Russell I would have laughed at you. And it wasn't always easy. He had mentioned having some health issues on the phone, but I didn't realize how sick Leon was until he arrived at the studio in LA. He looked like the ailing patriarch in a Tennessee Williams play: a long white beard, dark glasses and a cane. He struggled to walk. He would sit in a La-Z-Boy recliner in the studio for a couple of hours a day and sing and play. That was all he could manage, but what he did in those two hours was incredible. There were moments when I wondered if his contributions to the album were going to be released posthumously. One day, his nose started running: it was fluid leaking from his brain. He was rushed into hospital for surgery and treated for heart failure and pneumonia while he was there.

But we finished the record. We called it *The Union* and it went Top Five in the US. We toured together in the autumn of 2010, playing 15,000-seat arenas, places Leon said he'd never seen the inside of in decades. Some nights he had to come onstage in a wheelchair, but it didn't make any difference to how he sounded. He killed it every time.

And Leon finally got his due as a result of that album. He got a new record deal and was made a member of the Rock and Roll Hall of Fame. I was so pleased for him that I momentarily forgot my vow never to darken its doors again, and offered to give his induction speech. He made money and bought himself a new bus and toured around the world in bigger and better venues than he'd played for years. He was touring until the day he died in 2016. If you didn't see him, I'm sorry: you missed out. Leon Russell was the greatest.

sixteen

The first time it happened was in South Africa in 2009, at a drop-in centre for kids living with HIV and its after-effects. It was in the centre of Soweto, a place where orphaned children and kids who'd been forced to step up and become the head of their household could go and get things they needed, whether that was a hot meal, or counselling, or just help with their homework. We were visiting it because it was funded by the Elton John AIDS Foundation and they had put on a presentation for us: the women who ran the place and the children who benefited from it, explaining how it worked. A small boy wearing the kind of brightly patterned shirt that Nelson Mandela had made famous presented me with a little spoon, a symbol of the South African sugar industry. But then he wouldn't go back and sit with the other kids. I don't know why – he didn't have a clue who I was – but he just seemed to take a shine to me. He was called Noosa, and he stuck to my side for the rest of the visit. I held his hand and pulled faces and made him laugh. He was adorable. I wondered what his life in the outside world might be like: God, the horror stories you heard in South Africa about how AIDS had devastated lives that were no picnic to start off with. Where was he going when he left here? Back to what?

But looking at him, I realized I felt something that wasn't just pity or fondness. There was a flicker of something else there, something that was more powerful than just 'awww', something I couldn't quite put my finger on. I wandered over to David.

'This boy's just wonderful,' I said. 'He's an orphan. Maybe he needs support. What do you think?'

David looked completely baffled. He had broached the subject of starting a family before – the idea of a gay couple adopting children was nothing like as anomalous as it had once been. But every time he mentioned the idea, I had presented him with a list of objections so long it just wore him into submission.

I adored kids. I've got umpteen godsons and goddaughters – some of them are famous, like Sean Lennon and Brooklyn and Romeo Beckham, and some of them aren't known at all, like the son of my AA sponsor – and I love them very much. But having your own children was a different matter entirely. I was too old. Too set in my ways. Too absent – always off on tour. Too keen on porcelain and photographs and modern art, none of which respond well to being knocked over, or drawn on with crayon, or smeared with Marmite, or any of the other things small children are famously keen on doing. Too busy to find the room in my life that was clearly needed to be a parent. I wasn't being grumpy, I was just being honest. But really, my own childhood was at the root of every objection. Bringing up children was an incredible challenge, and I knew from personal experience how awful it was if you fucked that challenge up. You obviously want to believe you wouldn't make the same mistakes as your own mum and dad, but what if you did? I couldn't live with the thought of making my own children as miserable as I had been.

All those protests, and now here I was suggesting we look into adopting an orphan from Soweto. No wonder David looked baffled; I was too. What the hell was going on? I had no idea, but *something* had definitely just happened, completely out of my control. It was almost as if a real paternal instinct had finally kicked in in my sixties, the same way my libido had unexpectedly arrived, years after everyone else's, when I was twenty-one.

Whatever it was, it didn't matter. We made some enquiries and quickly found out that the little boy was in a relatively good place. He lived with his grandmother and sister and another relation, and they were well looked after, a tight-knit family – so tight-knit that when Noosa attached himself to me, his sister had burst into tears, thinking we were going to take him away from her. That settled it. We wouldn't help him at all by uprooting him from his culture and his own identity and bringing him to the UK: it was better to invest in his future in his own country. I saw him a few more times, when I went back to South Africa to perform or to do work with the AIDS Foundation, and he was still completely adorable, and clearly very happy.

It was an odd incident, but I put it out of my mind, knowing that we had done the right thing. I retreated back to my usual position regarding children. I don't think either of us brought up the subject again. And then, that same year, we went to Ukraine.

The orphanage was in Donetsk, a big industrial city in the centre of the country. It was specifically for children aged one to eleven, a place where they could be monitored to see if they developed HIV – not every child born to a mother with HIV tests positive. If they did, they got antiretroviral treatment, care and support. We were being shown round, handing out food, nappies and school-books – not lavish gifts; stuff they really, really needed – to the care workers and the kids. I played 'Circle Of Life' for them, on a piano I'd donated. Just afterwards, a tiny boy ran straight over to me, and I picked him up and hugged him. They told me he was called Lev. He was fourteen months old but looked younger – he was so small. His story was horrendous. His father was a convicted murderer who'd strangled a teenage girl. His mother was HIV positive, a chronic alcoholic who had tuberculosis and couldn't look after her children. They didn't know whether he had HIV yet, although he had an older half-brother called Artem who had tested positive for the disease. Lev had blond hair and brown eyes, and a grin that seemed completely at odds with his surroundings and with the hand that life had dealt him. I just melted every time he smiled at me.

I didn't put him down for the rest of the time we were there. Whatever had happened in Soweto happened again, only more intensely: there was an immediate bond, some kind of very powerful connection. I was in a raw emotional state anyway. A few days before, Guy Babylon, who'd played keyboards in my band for eleven years, had suddenly died. He was only fifty-two, he seemed perfectly fit and healthy but had a heart attack while swimming. It was a reminder that you only get so long, that you never know what's around the corner. Maybe that gave me some real clarity about what was important to me about life. Why try and deny how you really feel, deep down, about something as fundamental as fatherhood?

The rest of the party moved on and I stayed behind in the room, playing with Lev. I didn't feel I could leave. Eventually David came back to see where I was. As soon as he walked into the room, I started gushing.

'This little boy is remarkable, he's called Lev, he's an orphan. He found me, I didn't find him. I think this is a calling. I think the universe is sending us a message, and we should adopt him.'

David looked even more stunned than he had in Soweto. Clearly, he hadn't expected his simple enquiry of 'what are you doing?' to be answered with a load of stuff about higher callings and messages from the universe. But he could see I was deadly serious. He told me to slow down and keep things low-key for the moment – we had to find out more about Lev's situation, about his family, about whether he could leave the orphanage before they knew whether or not he was HIV positive.

I carried Lev around for the rest of the day. I was still holding him when we were ushered outside for a press conference in a makeshift marquee. I deposited him in David's lap while I answered the reporters' questions. The last one was about the fact that I'd said I never wanted children: had seeing kids that needed homes in the orphanage changed my mind? Here was a perfect opportunity for me to demonstrate that I'd fully grasped what David had said about the need to keep any thoughts I had on Lev's future low-key. Instead, I blurted out that my mind had changed, that the little boy sitting with David in the front row had stolen our hearts, and that I would love to adopt him and his brother if it was possible.

You may recall a few chapters ago that I explained why I'm pleased I became famous in an era before record companies and managers forced artists to get media training and watch what they say: that I'm proud of always giving straight answers and speaking my mind. Perhaps now I should qualify that statement by noting that there are a couple of points in my career where media training has suddenly seemed like a very good idea indeed, where I've wished that, for once in my life, I just answered a question by saying something unbelievably boring and bland and evasive, rather than telling the truth. This was definitely one of those points. I realized I shouldn't have said it as soon as it came out of my mouth, not least because I noticed David lower his head, close his eyes and mutter something that looked very much like the words 'oh shit'.

'That comment,' he complained, as we were driven back to the airport, 'is going to go everywhere, in minutes.'

He was right. By the time we landed in Britain, his BlackBerry was packed with texts and voice messages from friends, congratulating us on our wonderful news, which meant it had already hit the media. Certain sections of the British press couldn't have reacted more negatively if I'd said I harboured a pathological hatred for children and was planning on personally burning down the Donetsk orphanage later that night. The *Daily Mail* and the *Sun* immediately dispatched journalists to Ukraine. One got hold of a government minister who said that adoption was impossible, because we were a gay couple and, besides, I was too old. Another visited Lev's mother, bought her vodka and took her to the orphanage for a photo opportunity, which automatically set any adoption process back by a year: in order for a child to become a ward of state, they had to have been in an orphanage for twelve months without a visit from any family member. The journalist either didn't know, or didn't care – they hadn't thought about it. There was something really horrible, if inevitable, about the way the story became entirely about me and David, and not the children involved. It was hard not to think that if I hadn't said anything at the press conference, none of this would have happened. Perhaps it would have made no difference at all. But we would never know.

We kept trying, looking at the logistics of adoption, but it became obvious that it wouldn't work. We could have appealed to the European Court of Justice, but there didn't seem to be much point – Ukraine wasn't part of the EU. We had contacted a psychologist, asking about the emotional process of introducing kids who'd lived in an orphanage into a family, and something he said really brought us up short. He told us he believed any child who had been in an orphanage for longer than eighteen months would be irreversibly psychologically damaged. They wouldn't have experienced real nurturing, they wouldn't have been picked up and held and loved enough, and that would affect them in a way they would never recover from. So we gave up trying to find a way to adopt Lev and Artem and, working with a charity in Ukraine, we concentrated on getting them out of there before their eighteen months was up. Their mother died, and their father went back to prison, but they had a relatively young grandmother and it was arranged that they should go and live with her.

Through the charity, we quietly provided them with financial support. We were advised to keep it anonymous – so anonymous that not even Lev and Artem's grandmother would know we were helping – because of the way the media had descended on them: if they found out I was their benefactor, there was a chance they would never leave the kids alone. The help we gave wasn't extravagant Elton John-scale support, which would have served only to isolate them more. But we made sure they had enough of the things that the charity told us they needed: decent furniture, food, books for school, legal support. When the Russians invaded that part of Ukraine, we worked with the same charity that had funded the orphanage to evacuate them to Kiev. We'll always keep an eye on them.

Last year, when I went back to Ukraine with the AIDS Foundation, I saw Lev and Artem. They walked into the room in their matching hoodies and we hugged and cried and talked and talked. So much time had passed. Lev was grown up now. He was a funny, cheeky, charming ten-year-old. But in one way, nothing had changed at all: I still felt exactly the same connection to him as I had the day I first met him. I still wished we could have adopted him. But I knew his grandmother had done a great job.

We'd tried and failed to become adoptive parents. It was disheartening but, this time, the paternal feeling didn't fade at all. It was like someone had jammed a switch on: I now wanted to have kids as much as David. But it wasn't a straightforward process. Adoption was still incredibly tricky for a gay couple, and the other option, surrogacy, was pretty fraught too.

Transactional surrogacy is technically against the law in the UK, although you can have a child in a country where it's legal, then bring them back to live in Britain. We spoke to our doctor in California and were introduced to a company called California Fertility Partners. The process is incredibly convoluted: there are egg donor agencies and surrogacy agencies, and there are tricky legal processes involved, especially if you live abroad. The more we looked into it, the more complicated it seemed to become. After a while, my head was swimming with hormone therapies and blastocysts, embryo transfers and parenting orders and egg donors.

We were advised to find a surrogate who was unmarried – there were cases in the past of married surrogates' husbands making a legal claim to the child even though they had no biological connection. We decided to both contribute to the sperm sample, so we wouldn't know which one of us was the biological parent. We were advised that everything had to take place under a veil of strict secrecy. We were to remain anonymous to the surrogate, adopting the guise of Edward and James, an English gay couple who were vaguely described as 'working in the entertainment business', while everyone else involved had to be bound by strict legal non-disclosure agreements. Having recently received a powerful lesson in the benefits of keeping my mouth shut, I thought that made perfect sense. When the media had found out the identity of Matthew Broderick and Sarah Jessica Parker's surrogate, the poor woman had been forced into hiding: the last thing anyone wanted was an expectant mother being harassed by the press.

Surrogacy involves a real leap of faith. Once you've selected your egg donor and left your sperm sample at the fertility clinic, your fate is entirely in the hands of others. We were incredibly lucky. We found an amazing doctor called Guy Ringler, a gay man who specializes in fertility for LGBT parents. And we found the most remarkable surrogate. She lived north of San Francisco and had been a surrogate before. She was completely uninterested in celebrity or money: all she cared about was helping loving couples to have children. She worked out who Edward and James really were about three months into her pregnancy and she didn't bat an eyelid. David drove up to meet her, outside of her hometown in case he was recognized. It was when he came back, gushing about how incredible she was, that everything suddenly became very real. I didn't feel any trepidation or doubt about our decision; no panic, no 'what have we done?' – just excitement and anticipation.

The rest of the pregnancy passed in a blur. The baby was due on 21 December 2010. We became very close to the surrogate, her boyfriend and her family. The more I got to know them, the more I started to hate the phrase 'transactional surrogacy'. It sounded so clinical and mercenary, and there was nothing clinical or mercenary about these people at all: they were kind and loving and genuinely delighted to be helping us achieve a dream. We arranged to hire a nanny, the same one who had looked after our friend Elizabeth Hurley's son. We knew her because Liz had stayed at Woodside after she had given birth to keep out of the media's glare. We began creating a nursery at our apartment in LA, but it all had to be done under the veil of secrecy: everything we bought was sent to our office in LA, taken out of its packaging and wrapped so it looked like a Christmas present for David or me when it arrived at our home.

When the due date drew close, the surrogate and her family moved to a hotel in LA. Ingrid and Sandy, who we had asked to be godparents, flew in for the birth. We had planned to make a surprise announcement that we had become a family at a Christmas lunch for our friends in LA, but we had to keep putting the lunch off because the baby was late. Eventually, the surrogate got sick of sleepless nights, back pain and swollen ankles and took decisive action. There was a restaurant in LA, on Coldwater Canyon, that served a watercress soup reputed to induce labour. The reputation was obviously fully deserved: we got a phone call on the afternoon of Christmas Eve, telling us to rush to the Cedars-Sinai hospital.

Still concerned about the veil of secrecy, I arrived in disguise, dressed down and wearing a cap. As it turned out, I could have arrived at the hospital in the four-foot-high Doc Martens I wore in *Tommy* and my old glasses that lit up in the shape of the word ELTON and no one would have noticed, because no one was there. The place was absolutely deserted. The maternity ward looked like the hotel in *The Shining*. We learned that no one wants to have a baby at Christmas: they either induce or have caesareans to avoid being in hospital over the holidays. No one, that is, except us. We had deliberately tried to time the birth so that it would happen when I wasn't working or away on tour. So there wasn't a soul around, except for us and one other woman in the room next door, an Australian who had twins. And our son, who arrived at two thirty in the morning on Christmas Day.

I cut the umbilical cord – I'm normally incredibly squeamish, but the emotion of what had happened completely took over. We took our shirts off so the baby would have skin-to-skin contact. We called him Zachary Jackson Levon. Everybody always assumes the last name came from the song Bernie and I wrote on *Madman Across the Water*, but they're wrong: he's named after Lev. He had to be. Lev was like an angel, a messenger, who taught me something about myself that I didn't really understand. Lev was the reason we were there, on a maternity ward, holding our son, knowing that our lives had just completely changed forever.

As well as Ingrid and Sandy, we asked Lady Gaga to be Zachary's godmother. I had started collaborating with a lot of younger artists, everyone from the Scissor Sisters to Kanye West. It was always incredibly flattering to be asked to work with people who weren't even born when my career took off, but of all the young artists I collaborated with, I had a special bond with Gaga. I loved her from the moment I clapped eyes on her: the music she made, the outrageous clothes, the sense of theatre and spectacle. We were very different people – she was a young woman from New York, barely into her twenties – but as soon as we met, it was obvious we were cut from exactly the same cloth: I called her the Bastard Daughter of Elton John. I loved her so much, I got myself into yet more trouble with the press. I'd always got on fine with Madonna. I used to make fun of her for lip-synching onstage, but the problem really started when she ran Gaga down on an American chat show. I got that Gaga's single 'Born This Way' definitely sounded similar to 'Express Yourself', but I couldn't see why she was so ungracious and nasty about it, rather than taking it as a compliment when a new generation of artists was influenced by her, particularly when she claims to be a champion for women. I think it's just wrong – an established artist shouldn't kick down a younger artist right at the start of their career. I was furious and I said some pretty horrible things about her to a TV interviewer in Australia, a guy I'd known since the seventies called Molly Meldrum. You can tell from the footage that it wasn't part of the interview, that I was just sounding off to an old friend between takes – you can hear people moving cameras around to set up the next shot while we're talking – but they broadcast it anyway, which brought that particular old friendship to a very swift conclusion. Still, I shouldn't have said it. I apologized afterwards when I bumped into her in a restaurant in France and she was very gracious about it. Gaga turned out to be a great godmother: she would turn up backstage and insist on giving Zachary his bath while dressed in full Gaga regalia, which was quite an incredible sight.

In fact, everything about fatherhood is incredible. I haven't got any great insights into being a father that you haven't already heard a hundred times before. All those clichés about it grounding you, changing the way you look at the world, experiencing a love unlike any other love you've felt in your life, how awe-inspiring it is to see a person forming in front of your eyes – all are true. But perhaps I felt all those things more keenly because I never thought I would be a father until quite late on in my life. If you had tried to tell the Elton John of the seventies or eighties that he could find more fulfilment on a deep and profound level in changing a nappy than in writing a song or playing a gig, you would probably have had to exit the room at high speed immediately afterwards, with hurled crockery flying past your ears. And yet it was true: the responsibility was huge, but there is nothing about being a father that I don't love. I even found the toddler tantrums weirdly charming. *You think you're being difficult, my little sausage? Have I ever told you about the time I drank eight vodka martinis, took all my clothes off in front of a film crew and then broke my manager's nose?*

We knew we wanted another child almost straight away. It was largely because we loved being parents so much, but there was more to it than that. However normal we tried to make our child's life, the fact is that it was never going to be entirely normal, because of what one of his parents did for a living and everything that comes attached. Because, before he started school, Zachary always came with me on tour; he had been around the world twice by the time he was four years old. He'd been bathed by Lady Gaga and jigged up and down on Eminem's knee. He'd stood in the wings of shows at Las Vegas and had his photograph taken by paparazzi, which, to my delight, he endured rather than enjoyed: a chip off the old block, there. These are not the normal experiences of a toddler. There's obviously a degree of privilege that goes with being Elton John's son, but you would be fooling yourself if you didn't think there was also a degree of burden. I had hated being an only child, and it seemed right that he should have a sibling who he could share with, who would understand his experience of life. We used the same surrogate, same agencies, same egg donor and everything fell perfectly into place again: Elijah was born on 11 January 2013.

The only person who didn't seem delighted for us was my mother. My relationship with her had always been tough going, but it never really recovered after our civil partnership ceremony in 2005. As usual, things got smoothed over as best I could, but something about her had definitely changed, or at least been amplified. The drizzle of criticism turned into a constant downpour. She seemed to go out of her way to tell me how much she hated what I was doing. If I made a new album, it was a load of rubbish: why didn't I try to be more like Robbie Williams? Couldn't I write songs like that anymore? If I bought a new painting, it was bleedin' ugly and she could have painted something better herself. If I played a charity gig, it was the most boring thing she'd ever sat through in her life, the evening only saved from complete disaster by someone else's performance, which had stolen the show. If the AIDS Foundation held a glittering fundraising dinner packed with stars, it was evidence that I was only interested in fame and kissing celebrities' arses.

For variety, she threw in the occasional thunderclap of real anger. I never knew when they were coming or what was going to provoke them. Spending time with her was like inviting an unexploded bomb to lunch or on holiday with you: I was always on edge, wondering what was going to set her off. Once it was the fact that I'd bought a kennel for the dogs we kept at the house in Nice. Once it was *Billy Elliot*, apparently the only thing I'd done in about ten years that she thought was any good. The musical had really taken off in a way that no one involved in it had predicted, not just in the UK but in countries where people had barely heard of the Miners' Strike or the impact of Thatcherism on the British manufacturing industry: the story at its heart turned out to be universal. Mum went to see it in London dozens of times, until one afternoon, when the box office misplaced her tickets for the matinee and took five minutes to find them, something she decided I had deliberately, meticulously planned in an attempt to humiliate her. Luckily, I followed *Billy Elliot* up with *The Vampire Lestat*, a musical Bernie and I wrote together, which bombed – everything went wrong, from the timing, to the staging, to the dialogue – and normal service was resumed: it provided my mother with the unmissable opportunity to inform me that she had known from the start it would be a terrible flop.

I still tried to laugh it all off, or ignore it, but it wasn't that easy. If she wanted a row, Mum always knew which buttons to press, because she had installed the buttons in the first place. She still had the ability to make me feel as if I were a terrified ten-year-old back in Pinner, like everything was my fault: I was constantly in fear, metaphorically speaking, of getting a smack. The result was exactly what you would expect: I started to actively avoid her. On my sixtieth birthday, I had a huge party in New York at St John the Divine, the same cathedral where I later saw Aretha Franklin sing for the last time. Mum had been one of the guests of honour at my fiftieth, the famous fancy dress party where she and Derf came as the Queen and the Duke of Edinburgh, and I wore a Louis XVI costume with a train held by two men dressed as Cupid and a wig so huge I had to travel there in the back of a furniture van. I had ample time to reconsider the wisdom of this idea when the furniture van got stuck in a traffic jam for an hour and a half. This time, I decided not to invite her. I knew she would come and pour cold water on the whole event; she wouldn't enjoy herself and nor would I. I made an excuse about it being too far for her to travel – she hadn't been well – but the truth was, I just didn't want her there.

By the time Zachary was born, we weren't speaking at all. Mum had moved beyond just constantly criticizing, into going out of her way to try and be hurtful. She had delighted in telling me she was still friends with John Reid after our business relationship collapsed: 'I don't know what you're upset about,' she snapped, when I pointed out that this seemed a bit disloyal. 'It's only money.' That was certainly one way of describing what had happened. But the final row came when my PA, Bob Halley, left. We'd been together since the seventies but the relationship had become strained. Bob enjoyed a very lavish lifestyle by proxy, and he didn't like it at all when the management tried to rein in spending, to make my tours more cost-efficient: it's strange sometimes how fame affects the people around you more than it affects you. The flashpoint was an argument over which car service we should use. The management had brought in a more competitive company. Bob had got rid of them and employed a more expensive one. The management office overruled him and reinstated their choice of car service. Bob was furious. We had a big argument about it in the St. Regis hotel in New York. He said he'd been undermined, his authority had been challenged. I said we were just trying to save money. He told me he was going to leave and I lost my temper and told him that was fine with me. Later, after I had calmed down, I went back to speak to him again. This time he told me that he hated everyone at the Rocket office: apparently my entire management team were in his bad books. I didn't really know what to say to that: your entire team or your PA? It's not exactly the toughest choice in the world. Bob announced that he was quitting his job and stormed out, adding, as he left, that my career would be over in six months without him. Whatever Bob's talents were, clairvoyance was clearly not among them. The only change in my career after he quit was that the bills for touring expenses got noticeably smaller.

My mum was absolutely livid when she heard Bob had left – they had always got on well. She didn't want to hear my version of events, and told me that Bob had been more of a son to her than I had ever been.

'You care more about that fucking *thing* you married than your own mother,' she spat.

We didn't speak again for seven years after that phone call. There comes a point where you realize you're just banging your head against a brick wall: no matter how many times you do it, you're never going to break through, you're just going to end up with a constant headache. I still made sure she was looked after financially. When she said she wanted to move to Worthing, I bought her a new house. I paid for everything; made sure she had the best care when she needed a hip operation. She auctioned every gift I'd ever given her – everything from jewellery to platinum discs I'd had specially inscribed with her name – but she didn't need money. She told the papers she was downsizing, but it was just another way of telling me to fuck off – like hiring an Elton John tribute act for her ninetieth birthday party. I ended up buying back some of the jewellery myself, stuff that had sentimental value to me, even if it no longer had for Mum.

It was sad, but I didn't want her in my life anymore. I didn't invite her to the ceremony when the law around gay partnerships changed again and David and I got married in December 2014. It was a much smaller, more private event than the civil partnership. We went to the registry office in Maidenhead alone, then the registrar came back to Woodside and performed the ceremony there. The boys were ring-bearers: we tied the same gold bands we had used in the civil partnership – the ones we had bought in Paris years before – to a couple of toy rabbits with ribbon, and Zachary and Elijah carried them in.

I would say Mum missed out on her grandsons growing up – my auntie Win and my cousins flocked around, the way normal families do when there are babies and toddlers to be fussed over and played with and treated – but honestly, she didn't care. When Zachary was born, a tabloid journalist doorstepped her and asked her how she felt about not seeing her first grandchild, looking for a scoop about the callously abandoned grandmother. He didn't get it. She told him she wasn't bothered, and that she didn't like, and had never liked, children. I laughed when I read it: no points for winning yourself sympathy, Mum, but ten out of ten for honesty.

I got back into contact with her when I found out she was seriously ill. I sent her an email with some photos of the kids attached. She barely acknowledged them: 'You've got your hands full' was the only mention of them in her reply. I invited her to lunch. Nothing much had changed. She walked into Woodside and the first thing she said was, 'I'd forgotten how small this place is.' But I was determined not to answer back, not to rise to the bait. The kids were home, playing together upstairs, and I asked if she wanted to see them; my mum said no. I told her that I didn't want to talk about John Reid, or Bob Halley, that I just wanted to tell her after all we'd been through that I loved her.

'I love you too,' she said. 'But I don't like you at all.'

Oh well – at least things stayed cordial otherwise. We would talk on the phone occasionally. I never asked her what she thought of anything I had done, and if I mentioned the kids she always changed the subject. I managed to get her and Auntie Win talking again – they had fallen out when Derf died in 2010 and Mum had refused to let Win's son Paul come to the funeral, telling her that 'Fred never liked him' – so that was something. No luck building bridges between her and Uncle Reg, though. I can't even remember what that argument had been about, but they still weren't talking when she died in December 2017.

I was incredibly upset when Mum died. I had gone down to Worthing to see her the week before – I knew she was terminally ill, but she hadn't seemed like someone who was at death's door that afternoon. It was an odd meeting: when I knocked on the door of her house, Bob Halley answered. We said hello and shook hands, which seemed to be the highlight of the afternoon as far as Mum was concerned.

Mum was never one of life's tactile, nurturing, come-here-and-give-me-a-hug mothers, and there was a mean streak to her that went beyond just being prone to bad moods, or a victim of the Dwight Family Temper, into something else entirely, something I didn't like to think about too deeply, because it frightened me. She seemed to actively enjoy picking fights, and not just with me: there wasn't a member of the family she didn't fall out badly with over the years. And yet there had been times when she was supportive, and there were times, at the start of my career, when she was really good fun. That's how people who knew her in the early seventies remembered her to me after she died: oh, your mum was such a laugh.

We held a private family funeral for her in the chapel at Woodside: I wanted to remember the good things, with just relations around me. I talked about her at the service and I cried. I missed the person I was describing terribly, but I'd started missing her decades before Mum died; she just seemed to vanish as quickly and unexpectedly as she turned up. At the end, her coffin was taken away in a hearse. We all stood there, what was left of the Dwights and the Harrises, watching it go down the long drive at Woodside in silence. It was broken by my uncle Reg, addressing his sister for the last time.

'You can't answer anyone back now, can you, Sheila?' he muttered.

seventeen

I've been a professional musician for my entire adult life, but I've never got bored with playing live. Even when I thought I had – when I was playing the cabaret circuit with Long John Baldry, or in the mid-seventies, when I was just exhausted – I obviously hadn't. You could tell by the way I would grandly announce my retirement, then end up back onstage weeks later. Throughout my life that feeling I get before I go on each night, the mix of adrenalin and anxiety, has never changed, and thank God it hasn't, because that feeling is fucking great. It's addictive. You might get sick of the travelling, the promotion, all the stuff that surrounds playing live, but that feeling will always keep you coming back for more. That, and the knowledge that even at the worst show – bad sound, dull audience, lousy venue – something amazing will always happen onstage: a spark, a flash of inspiration, a song you've played a thousand times that unexpectedly causes a long-forgotten memory to reappear in your mind.

So the music will always surprise you, but after fifty years you do start to feel as if nothing else that happens at a gig can. It's easy to think that you've done pretty much everything it's possible to do onstage except keel over and die. I've performed sober, I've performed drunk and I have – to my shame – performed high as a kite. I've done gigs that made me feel as elated as it's possible for a human being to feel, and struggled through shows in the pits of despair. I've played pianos, I've jumped on pianos, I've fallen off pianos and I've pushed a piano into the crowd, hit a member of the audience with it and spent the rest of the night frantically apologizing to them. I've played with my childhood heroes and some of the greatest artists in the history of music; I've played with people who were so hopeless they had no business being onstage and I've played with a group of male strippers dressed as Cub Scouts. I've done gigs dressed as a woman, a cat, Minnie Mouse, Donald Duck, a Ruritanian general, a musketeer, a pantomime dame and, very occasionally, I've played gigs dressed like a normal human being. I've had gigs that were disrupted by bomb scares, gigs disrupted by student protests against the war in Vietnam and gigs that were disrupted because I flounced offstage in a huff and then came scuttling back shortly afterwards, contrite about losing my temper. I've had hot dogs thrown at me in Paris; I've been knocked unconscious by a hash pipe while wearing a giant chicken outfit in North Carolina – my band thought I'd been shot – and I've run onstage in a gorilla costume in an attempt to surprise Iggy Pop. That wasn't one of my better ideas. It was 1973 and I had been to see The Stooges the night before. It was just the greatest thing I'd ever seen – 180 degrees away from my music, but incredible, the energy of it, the sheer noise they made, Iggy climbing all over the place like Spider-Man. So the next night I went to see them again – they were playing a week of shows at a club called Richards in Atlanta. I thought it would be funny if I hired a gorilla costume and ran onstage during their set – you know, just adding to the general mayhem and anarchy. Instead, I was taught an important life lesson, which is this: if you're planning to run onstage in a gorilla suit and surprise someone, always check first to see whether or not the person you're surprising has taken so much acid before the show that they're unable to differentiate between a man in a gorilla costume and an actual gorilla. I discovered this when my appearance was greeted not with gales of laughter but the sight of Iggy Pop screaming and shrinking away from me in terror. This was quickly followed by the realization that I was no longer on the stage but flying through the air at high speed. Sensing the need for decisive action, another member of The Stooges had stopped playing, picked me up and thrown me into the crowd.

You can see why I might occasionally think that I've covered the full panoply of live incidents, that there isn't really anything left to do during a gig that I haven't already done. But of course, when you do start thinking that, life has a habit of letting you know you're wrong. Which brings us to the night in Las Vegas in 2017 when I found myself leaping up from the piano as the last chord of 'Rocket Man' died away and walking across the stage of the Colosseum, basking in the crowd's applause, punching the air and pointing at fans who were going particularly wild. Nothing unusual in itself, save for the fact that, as I was walking across the stage, basking in the crowd's applause and punching the air, I was also, unbeknown to the audience, copiously urinating into an adult nappy concealed beneath my suit. Pissing myself in front of an audience while wearing a giant nappy: this was definitely hitherto uncharted territory. There aren't a huge number of positives about contracting prostate cancer, but at least it had enabled me to have an entirely new and unprecedented experience onstage.

My life is never quiet, but the preceding few years had been even more tumultuous than usual. Some aspects of them had been really positive. I settled into fatherhood far more easily than I would ever have expected. I loved doing everyday stuff with the boys – taking them to the cinema on a Saturday; going to Legoland and to meet Father Christmas at Windsor Great Park. I loved taking them to see Watford. They're football-mad. I can spend hours talking about it with them, answering their questions about its history: 'Who was George Best, Dad?' 'Why was Pelé such a great player?' They came to Vicarage Road for the opening of a stand named after me, something I'm incredibly proud about; there's a stand there named after Graham Taylor, too. Since then, they've been mascots at matches and they go to games all the time.

And I loved how having kids rooted me in the village nearest to Woodside. I'd lived there since the mid-seventies, without ever really getting to know anyone locally. But when the boys started nursery and school, they made friends, and their friends' parents became our friends. They didn't care about who I was. A harassed mum at the school gates is less interested in asking you how you wrote 'Bennie And The Jets', or what Princess Diana was really like than in talking about uniforms and packed lunches and the difficulty of assembling a costume for the nativity play at forty-eight hours' notice – which was fine by me. We ended up with a whole new social circle we never would have had when David and I were just a famous, jet-setting gay couple.

I had opened a new Vegas show, *The Million Dollar Piano*, in 2011. It was less controversial than its predecessor, but just as spectacular and successful. I brought Tony King in to act as creative director – he'd been working for The Rolling Stones for years, travelling around the world with them on their tours – and he did an incredible job. He's been part of my organization ever since: his official job title is Eminence Grise, which just fits Tony perfectly. The following year, I made *Good Morning to the Night*, an album unlike anything I had done before, that went to Number One. Or rather, I didn't make *Good Morning to the Night*: I handed over the master tapes of my seventies albums to Pnau, an Australian electronic duo that I loved, and told them to do whatever they wanted with them. They remixed different elements from old songs into entirely new tracks, making me sound like Pink Floyd or Daft Punk in the process. I thought the results were fantastic, but I didn't understand the process they used; there was an album with my name on it at Number One and I had no idea whatsoever how it had been made. We played together at a festival in Ibiza, which was fantastic. I always feel nervous before a gig – I think the day you stop feeling nervous is the day you start phoning it in – but this time, I was genuinely terrified. The crowd were so young; they could theoretically have been my grandkids, and the first part of the show was just me and a piano. And they loved it. There's something incredibly gratifying about seeing an audience that's completely different from the people who normally come to see you enjoying what you do.

Pnau weren't the only people I collaborated with. I worked with all sorts of different people: Queens of the Stone Age, A Tribe Called Quest, Jack White, the Red Hot Chili Peppers. I love going into the studio with artists people wouldn't ordinarily expect me to play with. It reminds me of being a session musician in the late sixties: that challenge of having to adapt your style and think on your feet musically is still really exciting to me.

I was in the studio with Clean Bandit when I was called to the phone: apparently Vladimir Putin wanted to speak to me. There had been a lot of publicity about a couple of gigs I'd done in Russia, where I spoke out about LGBTQ rights onstage. I'd dedicated a show in Moscow to the memory of Vladislav Tornovoi, a young man who had been tortured and murdered in Volgograd for being gay, and in St Petersburg I'd talked about how ridiculous it was that a monument to Steve Jobs in the city had been taken down when his successor as Apple CEO, Tim Cook, came out. It turned out to be a prank call, by two guys who'd done the same thing to all sorts of public figures, including Mikhail Gorbachev. They recorded the whole thing and broadcast it on Russian TV, but, fuck it, I wasn't embarrassed at all, because I hadn't said anything stupid to them; I'd just said how grateful I was and how I'd love to meet face to face to discuss civil rights and provision for AIDS treatment. Besides, the real Vladimir Putin rang me at home a few weeks later to apologize and said he wanted to set up a meeting. The meeting hasn't happened – I've been back to Russia since, but my invite to the Kremlin seems to have got lost in the post. But I live in hope.

You don't achieve anything by cutting people off. It's like when I played at the wedding of the right-wing talk show DJ Rush Limbaugh in 2010. I was surprised to be asked – the first thing I said onstage was 'I expect you're wondering what the fuck I'm doing here' – and I got really hauled over the coals in the media: he said some incredibly stupid things about AIDS, how can you possibly perform for him? But I'd rather try and build a bridge to someone on the opposite side to me than put up a wall. And in any case, I donated my fee for the performance – and I assure you that, as a wedding singer, I don't come cheap – to the Elton John AIDS Foundation. So I managed to turn a right-wing talk show DJ's wedding into a fundraising benefit for AIDS.

But a lot of awful things happened in those years, too. Bob Birch, who had played bass in my band for over twenty years, committed suicide. He had been unwell since a car accident in the mid-nineties – a truck had hit him in the street before a gig in Montreal, and he never really recovered from his injuries – but I don't think I fully grasped how much pain he was in or the psychological toll it was taking on him. He seemed incredibly resilient – at first they told him he would never walk again, but he was back on tour within six months. His playing never faltered and he never complained, even when he had to perform sitting down. But then, during the summer break in our 2012 touring schedule, his injuries got worse until it must have become unbearable. I got the phone call from Davey at six o'clock in the morning in Nice, telling me Bob had shot himself outside his home in Los Angeles. I wished he'd reached out; I wished he'd said something. I don't know what I could have done, but I couldn't stop the thought haunting me after his death that he had suffered in silence.

Then Ingrid Sischy died. She'd had breast cancer before, in the late nineties: she'd called me up in tears in Nice, asking if I could help her get an appointment with a top oncologist called Larry Norton, the same doctor that had treated Linda McCartney. The cancer went into remission but, from that point, Ingrid was terrified of it returning. She was so paranoid about it, looking for signs that it had returned in the most bizarre places, that it became a running joke between us.

'Elton, look, my hands are shaking, do you think I have cancer of the hand?'

'Oh, yeah, Ingrid, you've got cancer of the hand now. You've probably got cancer of the teeth and the hair as well.'

It seemed funny at the time, because I couldn't imagine her actually dying. I'd never met anyone with that much vitality; she was always doing something, a million projects on the go at once. And she was so present in my life: I would literally ring her every weekday, Monday to Friday, for a chat and gossip and to ask for her opinions, of which she had an apparently fathomless supply. When someone has that much life force inside them, when someone takes up so much space, it just seems impossible that life could be snuffed out.

Until it was. The cancer returned in 2015 and she died very suddenly – so suddenly that I had to race from Britain to America to see her before she passed away. I just made it. I got to say goodbye, which hadn't happened with a lot of my friends who had died. In a way, I was pleased it was so sudden: Ingrid was so scared of cancer, so scared of dying, and at least she didn't have to spend weeks or months facing death. But it wasn't really any consolation. I'd lost Gianni; now I'd lost another best friend, another almost-sibling. I never stop thinking about her: there are photos of her all over my houses, so she's always there. I miss her advice, I miss that intelligence, I miss her passion, I miss the laughs. I miss *her*.

And then there was David. I can't say I hadn't noticed he was drinking a lot more, maybe too much. He started coming to bed most nights with a glass of wine and would sip it while he was reading and chatting. Or he'd stay up much later than me, and the next morning, I'd see the empty bottle by the kitchen sink. Sometimes two. A couple of times when we were on holiday at the house in Nice, he didn't come to bed at all. I'd find him in the morning, spark out in front of his computer, or on the sofa in the living room. But I honestly didn't think he had any issues. Regardless of what had happened the previous evening, he would be up at seven and off to work. There were times when we were out, and he'd get drunk – after a joint birthday party I had with Sam Taylor-Wood, I remember having to grab his arm and guide him very firmly to the car, so he didn't weave about in front of the paparazzi – but he never made a fool of himself. Given that, after a few vodka martinis, I had been capable of anything from verbal abuse to violence to displays of public nudity, you can understand how I failed to notice David had a serious problem.

I didn't realize he was propping himself up with booze. I always thought David had slipped into Elton John World with remarkable ease and confidence, but it turned out that a lot of things I was completely used to living with, that I just saw as a fact of life, made him anxious. He didn't like being photographed all the time, or being under press scrutiny, or public speaking at AIDS Foundation events. He was always a nervous flyer, but, in my life, hardly a week goes by when you don't set foot on a plane. He found it all easier to deal with after a few drinks. Plus, there was the fact that we were often apart – I was away all the time doing gigs, and he was back at home. I don't want to make him sound like a kind of rock and roll touring widow – he had plenty going on in his life – but after a while, he got lonely and bored, and one way of feeling less lonely and bored is cracking open a bottle of nice wine or knocking back a few vodkas. And on top of everything else, there were the kids. As any new parent will tell you, however much you love it, there are moments when you feel shaken by the responsibility of it all. David wouldn't have been the first parent in history to race to the fridge after bedtime, in urgent need of a glass of something cold, alcoholic and relaxing. Obviously, we had help, but it doesn't really matter if you've got the best nannies in the universe: every new parent who cares about their children has points where they feel overwhelmed by the idea of bringing new humans into the world and ensuring their lives are as good as they can be.

If you treat your anxieties with booze, it usually works, at least while you're drinking: it's the next morning that you find yourself feeling more anxious than ever. And that's what happened to David. It all came to a head in Los Angeles in 2014, two days before I was due to start a US tour. I was leaving that night for Atlanta: Tony King was flying in, and I was looking forward to catching up before the tour began. David was feeling low and wanted me to stay the extra night with him. I said no. We had a huge row. I went anyway. The next morning, David called and we had a row that made the previous day's row look like a light-hearted disagreement over what to have for lunch: the kind of argument where you come off the phone teary and reeling, where things are said that make you wonder whether the next time you communicate, it'll be through lawyers. In fact, the next time I heard from David, he had checked himself into a rehab clinic in Malibu. He told me that after he had come off the phone, he had lain in bed. He could hear Elijah and Zachary playing just down the hall, but he was too depressed and anxious to get up and see them. That was it:

he contacted the doctor, told her he had had enough, that he needed help.

I was pleased he was getting treatment. I felt bad that I hadn't noticed things had got as out of hand as they had: once I did, I just wanted David to get better. But I was also weirdly nervous. The world doesn't have a bigger advocate for getting sober than me, but I also know that it's a huge undertaking: it can change people completely. What if the man I loved came home a different person? What if our relationship changed – the way my relationship with Hugh had changed when we got sober – and became unworkable? It was enough to keep me up at night, but when David came back, he didn't seem that different, although he had more energy and more focus, and he was dedicated to working on his recovery in a way that affected me. I started going to AA meetings again. I hadn't been since the early nineties and I only went to keep David company and show support, but when I got in there, I found I really enjoyed it. You always hear something inspiring; you always come out with your spirits lifted. We started hosting a meeting at home, every Sunday, inviting friends who are also in recovery, like Tony King. I suppose it's a little like going to church – just being thankful for your sobriety. I always come out bouncing.

David seemed to be bouncing, too. Not long after he got sober, I parted company with Frank Presland, who'd gone from being my lawyer to my manager. I'd had a succession of different managers since John Reid, but none of them had really worked out. I thought about different options, then found myself wondering if David couldn't do it. Before we had met, he was a hot-shot advertising executive. He oversaw huge campaigns, worked with budgets – the skills you needed to do that didn't seem so different to the skills you needed in rock management. There were obviously reservations about having a business relationship with your partner, but I liked the idea of us working together: we had kids, it would be like a family business. David was nervous about taking the role on, but eventually he agreed.

He really ran at the task: never underestimate the zeal of the newly sober. He streamlined the company and made financial savings. He started changing things to suit the way the music business was changing: taking streaming into account, and social media. I didn't know anything about that stuff. I've never owned a mobile phone. As you might expect, given my collector's mentality, I'm not really interested in streaming music: I like to own albums, lots of them, preferably on vinyl. And, having taken into account both my temper and my impressive track record of expressing what you might call robust and forthright opinions, I realized that my going anywhere near something like Twitter was likely to end in complete bedlam, at best.

But David worked it all out. He built up a great team. He seemed genuinely interested in areas of the music industry that I couldn't have been more bored by. He started really pushing to get a biopic made of my life. The idea had started years before, with the films David LaChapelle made for *The Red Piano* shows in Vegas: if a film was going to be made about me, I wanted it to look like them. They were gritty, but they were fantastical and surreal and over-the-top, and my career's been fantastical and surreal and over-the-top, so they fitted perfectly. We got Lee Hall, who wrote *Billy Elliot*, to write the screenplay, which I loved, but it took years and years to get it off the ground. Directors and lead actors came and went. David LaChapelle was supposed to direct it initially, but he wanted to concentrate on his fine art career. Tom Hardy was going to play me, but he couldn't sing, and I really wanted whoever was going to be me to perform the songs, rather than lip-synch them. There was a lot of wrangling with studios over budgets and over the content of the film. People kept asking us to tone the gay sex and drugs down so it would get a PG-13 rating, but, you know, I'm a gay man and a recovering addict: there doesn't seem to be a lot of point in making a sanitized film about me that leaves out the sex and the coke. There was a time when I didn't think it was going to happen, but David kept plugging away, and eventually it did.

And he had some radical new ideas. I discovered just how radical one morning in LA, when he presented me with a sheet of paper. He had written down a load of dates relating to Zachary and Elijah's school life – when each term would start, how long the holidays were, the years they would be moving up from infants to juniors and then secondary school, when they would be sitting exams.

'How much of this do you want to be around for?' he asked. 'You can work your tour schedules around it.'

I looked at the sheet of paper. It effectively mapped out their lives. By the time they reached the final dates on it, they wouldn't be children anymore, they would be teenagers, young men. And I would be in my eighties.

'All of it,' I said finally. 'I want to be there for all of it.'

David raised his eyebrows. 'In which case,' he said, 'you need to think about changing your life. You need to think about retiring from touring.'

It was a huge decision. I've always thought of myself as a working musician, just as I was when Bluesology were going up and down the motorway in the van that Arnold Tendler had forked out for on our behalf. That's not false modesty. Fairly obviously, I'm not exactly the same as I was in the sixties – I can assure you it's a very long time indeed since I arrived at a gig in the back of a transit van – but the underlying philosophy, if you like, has never changed. Back then, if you got a gig, you went and played it: that's ultimately how you earned your living; that's how you defined yourself as a musician. I prided myself on the fact that my schedule now wasn't that different from my schedule in the early seventies. Bigger venues, obviously, more luxurious accommodation and travel arrangements, and less time spent locking myself in the lavatory backstage to avoid the attentions of female groupies. Even the most ardent among them had long ago got the memo regarding the improbability of Elton John being swayed by their charms. But I played roughly the same number of gigs: 120 or 130 a year. However many shows I did, I wanted to do more the following year. I kept a list of countries I still wanted to play – places I hadn't visited yet; countries like Egypt, where I'd thus far been banned from performing because I was gay. I was fond of saying I would be happy to die onstage.

But David's list of school dates had thrown me. My kids were only going to grow up once. I didn't want to be in Madison Square Garden, or the Los Angeles Staples Center, or the Taco Bell Arena, Boise, while it happened, much as I loved the fans who came to see me there. I didn't want to be anywhere other than with Zachary and Elijah. I'd finally found something that matched the lure of the stage. We started making plans for a farewell tour. It had to be bigger and more spectacular than anything I had done before, a big celebration, a thank-you to the people who'd bought albums and tickets over the years.

The plans for the farewell tour were already underway when I found out I had cancer. They discovered it during a routine check-up. My doctor noticed that the level of prostate-specific antigens in my blood had gone up slightly, and sent me to an oncologist for a biopsy. It came back positive. It was strange: I wasn't as shocked at hearing the word 'cancer' as I had been back in the eighties, when they thought I had it in my throat. I think it was because it was prostate cancer. It's no joke, but it's incredibly common, they had caught it very early, and besides, I'm blessed with the kind of constitution that just makes me bounce back from illnesses. I'd had a couple of serious health scares before, and they didn't really slow me down. In the nineties, I was taken ill en route to David and Victoria Beckham's wedding. I felt faint that morning when I was playing tennis, and passed out in the car on the way to the airport. I missed the wedding, went to the hospital, they monitored my heart and told me that I had an inner-ear infection. The next day, I was playing tennis again, when David came thundering down from the house yelling that I had to stop immediately. My feelings about being interrupted while I'm playing tennis are a matter of public record – you may recall the incident in *Tantrums and Tiaras* where I announced I was leaving France immediately and never coming back, because a fan had waved at me and shouted 'yoo-hoo!' while I was trying to serve. I had just begun telling David to fuck off in no uncertain terms, when he shouted that the hospital had called; they had made a mistake – I had a heart irregularity and I had to fly to London immediately to get a pacemaker fitted. I was only in the hospital for one night and, rather than feeling debilitated, I thought the pacemaker was fantastic. It seemed to give me more energy than before.

More recently, I'd managed to play nine gigs, take twenty-four flights and perform with Coldplay at a fundraising ball for the AIDS Foundation with a burst appendix: the doctors told me I had a colon infection and I felt exhausted, but I just kept going. I could have died – normally when your appendix bursts it causes peritonitis, which kills you within a few days. I had my appendix out, spent a couple of days in hospital on morphine, hallucinating – I'm not going to lie, I quite enjoyed that part – and a few weeks in Nice recuperating, then went back on the road. It's just how I am. If I hadn't got the constitution I have, all the drugs I took would have killed me decades ago.

The oncologist told me I had two options. One was surgery to remove my prostate. The other was a course of radiation and chemotherapy that meant I would have to keep going back to hospital dozens of times. I went straight for the surgery. A lot of men won't have it, because it's a major operation, you can't have sex for at least a year afterwards and you can't control your bladder for a while, but effectively my kids made the decision for me. I didn't like the idea of cancer hanging over me – us – for years to come: I just wanted rid of it.

I had the surgery done in Los Angeles, quickly and quietly. We made sure that news of my illness didn't reach the press: the last thing I wanted was a load of hysterical stories in the papers and photographers outside my house. The operation was a complete success. They discovered that the cancer had spread to two lobes in my prostate; targeted radiotherapy wouldn't have caught that. I had made the right decision. I was back onstage at Caesar's Palace within ten days.

It wasn't until I arrived in Las Vegas that I noticed something wasn't right. I woke in the morning feeling a little uncomfortable. As the day progressed, the pain got worse and worse. By the time I was backstage at the gig, it was indescribable. I was in tears. The band suggested we should cancel the show, but I said no. Before you start marvelling at my bravery and nonpareil professionalism, I should point out that I didn't agree to play out of any show-must-go-on stoicism or sense of duty. Weirdly, getting onstage seemed preferable to sitting at home with nothing to do in exactly the same pain. So we went on. It sort of worked. At least the gig gave me something else to think about other than how ill I felt, not least at the aforementioned moment when I realized that the radical prostatectomy's after-effects on my bladder were making themselves known.

That was pretty funny – *if only the audience knew* – but nevertheless, if pissing yourself in front of 4,000 people constitutes the highlight of your day, you're clearly in a bad way. It turned out that I was suffering a rare and unexpected complication from the operation: fluid was leaking from my lymph nodes. I had it drained at the hospital and the pain went away. The fluid built up again and the pain came back. Fabulous: another thrilling evening of agony and incontinence onstage at Caesar's Palace. The cycle went on for two and a half months, before they cured it by accident: a routine colonoscopy shifted the fluid permanently, days before my seventieth birthday.

My party was at the Red Studios in Hollywood. David brought Zachary and Elijah over from London as a surprise. Ryan Adams, Rosanne Cash and Lady Gaga performed. Prince Harry sent a video, wishing me all the best while wearing a pair of Elton John glasses. Stevie Wonder played for me, having either forgotten about, or forgiven me for refusing to come out of my bedroom the last time he'd tried to sing 'Happy Birthday' to me, on board the Starship, forty-four years previously. And Bernie was there, with his wife and two young daughters in tow – it was a kind of dual celebration, because it was fifty years since we'd first met, in 1967. We posed for photographs together – me in a maroon suit with satin lapels, a shirt with a ruff and velvet slippers; Bernie dressed down in jeans, his hair cropped and his arms covered in tattoos. We were as much a study in opposites now as we had been the day Bernie first turned up in London from Owmby-by-Spital. Bernie had ended up back in the countryside, on a ranch in Santa Barbara: he'd half gone back to his roots and half turned into one of the Old West characters he loved to write about, like something off *Tumbleweed Connection*. He literally won competitions for roping cattle. I collected porcelain, and the Tate Modern was staging an exhibition drawn from the vast selection of twentieth-century photography I had amassed: one of the star exhibits was the original Man Ray photograph Bernie and I had bought a poster of when we were trying to decorate our shared bedroom in Frome Court. We were worlds apart. I don't know how it all still worked between us, but then, I never understood how it worked in the first place. It just did. It just does.

It was a magical evening. I can usually live without the kind of event that revolves around everyone telling me how wonderful I am – I've never been good at taking a compliment – but I was in a fantastic mood. I was cancer-free, and pain-free. The operation had been a success. The complications had been fixed. I was about to go back on tour, down to South America to play some shows with James Taylor. Everything was back to normal.

Until I nearly died.

It was on the flight back from Santiago that I started feeling ill. We had to change planes in Lisbon, and by the time I got on board, I felt feverish. Then I felt freezing cold. I couldn't stop shaking. I wrapped myself up in blankets and felt a little warmer, but something clearly wasn't right. I got home to Woodside and called the doctor. My fever had subsided a bit, and he advised me to take some rest. The next morning I woke up feeling worse than I ever had in my life. I was taken to King Edward VII's Hospital in London. They gave me a scan and noticed that something was terribly wrong. I was told that my condition was so serious, the hospital didn't have the equipment to cope with it. I had to be moved to the London Clinic.

I arrived at midday. My last memory is of hyperventilating while they were trying to find a vein to give me an injection. I have really muscular arms, so it's always been difficult, compounded by the fact that I hate needles. Eventually they brought in a Russian nurse, who looked like she had just changed into her uniform after a morning's training with the Olympic shot put team, and by two thirty I was on the operating table: there was more lymphatic fluid leaking, this time in my diaphragm, and it had to be drained. For two days afterwards, I was in intensive care. When I came round, they told me I had contracted a major infection in South America, and that they were treating it with massive doses of antibiotics, intravenously. Everything seemed to be fine, and then the fever came back. They took a sample of the infection and grew it in a Petri dish. It was much more serious than they had first realized;

they had to change the antibiotics, up the dosage. I had MRI scans and God knows how many other procedures. I just lay there feeling terrible, being wheeled here and there, having tubes stuck in me and taken out again, not really taking in what was going on. The doctors told David I was twenty-four hours away from death. If the South American tour had gone on for another day, that would have been it: brown bread.

I was incredibly lucky – I had a fantastic team around me and the best possible medical care – although, I have to say, I didn't exactly think of myself as terribly lucky at the time. I couldn't sleep. All I can really remember is lying in bed, awake all night, wondering if I was going to die. I didn't know the details, didn't know how close I really was to dying – David had very wisely kept that information to himself – but how ill I felt in itself was enough to get me thinking about mortality. This wasn't how or when I wanted to go. I wanted to die at home, surrounded by my family, preferably having lived to an enormously advanced age first. I wanted to see the boys again. I needed more time.

After eleven days I was allowed to leave. I couldn't walk – there were shooting pains down my legs – and the sheer quantity and power of the antibiotics I had to take wiped me out completely, but at least I was home. I spent seven weeks recuperating, learning to walk again. I never left the house unless it was to see a doctor. It was the kind of forced leisure that would ordinarily have driven me up the wall – I couldn't remember the last time I'd spent this long at home – but, as ill as I felt, I found I really enjoyed it. It was springtime, and the gardens at Woodside looked beautiful. There were far, far worse places in the world to be trapped. I settled into a kind of domestic routine, pottering around the grounds and enjoying the garden during the day, waiting for the boys to come home from school and give me their news.

In the hospital, alone at the dead of night, I'd prayed: please don't let me die, please let me see my kids again, please give me a little longer. In a strange way, it felt like the time I spent recuperating was the answer to my prayers: if you want more time, you need to learn to live like this, you have to slow down. It was like being shown a different life, a life I realized I loved more than being on the road. Any lingering doubts I might have had about retiring from touring just evaporated. I knew I had made the right decision. Music was the most wonderful thing, but it still didn't sound as good as Zachary chattering about what had happened at Cubs or football practice. I couldn't carry on pretending I was twenty-two anymore. Pretending I was twenty-two was going to do what drugs and alcohol and cancer had failed to achieve, and kill me. And I wasn't ready to die yet.

epilogue

The farewell tour kicked off on 8 September 2018 in Allentown, Pennsylvania. David had pulled together exactly the lavish celebration I wanted. There was an incredible set, and he had commissioned a series of amazing films to accompany the songs: animations that made the cover of *Captain Fantastic* come to life, old footage of me from every stage of my career and edgy films made by contemporary artists. Tony King was on hand to cast his eye over them, and ensure they all looked perfect: half a century after he first wafted into my life, looking extraordinary, I still trusted his aesthetic sense implicitly. The reviews were incredible – the last time I'd had notices like that, I had a full head of hair and the critic had to spend half the piece explaining who I was. The loveliest thing was the sense of affection about them, a real sadness that I'd decided to stop touring, that an era was drawing to a close.

Midway through the first dates, I saw a rough version of the biopic, *Rocketman*, for the first time. David was visibly incredibly nervous about my reaction. I knew that Taron Egerton was the right man to play me when I heard him sing 'Don't Let The Sun Go Down On Me' – he managed to get through it without threatening to murder anyone or screaming about Engelbert

Humperdinck, which was certainly an improvement on the first time I sang it. I'd invited Taron to Woodside and chatted with him over a takeaway curry, and I let him read some of the old diaries I'd kept in the early seventies to give him a sense of what my life was like then. Those diaries are inadvertently hilarious. I wrote down everything in this incredibly matter-of-fact way, which just makes it seem even more preposterous. 'Got up. Tidied the house. Watched football on TV. Wrote "Candle In The Wind". Went to London. Bought Rolls-Royce. Ringo Starr came for dinner.' I suppose I was trying to normalize what was happening to me, despite the fact that what was happening to me clearly wasn't normal at all.

But I'd kept away from the set and tried to avoid looking at the rushes: the last thing you want is the person you're playing gawping at you while you're pretending to be him. But watching the film was like the first time I saw *Billy Elliot* all over again: I started sobbing during the scene set in my gran's house in Pinner Hill Road, where my mum and dad and gran are singing 'I Want Love'. That was a song Bernie had written about himself, a middle-aged man with a few failed marriages behind him, wondering if he'll ever fall in love again. But it could have been written about the people who lived in that house. It felt right, and that was the really important thing to me. It's the same as this book: I wanted something my kids could watch or read in forty years' time, and find out what my life was like, or what it felt like to me.

When the farewell tour was announced, a number of journalists had written pieces suggesting that there was absolutely no way I would really retire. They supported this argument with extensive knowledge of my history and impressive psychological insights into my character: tried to retire before, addictive personality, born entertainer, music obsessive. They could have supported it even more strongly by repeating what I'd said at the press conference, which was that I had no intention whatsoever of actually retiring from music, or even live performances. All I said was that I wasn't going to schlep around the world any more: one last huge tour – 300 gigs over three years, covering North and South America, Europe, the Middle East, Asia and Australasia, the kids getting a tutor and coming with us – and that's that.

It isn't the end. I was excited by the fact that stopping touring would give me more time to do different things. I want to write more musicals and more film scores. I want to spend time working with the AIDS Foundation, especially in Africa. I want to stand up for the LGBTQ community there, to try and talk to politicians in Uganda or Kenya or Nigeria and do something to change the way people are treated. I want to collaborate with different artists. I want to stage a huge exhibition, covering my whole career, maybe even think about opening a permanent museum, so people can see some of my art and photography collections. I want to spend more time making albums, and to make them in the way I used to at the start of my solo career: get Bernie to spend time writing a lot of lyrics and develop a stockpile of material. I haven't gone into the studio with a big hoard of songs to choose from since *Madman Across the Water*, forty-eight years ago – I've just turned up and written on the spot, like the musical version of a painter with a blank canvas. I want to go back to writing without recording what I'm doing, the same way we made *Captain Fantastic*, memorizing what I come up with as I go along. I want to play live, but much smaller shows, where I can concentrate on playing different material. If there's a problem with writing songs like 'I'm Still Standing', or 'Rocket Man', or 'Your Song' it's that they become so huge; they develop a life of their own and overwhelm everything else you do. I love those songs to death, but I've written other songs I think are as good as them, that exist in their shadow, and I'd like to give those other songs a moment in the spotlight.

But most of all, I want to spend time being . . . well, normal, or as normal as I can ever hope to be. Less time on the road means more time doing the school run, more Saturday afternoons taking the kids to Pizza Express, or round Daniel's, the department store in Windsor – things the boys enjoy, things I would once never have thought of doing. I spent my whole life trying to run away from Reg Dwight, because Reg Dwight really wasn't a happy budgie. But what running away from Reg Dwight taught me is that when I got too far from him, too removed from the normal person I once was, things went horribly wrong; I was more miserable than ever. I need – *everybody* needs – some connection to reality.

I live and have lived an extraordinary life, and I honestly wouldn't change it, even the parts I regret, because I'm incredibly happy with how it has turned out. I obviously wish I'd just kept walking when I saw John Reid chopping out coke in the studio, rather than sticking my nose in – in every sense of the phrase – but then, maybe I had to go through all that to end up where I am now. It's not where I expected to be at all – married to a man, a father of two, both things that seemed impossible to me not that long ago. But that's the other lesson my ridiculous life has taught me. From the moment I was ushered out of a failed audition and handed an envelope of Bernie's lyrics as I got to the door, nothing has ever really turned out how I thought it would. My history is full of what ifs, weird little moments that changed everything. What if I'd been so upset by failing my audition that I'd dumped Bernie's envelope in a bin on the way to the station? What if I'd stood firm and not gone to America when Dick James told me I should? What if Watford had beaten West Bromwich Albion that Saturday afternoon in the early nineties and lifted my spirits, so that I didn't feel the need to call a friend and beg him to bring some gay men to dinner? What if I hadn't noticed Lev at the orphanage in Ukraine? Where would I be now? *Who* would I be now?

You can send yourself crazy wondering. But it all happened, and here I am. There's really no point in asking what if? The only question worth asking is: what's next?

acknowledgements

T hank you to everyone who jogged my memory and who contributed to my amazing life.

index

picture acknowledgements

All photographs are from the author's family or personal collection,
  with the exception of the following:

Page 3 top left © Edna Dwight

Page 3 bottom © Mercury Records Ltd

Page 5 top © Mike Ross / Lickerish Syndication

Page 5 bottom © Barrie Wentzell

Page 6 top, page 10 middle, left and right, photographs courtesy
  of Rocket Entertainment

Page 6 middle, photograph by David Larkham

Page 6 bottom, photograph by Don Nix © OKPOP Collection /
  Steve Todoroff Archive

Page 7 top © Bob Gruen / www.bobgruen.com

Page 7 bottom © Anonymous / AP / Shutterstock

Page 8 top © Michael Putland / Getty Images

Page 8 bottom © Bryan Forbes

Page 9 top © MARKA / Alamy Stock Photo

Page 9 bottom right, page 11 top and bottom, page 12 top and
  bottom © Sam Emerson (courtesy of Rocket Entertainment)

Page 10 top © May Pang

Page 10 bottom © Mike Hewitson

Page 13 top © Terry O'Neill / Iconic Images

Page 14 top © Ron Galella / WireImage

Page 14 bottom © Northcliffe Collection / ANL / Shutterstock

Page 15 top © Chris Morris / Shutterstock

Page 15 bottom © Alan Cozzi / courtesy of Watford FC

Page 16 top © Richard Young

Page 16 bottom © Pete Still / Redferns

Page 17 top © Alan Berliner / Berliner Studio

Page 17 bottom, photograph by Eugene Adebari

Page 18 top, photograph by Herb Ritts © Herb Ritts Foundation

Page 18 bottom left © Richard Young / Shutterstock

Page 18 bottom right © AF archive / Alamy Stock Photo

Page 19 top left © Greg Gorman

Page 19 bottom © KMazur / WireImage

Page 20 © Mario Testino, David Furnish and Elton John, Paris, 1997

Page 21 top, photograph by Charles Green

Page 21 bottom, page 23 top right, bottom left and bottom right and page 24 middle © David Furnish

Page 22 top left and right © Sam Taylor-Johnson

Page 22 bottom © Johnnie Shand Kydd

Page 23 top left © Matthew Baron

Page 24 top © James Turano

Page 24 bottom, photograph by Greg Gorman © HST Global (courtesy of Rocket Entertainment)